AFTER THE FACT

AFTER THE
FACT

THE EROSION OF TRUTH
AND THE INEVITABLE
RISE OF DONALD TRUMP

NATHAN BOMEY

Prometheus Books

59 John Glenn Drive
Amherst, New York 14228

Published 2018 by Prometheus Books

Cover design by Nicole Sommer-Lecht
Cover design © Prometheus Books

Inquiries should be addressed to
Prometheus Books
59 John Glenn Drive
Amherst, New York 14228
VOICE: 716–691–0133 • FAX: 716–691–0137
WWW.PROMETHEUSBOOKS.COM

22 21 20 19 18   5 4 3 2 1

Library of Congress Cataloging-in-Publication Data

Names: Bomey, Nathan author.
Title: After the fact : the erosion of truth and the inevitable rise of Donald Trump / Nathan
    Bomey.
Description: Amherst, New York : Prometheus Books, 2018. | Includes index.
Identifiers: LCCN 2017057839 (print) | LCCN 2017060773 (ebook) |
    ISBN 9781633883789 (ebook) | ISBN 9781633883772 (hardback)
Subjects: LCSH: Journalism—United States—History—21st century. | Journalism—Political
    aspects—United States. | Journalism—Objectivity—United States. | Social media—
    Political aspects—United States. | BISAC: SOCIAL SCIENCE / Media Studies. |
    LANGUAGE ARTS & DISCIPLINES / Journalism.
Classification: LCC PN4867.2 (ebook) | LCC PN4867.2 .B68 2018 (print) |
    DDC 071/.309051—dc23
LC record available at https://lccn.loc.gov/2017057839

Printed in the United States of America

To Mom and Dad

CONTENTS

THE NEW GATEKEEPERS

Adam Schrader arrived for his secret job at Facebook one Friday morning in late August 2016 without realizing that his hours there were numbered. After taking the elevator to the seventh floor of the social media giant's gleaming office in lower Manhattan, the former *Dallas Morning News* community publication editor strode by inspirational posters, white desks, and then by TVs that blared the latest news from the presidential campaigns of Donald Trump and Hillary Clinton.[1]

Having completed his daily trek to his workspace in the former Wanamaker department store overlooking Broadway, Schrader took his place among a crew of contractors who had been sworn to secrecy over the existence of their jobs.

Their role? To authenticate and select "trending" news stories for display to hundreds of millions of Facebook users who encountered the items whenever they logged on. The team of about twenty-five news curators primarily consisted of journalists skilled in the art of determining source credibility, ascertaining truth, and applying news judgment. Facebook had provided extra training on journalism ethics and given the curators a suite of software to help them pick out news stories that were captivating users. Unlike an individual user's algorithmically filtered News Feed, the software removed the personalization factor for the curators and showed them what the masses were discussing and reading.[2] The result was a window into Facebook's grisly underworld—a swirling vortex of fabricated news stories and highly distorted partisan content.

"If you're looking at your own personal Facebook account, Facebook might look one way. You're not going to necessarily see all these fake news articles being shared," Schrader said. "We had a backside view of what people are talking about outside of our own Facebook bubbles."[3]

Every day, the curators sought to contain the inferno of deception by dousing the blaze with journalistic sensibility, ensuring false and extremely skewed stories did not reach the trending topics list for the entire nation to see.

"The main thing that we had to confirm was that there was not a fake story that would go up. You would have really [messed] up if you allowed a fake story to trend," said Benjamin Fearnow, another former Facebook trending-news curator.[4]

The curators addressed what Fearnow called a "bombardment of fake news" by taking a fairly clinical approach. A panel on the left-hand side of their screens would display trending topic candidates in descending order of popularity. When they clicked on a topic, it would pop up into a review pane on the right-hand side. The curators would write headlines and short descriptions and pair them with links to credible articles by trustworthy news organizations.

"That's all we had room for," Schrader said. "Our goal was to be as dry as possible. No sensational headlines. Nothing like that."[5]

After a team editor screened each selection and approved the proposed wording, the trending topic would splash onto the public site. It was not much different from the vetting process that occurs every day in a traditional news-room. But that labor-intensive journalistic procedure was not Facebook's long-term plan. At a meeting several months earlier, the news curators had been told that the company's ultimate goal was to use artificial intelligence to select popular news stories for display in the trending field.[6]

"The writing was on the wall," Fearnow said. "We literally were going to be replaced by the algorithm eventually."[7]

WHAT'S TRENDING

Although the news curators worked on the same floor as official Facebook employees—such as people working on the site's live video platform—they were mostly third-party contractors.[8]

In fact, Facebook intentionally kept them "hidden" from the news companies it was simultaneously wooing to post more content to the platform, said a former Facebook executive who requested anonymity to speak freely about the matter. "They thought it would make the [news] industry nervous to know that they were doing that—to know they had editorial talent in-house making editorial decisions about the platform," the former executive said.[9]

But plans to hide the curators imploded in early May 2016 when tech blog *Gizmodo* published stories revealing the secret team's existence and alleging that the curators "routinely suppressed news stories of interest to conservative readers."[10]

The claim drew intense criticism from conservatives, prompting US senator John Thune (R-SD) to fire off a letter demanding accountability. "Facebook must answer these serious allegations and hold those responsible to account if there has been political bias in the dissemination of trending news," Thune wrote. "Any attempt by a neutral and inclusive social media platform to censor or manipulate political discussion is an abuse of trust and inconsistent with the values of an open Internet."[11]

Facebook executives panicked. The accusations threatened their priority of keeping people of all political persuasions clicking, sharing, posting, scrolling, and commenting. Any perception that Facebook was biased could have undermined the company's carefully manicured reputation for political neutrality. That deliberately evenhanded strategy had been tailored to bolster the bottom line, according to a second former Facebook executive. By rewarding content with visibility in the News Feed based on an algorithmic gauge of engagement, Facebook had staked out what the former executive described as the "most defensible" position possible—that its system circulated posts based on a coldly mathematical calculation that ignored politics.[12]

"If it gets good engagement and it gets good feedback, it gets displayed more—and if it gets bad feedback, it gets displayed less. It's almost a complete meritocracy," the former executive said, describing the company's fierce commitment to political neutrality.[13]

As a business plan, it made sense. Engagement fuels traffic, which draws advertisers, which stokes profits, which thrills investors. But the accusations of political bias threatened to disrupt that bulletproof formula and generate unwanted scrutiny.

After Thune demanded answers, Facebook CEO and cofounder Mark Zuckerberg quickly lined up a listening session with conservative journalists to hear their concerns. The company also promptly launched an internal investigation to determine whether there had been any systemic bias.[14]

The probe revealed nothing scandalous or even remotely awry.[15] The curators had, in fact, vigorously embraced their role as politically neutral arbiters of news trends. And the layered journalistic structure installed to prevent their personal biases from seeping onto the site was effective in blocking any potential attempts to circumvent the system.

The curators had even taken extra steps to verify stories before releasing them for all to see. To confirm that a trending-topic candidate was circulating in the mainstream press, lending it a measure of legitimacy, Facebook's curators would check a predetermined list of ten different news sites—the BBC, CNN, Fox News, NBC, the *Guardian*, the *New York Times*, *USA Today*, the *Wall Street Journal*, the *Washington Post*, and BuzzFeed—for similar coverage before featuring the story.[16]

"As a journalist you want to be as ethical as possible, and you pause and think, 'Hey, are we actually doing anything unethical?' The conclusion was no. We all reviewed our policies," Schrader said. "All of us were trained journalists. Some of us had had long careers already. We're not these fresh-out-of-college people. All of us had racked up experience already. Some people were fact-checkers at the *New York Times* previously. We had people of liberal and conservative backgrounds on the team. And it was pretty balanced between those two points of view, which is good. You don't always get that in a newsroom, but it definitely adds to a newsroom's credibility when you can make sure that there's a decent balance."[17]

After concluding its investigation, Facebook publicly cleared the curators of any anti-conservative bias—and reporting for this book also uncovered no such agenda. "Our analysis indicated that the rates of approval of conservative and liberal topics are virtually identical in Trending Topics," Facebook general counsel Colin Stretch told Thune in a late-May 2016 letter summarizing the company's internal probe. "Moreover, we were unable to substantiate any of the specific allegations of politically-motivated suppression of subjects or sources, as reported in the media. To the contrary, we confirmed that most of those subjects were in fact included as trending topics on multiple occasions, on dates and at intervals that would be expected given the volume of discussion around those topics on those dates."[18]

Despite exonerating the news curators, Facebook announced weeks after

Thune's inquiry that it would nonetheless alter the team's policies. "We believe that assessing whether a source is 'unreliable' places more discretion in the hands of [the] reviewer than we intended, and we will be eliminating this from the Guidelines," Stretch told Thune. The company also ordered the news curators to cease considering the list of ten popular news sources to gauge the validity of trending topics.[19]

RUMOR CASCADES

It was particularly ironic that the news curators were battling deception in a complex that once housed John Wanamaker's department store. Wanamaker is regarded for having printed an advertisement in 1874 that introduced the concept of "truth in advertising," which "earned him the public's trust," according to PBS.[20] These days, a street intersecting Broadway outside Facebook's office is named after Wanamaker. But the retail legend's heritage as a purveyor of truth was not top of mind when the news curators received an ominous message at about 4:00 p.m. on August 26, 2016.

"There's an email saying, 'Hey we're going to have a meeting in the board-room upstairs,'" Schrader said.[21]

After gathering together, the curators were summarily informed that they had all been fired. "They literally had security escort us out of the building almost immediately after we were told that we were let go," Schrader said.[22]

Although political consternation over the trending-news team had already died down, Facebook had still decided in the weeks following the controversy that it was ready to hand the verification process over to technology—as it had long planned. The company said afterward in a statement that it would still have a handful of real people "involved in this process to ensure that the topics that appear in Trending remain high-quality—for example, confirming that a topic is tied to a current news event in the real world." But the social network emphasized that it treasured its role as "a platform for all ideas" and seemed to breathe a sigh of relief that "we no longer need to do things like write topic descriptions and short story summaries, since we're relying on an algorithm to pull excerpts directly from news stories."[23]

The move reflected a bet on technology over human journalists. Yet two months earlier Zuckerberg had publicly acknowledged that the company's artificial intelligence capability remained limited. "There are millions of posts, right, that are available for you that people share publicly every day," he told investors in June 2016. "And right now, we don't understand the meaning of those posts."[24]

He didn't know how right he was.

Trusting artificial intelligence turned out to be a huge blunder. As the news curators exited the Wanamaker building for the last time, Facebook's frontline defense against fake news withered. Almost immediately, fabricated stories that the curators had been shielding from national exposure suddenly burst into the spotlight.

As Americans logged on to Facebook the next Monday, they were greeted with the technologically composed list of curated topics. On that particular morning, then Fox News host Megyn Kelly was trending. One click revealed the culprit: "BREAKING: Fox News Exposes Traitor Megyn Kelly, Kicks Her Out for Backing Hillary," blared the bogus headline by fringe conservative website Ending the Fed. The false item lingered for several hours before Facebook finally removed it.[25]

No fewer than two years earlier, the company's own researchers knew the site had a problem with misinformation and that it was extremely difficult to stop. In 2014, Facebook data scientists had concluded in their own study of the platform that bogus content reverberated through what they called "rumor cascades," even when it was debunked, or publicly corrected by another user.[26] The researchers calculated that Facebook users shared false rumors an average of 108 times per item.[27]

In fact, the company itself had been the victim of a misinformation explosion beginning in July 2011, when users spread a false rumor that Facebook would implement a usage fee. "It's official," the bogus post proclaimed. "Facebook will start charging this summer. If you copy this on your wall your icon will turn blue and Facebook will be free for you."[28] Users published 12.7 million posts circulating the original rumor, 8.6 million posts spoofing it, and only 5,000 posts directly debunking it.[29]

It was wishful thinking—at best—for Facebook to believe that technology was suddenly ready to assume the journalistic process of distinguishing between fact and fiction. Facebook's decision was "unjustifiable" because it "should have known better that AI is nowhere close to being able to defend itself against human ingenuity," said computer scientist Panagiotis Takis Metaxas, a Wellesley College professor who has studied how fabricated content spreads through social media.[30]

"To those of us who are doing research in this area, this is known," said Metaxas, who is also a scholar at Harvard University's Center for Research on Computation and Society. "Humans are not predictable. You see, the moment somebody knows they are observed they might change their behavior."[31]

The bloodletting of the curators brought into full view the sharp cultural conflict between Silicon Valley and the news industry. Whereas professional, mainstream journalists have historically taken responsibility for selecting, reporting, and presenting accurate information to the public—at least in the post–Vietnam War era—Facebook has delegated that responsibility to powerful algorithms and sterile digital platforms, retaining scarcely any hands-on role in discriminating based on legitimacy, meaning, quality, and impact.

Facebook's abdication of this responsibility was emblematic in Zuckerberg's now infamous proclamation—on the same day the fake Megyn Kelly story blew up—that "we are a tech company, not a media company."[32] While the news industry reacted to Zuckerberg's assertion with scorn, believing that he should assume accountability for Facebook's impact on democracy, the statement reflected his sweeping ambition to change the world through advancements like telepathic communication, virtual reality, and internet access for everyone. For him, admitting Facebook was a media company was a nonstarter.

"He didn't want to say that, or position Facebook in that way, because it saddles Facebook with a ton of responsibility that they were not well-equipped for, obviously, we've discovered," said the first former Facebook executive. "It constrains the company. Zuckerberg is like this huge visionary. He's had a huge impact on the world already, and he just keeps going bigger. I think the idea of saddling Facebook with that frame was infeasible for that reason because it limits what it can be. But Facebook knows they are not well-equipped to do what media does. And I don't know if anyone exactly is well-equipped at that scale."[33]

With two billion people using the site on at least a monthly basis as of summer 2017, Facebook's influence extends into all walks of life, completely reshaping the way people interact with each other.[34] Its profound effect on how people perceive the world dwarfs the impact of any single news outlet or social institution. The average user spends an extraordinary fifty minutes a day on Facebook, the company's Instagram app, or its Messenger feature.[35]

"The scale is just mind-boggling when you really think about it," the first former Facebook executive said. "Each one of [Facebook's users] is getting a personalized experience. All over the world there's mainstream and non-mainstream outlets contributing to it, and it's all driven by humans. It's so hard to really imagine how they would actually act responsibly as a media company."[36]

"THEY'RE UNTOUCHABLE"

In 1964, Marshall McLuhan famously declared that "the medium is the message." He wrote, "The 'message' of any medium or technology is the change of scale or pace or pattern that it introduces into human affairs. The railway did not introduce movement or transportation or wheel or road into human society, but it accelerated and enlarged the scale of previous human functions, creating totally new kinds of cities and new kinds of work and leisure."[37]

The change of scale or pace or pattern that Facebook has introduced into human affairs is visible in how it has redirected the flow of information and enlarged our collective capacity for mistruth. That change was well underway by the time Facebook axed its team of news curators. But kicking the news curators out the door fanned the flames of fabricated content that had already ignited on the platform, largely without the knowledge of Facebook's senior executives, according to the first of the former company officials.[38]

From August 1, 2016, through Election Day—roughly coinciding with the campaign period in which the contracted news curators were gone—the top twenty false election stories on Facebook accumulated more combined shares, reactions, and comments than the top twenty authentic election stories from mainstream news sites, according to an analysis conducted by BuzzFeed using content analysis tool BuzzSumo. The fake stories received some 8.7 million instances of engagement, such as comments and likes, topping the real stories' 7.4 million. In the six-month period leading up to August, fake stories had gotten only 6.2 million engagements, far below the 21.9 million for real stories. Facebook argued that the fake stories that topped the charts didn't reflect the preponderance of legitimate content shared on its platform.[39]

To be sure, the increased engagement with fake stories cannot be fully blamed on the ouster of the curators. In the grand scheme of Facebook's impact, the curators only had influence over a portion of the billions of posts published daily on the social media site.[40] Plus, there's reason to believe that the period with the most fake news was always likely to immediately precede the election. That's when the most people were paying attention, and thus, that's when the most money could be made and the most influence could be exerted by foreign forces and partisan actors. But that paradigm simply underscores the fact that when the stakes were the highest, Facebook willingly relinquished one of its most powerful tools in the war against bogus content.

Facebook did not agree to interviews for this book.

"They tried to bend over backward so hard to pretend that they weren't a news source," former curator Fearnow said. "Then they ended up saying 'laissez-faire' and opening up the floodgates for whatever [fakery] was out there. Because from a business perspective Zuckerberg is not going to want to offend 50 percent of his customer base. So they pulled out all the restrictions and just let the [garbage] flow. And the result was the fake-news bombardment, which particularly sided against Hillary Clinton."[41]

He is right about the slanted nature of the fabricated content. Bogus stories that flourished on the site from August through Election Day included whoppers like, "Pope Francis Shocks World, Endorses Donald Trump for President, Releases Statement," from Ending the Fed, and, "WikiLeaks CONFIRMS Hillary Sold Weapons to ISIS . . . Then Drops Another BOMBSHELL! Breaking News," from the Political Insider. All but three of the top twenty fake stories during that period boosted Trump or sought to undermine Clinton.[42]

Although Facebook repeatedly pledged months after the election to combat bogus stories and play a more active role in promoting authentic content—with Zuckerberg suddenly acknowledging that the company could no longer sit on the sidelines—the former curators were skeptical that much would change in the long run. After all, Facebook has little incentive to take aggressive action. Even after it became clear in fall 2017 that Russian forces had infiltrated the site by using skilled trolls to organically provoke political division and using paid ads to target specific audiences, the public's faith in the service didn't waver—at least not if measured by engagement. Facebook usage continued to rise unabated.[43]

"People cannot function without Facebook. I've even tried," Schrader said. "I've tried deleting my Facebook account several times over the years. It's just—in this day and age, until Facebook gets replaced by something else—it is the most efficient way to communicate with businesses, with news publishers, with your friends, with your family. And Facebook knows that they don't really have to change. They're so big now that nothing can touch them. They're untouchable. So it's easier for them to lay off twenty-five journalists than it is to acknowledge the problem and move forward appropriately."[44]

Facebook's dismissal of the news curators—although limited in its long-lasting effects—was a microcosm of a much broader issue. It symbolized a wholesale shift that was already well underway across society—an indiscriminate and subconscious transfer of trust from news professionals to secretive algorithms and ideologically motivated groups. The resulting upheaval has gravely undermined our collective grasp of reality.

"What I thought was weird was that people were more up in arms about this 'group of liberal journalists' dictating their stories than they were about four engineers in a room in Menlo Park who are creating this algorithm that is inevitably deciding what you would see—what anyone would see," Fearnow said, referring to the California town where Facebook is headquartered. "How is that not scarier—that these unnamed engineers at Facebook are the ones who are the gatekeepers to how this works? The culture at Facebook is, the engineers there are like the editors. They're like God—because no one really knows what . . . they do."[45]

INTRODUCTION

THE POST-FACT ERA

I'm a truth-teller. All I do is tell the truth.
—Donald Trump on CNBC's *Squawk Box*, August 11, 2016

My childhood Sunday school teacher liked to say that the most dangerous lies are the ones that contain the most truth.

He was right. Yet some measure of manipulation is normal in a healthy democracy. In America, free speech gives us the right to skew reality—short of slander, libel, perjury, or shouting "fire" in a crowded theater.

We have entire professions devoted, at least to some degree, to spinning the facts. Public relations. Marketing. Lobbying. Law. Politics. People in those fields are paid to present a filtered version of the truth to their target audiences. And we need them to do their jobs effectively. They should not have to give up their right to bend the truth.

But how much can you bend the truth before it breaks?

As former US senator Daniel Patrick Moynihan is often said to have decreed, "everyone is entitled to his own opinion but not to his own facts."[1] He was right, too. With all due respect to the late Moynihan, however, few of us live by that standard. For most of us, facts are fungible and shapeable. There's no one who better exemplifies this than President Donald Trump, who trampled the truth en route to the White House.

During his 2016 campaign—and during the first year of his presidency—Trump repeatedly skewed the facts, evaded the truth, and stirred up dissension based on rumors, innuendo, and outright concoctions. He spun falsehoods about the threats posed by refugees, Muslims, criminals, and innumerable other boogeymen.[2] He fibbed about his own achievements, misled voters about his opponents, circulated conspiracy theories, deceived the public about legitimate journalism, and grossly mischaracterized a multitude of political issues.

You can argue, as many do, that the facts have never formed the foundation of political discourse. And that's fair—to an extent. But "in saying that all politicians lie, dissemble, and spin, we didn't take seriously the extremes to which that notion could be taken," said political scientist Brendan Nyhan, a Dartmouth College professor who has researched political misperceptions. "So when a politician like Donald Trump appears, the disincentives for promoting misinformation are a lot weaker than we think."[3]

Those disincentives have actually morphed into incentives. Promoting and capitalizing on misinformation is easier and more rewarding than ever. Trump simply exploited that new reality. And it helped him win the election. "People who tend to agree with him will often believe his claims, even though they're not based on any evidence or are directly disproven by the facts," Nyhan said. "The immune system of democracy is weaker than we'd like to think."[4]

Trump has always understood the power of tinkering with the truth. After all, he famously articulated in his 1987 book, *Trump: The Art of the Deal*, precisely how he manipulates the press and the public. "I play to people's fantasies. People may not always think big themselves, but they can still get very excited by those who do," he wrote. "That's why a little hyperbole never hurts. People want to believe that something is the biggest and the greatest and the most spectacular. I call it truthful hyperbole. It's an innocent form of exaggeration—and a very effective form of promotion."[5]

It's tempting and perhaps even reassuring to describe Trump as an outlier. That's understandable. But the truth is there's a little bit of Donald Trump in all of us—a willingness to misrepresent reality to achieve selfish goals, deny irrefutable facts that make us uncomfortable, and cling to our own preconceived notions of the world.

Donald Trump did not usher the post-fact era into existence. He was a product of it. He was its inevitable outcome.

To understand how this happened, we must relinquish any pretense that this is a one-sided problem. It's a bipartisan epidemic. Democrats are also guilty, albeit not to the same degree as Republicans during the 2016 campaign. But this isn't a purely political book because the problem transcends politics. In fact, politics is simply a reflection of our "post-truth" society, which the Oxford Dictionaries named the 2016 word of the year.[6]

Most people who use social media are contributing to this crisis, myself included. Social media has given us the ability to twist the facts on a sweeping scale, transforming us into our own personal publicists and political spin doctors while provoking deep-seated misunderstanding and interpersonal division. Through tools like Facebook and Instagram, we cultivate false impressions, purposely or inadvertently deceiving others about our lives. This increases the likelihood that our family, friends, and acquaintances will fall prey to depression, resentment, vulnerability, and isolation—which collectively make up the building blocks of distrust and even hate.

Nearly half a century before Mark Zuckerberg cofounded Facebook in a Harvard University dormitory, sociologist Erving Goffman warned about the societal risks of people misrepresenting themselves. "A discrepancy between fostered appearances and reality" provokes social distance, Goffman wrote in 1956 in *The Presentation of Self in Everyday Life*. "Paradoxically, the more closely the impostor's performance approximates to the real thing, the more intensely we may be threatened."[7]

That sounds a lot like my Sunday school teacher's warning.

GOODBYE, WATCHDOGS

Meanwhile, the broader digital ecosystem has recomposed our traditional relationship with facts and news. Whereas we once shared a few common, trusted sources for information about the world—namely network TV news, newspapers, periodicals, books, and radio—the internet has brought us innumerable outlets to mine for material to support our biases and preconceptions.

The gatekeepers we once trusted implicitly to handle the information-filtering process on our behalf have declined precipitously in stature, number, quality, and influence. In many cases, entire areas are going largely uncovered. Small towns where reporters once tracked government officials, formed relationships with community members, and explained arcane issues to the public have entered a post-fact world in which scarcely any independent presence exists to actively guard against the threat of corruption and deceit.

"You can go twenty years covering a school board without there being a scandal, but on the one day that the school board is actually selling the kids in return for a major fortune in something else, it's really nice to have someone there," said Fred Vultee, a former news copy editor who is now a journalism professor at Wayne State University. The reporter "who covers the school board all night is your friend."[8]

Journalists who have managed to survive the industry's crushing contraction are stretched thin. It's common for reporters at small- to mid-size publications to be required to cover several unrelated stories on a daily basis, shoot and edit videos, take photos, upload their own stories, stay active on Twitter, interact with readers on Facebook, cultivate sources, and monitor competition. Most reporters no longer have time to dive deeply into stories or become experts on narrow topics. The ones who do—at institutions such as the *New York Times*, the *Wall Street Journal*, the *Washington Post*, and *USA Today*—are the exceptions to the rule. And they can only cover a sliver of what happens in this country.

"The only news organizations that are well positioned to succeed are on the coasts," said Nikki Usher, a George Washington University journalism professor who has studied the industry's crisis.[9]

In their quest for relevancy and revenue amid digital upheaval, thousands of news outlets have embraced real-time metrics to track story readership, photo gallery clicks, video views, and other measures of audience engagement. But access to raw data on what readers want has tipped the scales in favor of more controversial topics, sensational headlines, and buzzy tweets. With some obvious exceptions, the news is increasingly hyperbolic and light on nuance.

These trends have played a key role in severing the bonds of trust between journalists and folks in Middle America, many of whom voted for Trump as he repeatedly bashed the industry. To be sure, Trump's attempts to discredit legitimate reporting have been disheartening because of his profound influence on millions and because, despite extraordinary financial challenges, some reporters have managed to churn out exceptional watchdog reporting on the president's rise. But his accusations have nonetheless struck a chord with Americans who have noticed the negative effects of the industry's desperate scramble to survive. That scramble has narrowed the gap between what's real and what's fake. Suddenly the implausible looks plausible.

Therefore we should not be surprised that people fell for false headlines, photos, videos, and social media posts like those that flourished on Facebook during the 2016 campaign.

"REALITY IS INCONVENIENT"

In a world riddled with disappointment, heartache, and discontent, fake news often resonates with readers because it's reassuring. Many people would simply prefer not to face the facts, said Neil McGinness, editor in chief of the *Weekly World News*, a tabloid that has long trafficked in fake news. "I don't think the truth is convenient," McGinness said. "Reality is inconvenient on a lot of different levels for people—the reality of economic decline, the reality of uncertainty of where you're headed and what it might bring."[10] Ultimately, "it's easier to look at some sort of alternate version of the story," he said. "I think the appeal, at least politically, for a lot of what is being labeled as fake news now is convenience."[11]

And avoiding reality is more convenient than ever. Before the internet, it was difficult to completely dodge information that made you uncomfortable. To stay up to speed, you might have had to read a newspaper column written by someone you disagreed with or had to watch a newscast that presented viewpoints that challenged your beliefs. That form of incidental interaction with information has faded in the age of digital customization, as Eli Pariser documented in his 2011 book, *The Filter Bubble*.[12]

It would be natural to conclude that overwhelmingly easy access to basic facts would provide the foundation for a well-informed society that's less susceptible to manipulation. But while access to abundant information is something worth fighting for, the side effect is that our fundamental process of fact discovery has been forever altered.

This wholesale shift in how we encounter information has also made it unnecessary to remember certain important facts. We can just search for them on Google. The internet has become a substitute for our brains, a digital extension of our gray matter that redefines how we think, recall facts, form arguments, and draw conclusions. In past eras, such as the Industrial Revolution, technology came along and made certain skills obsolete. In the digital revolution, technology has made memory obsolete.

But most of us were never taught how to vet facts in the same way we were taught basic multiplication, sentence structure, or state capitals. We historically relegated that responsibility to journalists who did it as a public service in exchange for our subscriptions and our attention. Without those professional authenticators—however flawed they were at times—to protect us from misinformation, we have subsequently become more susceptible to deception.

"Most people overrate their skills at lie detection," said Leonard Saxe, a Brandeis University social psychologist and an expert on lying and polygraph tests. "One problem in detecting lies is that liars may believe in the lie. They have constructed a reality in which the lie makes sense. . . . And the more they repeat it, the more they believe it."[13]

To be sure, instant access to information makes everyday life easier. But it also gives us a clear route to materials that provide dubious support to crackpot theories, ideologies, and ideas.

Conspiracy theories are certainly nothing new. Ever since President John F. Kennedy's death in 1963, people have believed that assassin Lee Harvey Oswald had help, despite investigators' conclusion that he acted alone. That will never change. But comprehensive access to details about conspiracy theories fans the flames of misinformation, expanding the reach of cockeyed beliefs. And social media helps people with fringe views find like-minded believers more easily, exacerbating the situation.

Those who skew the truth about scientific issues such as climate change, genetically modified organisms, and vaccines can easily cluster together and share evidence to support their views, posing cataclysmic consequences for society.

"Yes, we live in a post-factual world, but that only affects us insofar as how we interact with facts," said Katharine Hayhoe, a Texas Tech University atmospheric scientist and evangelical Christian who tries to bridge cultural divides to promote action on climate change. "Whether you believe in gravity or not, if you step off the cliff, you're going down. So facts are still true. But if we negate their validity, we are making decisions based on false and poor information that will have long-term, potentially catastrophic outcomes."[14]

Contrary to conventional wisdom, however, people don't necessarily deny the relevancy of science. In many cases, they legitimately believe the science is on their side. And this is not exclusive to uneducated people. In fact, intelligent citizens on both sides of the political aisle often fall into this trap, craving a sense of belonging more than the facts.

"People will selectively credit or reject the claim that somebody is an expert on something depending on whether the person's view is consistent with the one that predominates in their group," said Dan Kahan, a professor of law and psychology at Yale Law School and a scholar at the Cultural Cognition Project, which has researched people's tendencies to snub scientific data. "Their position is a badge of loyalty to the group, and at that stage, people are going to use their reason to form and persist in the kinds of beliefs that identify them as a good group member, rather than use their reason to figure out what the truth is."[15]

Fearing rejection among their peers for embracing the facts, people instead reject the truth. "That's usually something that doesn't have a big impact on them anyway," Kahan said. "I mean, think about it. What a person believes about climate change doesn't affect the climate. Your [individual] carbon footprint can't be big enough to make a difference, and your vote isn't going to change some critical election in which climate change policy is adopted. So any mistake you make in those settings is costless for you and for everybody else. But if you make a mistake about the position you should be taking within your group, then you could have pretty serious consequences for yourself."[16]

Elected officials, interest groups, and partisan media are particularly adept at exploiting this human desire for a sense of belonging, positioning group loyalty as a virtue to be cherished above all else. As leaders leverage strategically constructed us-versus-them narratives to perpetuate their respective ideologies, voters naturally gravitate toward politicians who emphasize pure political principles over compromise and pragmatism.

But the risks of relentlessly provoking division are significant. While trust among like-minded individuals may intensify, distrust widens between groups. This grouping effect threatens the underpinnings of American democracy by preventing legislative progress and fueling cultural and political divides. From 2006 to 2016, trust in ten of fourteen key American institutions fell, with several suffering double-digit percentage declines, according to polling firm Gallup.[17] This widespread breakdown in trust has paved the way for further deceit and fearmongering, which breeds bitterness, misunderstanding, and isolation. Isolation fuels self-segregation, disrespect, and a lack of conversation, preventing the free flow of ideas and distancing us from the truth. It's a destructive cycle.

Put simply, the more polarized we become, the more we ignore each other and the more we skew the facts to fit our own preferred worldview. Evidence suggests that this severe polarization is transcending the boundaries of politics and destabilizing personal relationships, disrupting the interconnectedness that's crucial to American democracy.

In one 2014 study, participants were told they would be given the opportunity to pick the winner of a $30,000 college scholarship funded by an anonymous donor whose selection committee had split over two student finalists. The researchers, Shanto Iyengar of Stanford University and Sean Westwood of Princeton University, gave the participants information about the academic achievements, extracurricular activities, and community involvement of each scholarship candidate.[18] Then, in separate tests, the candidates were identified to the participants by race and partisan affiliation. In the partisan test, one was described as president of the Young Republicans, while the other was described as president of the Young Democrats. To ensure a reliable outcome, the researchers randomized the academic qualifications of each candidate. Overall, study subjects who identified as Republicans awarded the scholarship to the Republican 80 percent of the time, while people who identified as Democrats gave the scholarship to the Democrat 79 percent of the time.[19]

"Even when the candidate from the opposing party was more qualified, partisans opted to award the scholarship money to the" person who shared their respective views, the researchers wrote. "Partisanship simply trumped academic excellence in this task."[20] In addition, "discrimination based on party affiliation exceeds discrimination based on race," they found.[21] Participants who professed to only lean in one political direction or another—and were not firmly committed to one side—were also "unresponsive to candidate qualifications," the researchers wrote.[22]

Their findings illustrate that partisanship has become a socially acceptable form of prejudice in American society. This culture of bitterness and personal animosity toward the other side weakens the American spirit of hopefulness and optimism that has historically made our country, despite all of its flaws, a beacon of light to the rest of the world.

Although this is not a book devoted to exploring neurological influences and changes—for that, it's worth reading Nicholas Carr's *The Shallows* or Jonathan Haidt's *The Righteous Mind*—evidence suggests that a widening disconnect with the truth poses disturbing biological consequences.

Aiming to gauge the neurological effects of perpetuating falsehoods, researchers at University College London's Affective Brain Lab instructed participants in a 2016 study to tell another person how much money was inside a glass jar filled with pennies. Incentives for lying or telling the truth varied with each test, and the researchers tracked the gap between what the participants had privately estimated versus what they disclosed to the other person.[23] Using functional magnetic resonance imaging, the scientists observed that activity in the brain's amygdala—which processes emotion—diminished as the participants grew increasingly dishonest. In other words, white lies gave way to bigger lies, while feelings registered in the brain became less intense.

"We observed clear evidence of escalation in self-serving dishonesty, such that the magnitude of dishonesty got larger and larger over the course of" time and with repetition, the researchers concluded. "Despite being small at the outset, engagement in dishonest acts may trigger a process that leads to larger acts of dishonesty further down the line."[24]

The title of their article said it all: "The Brain Adapts to Dishonesty."[25]

WHAT'S AHEAD IN THIS BOOK

My goal with this book is to explain why we should not be surprised by the rise of a powerful person who openly skews the facts, to discuss the threats posed by the post-fact era, and to suggest how we can begin reorienting back toward the truth.

In part 1, I'll trace the roots of the crisis, explain why it's disrupted our collective relationship with facts, and discuss how Trump took advantage of this. In chapter 1, I'll explore how a transfer of trust to search engines—namely Google—has affected our basic research process and our understanding of what's true and what's false. In chapter 2, I'll articulate the impact of journalism's decline and its pivot toward sensationalism and partisanship on the public's perception of the truth. And in chapter 3, I'll highlight the rise of false and distorted content in connection with our algorithmic age.

In part 2, I'll discuss how these changes have sparked a crisis of disconnectedness and threatened to undermine scientific and community values that were historically considered core to our well-being. In chapter 4, I'll cover the role of fiercely ideological politics in driving misperceptions and falsehoods, particularly about scientific issues. In chapter 5, I'll examine how social media has compromised our ability to recognize reality in each other as friends, family, acquaintances, and strangers. And in chapter 6, I'll analyze the effects of political division and digital disruption on our democratic values, health, and welfare.

In part 3, I'll explore the future of the post-fact era and how we need to rethink education, communication, journalism, and technology. In this section, I'll even propose a few potential solutions—perhaps naively but at least in good faith. In chapter 7, I'll explain the serious risk of a massive increase in fabrication via technology, social media, and online news. In chapter 8, I'll show how educators need to adapt to these challenges to begin preparing us for dynamic economic and social changes. In chapter 9, I'll delve into the ways in which altering how we talk to each other can help disparate groups break through barriers and restore trust. And in chapter 10, I'll discuss potential solutions for journalism and technology to help people reconnect with reality—and barriers that could prevent social media from changing.

Finally, in the conclusion, I'll explore why, amid a culture of distrust, so many people seem to be craving authenticity.

Throughout this book, I'll share a few personal experiences and observations as a professional journalist. But I'll primarily rely upon a comprehensive review of modern research, public reports, and extensive personal interviews with public figures, academics, technologists, psychologists, sociologists, entrepreneurs, educators, and others.

After all, as Winston Churchill once said, "It is a fine thing to be honest, but it is also very important to be right."[26]

PART 1

DISORIENTED

CHAPTER 1

MISINFORMATION OVERLOAD

O ne day around the dawn of the twenty-first century, internet pioneer Howard Rheingold sat down at a computer to help his daughter conduct research for a middle school paper. As they faced the screen together, the San Francisco–area technology critic considered the implications of an online universe that had already begun to disrupt the typical path to basic facts. "The ability to find so much information so quickly is a miracle that people fail to recognize, having started out as a freelance writer when my tools were a type-writer and a library card and a telephone," Rheingold said.[1]

But that miracle came with serious side effects.

Pondering a powerful lesson on digital trust, he turned to his daughter. "And I said, 'If you get a book out of the library for your research, there was an author and an editor and a publisher and a librarian, all of whom were gatekeepers that guaranteed the authenticity of the text. You could trust the authority of what was written,'" Rheingold said. But, "'the really miraculous advantages of the web are the cause of the problem with credibility, which is that you can ask any question, anytime, anywhere, and get a million answers.'"[2]

To demonstrate the risks of trusting online material without first verifying the validity of the source, Rheingold directed his daughter to MartinLutherKing.org. "For many years you could search Martin Luther King and the third or fourth hit that came up was MartinLutherKing.org," Rheingold said. "And it looks like it's a legitimate historic site about Martin Luther King, but the articles are about what a terrible person he was."

As they perused the site together, his daughter was puzzled. "Well, how can I tell what's real and what's not?" she asked.

"Well, let's look for some authors," Rheingold responded. After spotting the name of one of the site's originators, "we searched for the author's name, and it was pretty clear that the author was writing white nationalist stuff," he recalled.

"Let's look at whose website it is," the technologist instructed his daughter. Using an internet utility that reveals the registered owner of a website, they found the name Don Black.[3] "If you look up Don Black, the first hits you get are for an organization called StormFront.org. And if you look at Storm Front, it's a neo-Nazi site. So a little bit of investigation revealed that you can't trust everything you find online," Rheingold said.[4]

"That was many years ago," Rheingold added.[5] But on a Wednesday afternoon in June 2017, as I conducted research for this book, a Google search for "Martin Luther King Jr." turned up Black's MartinLutherKing.org as the eighth listing.[6]

Google did not respond to a request for interviews for this book.

IN GOOGLE WE TRUST

In the time since Rheingold taught his daughter about how to navigate the internet for facts about Martin Luther King, Google's rise to prominence has made it the central funneling point for information seekers. Without it or its lesser-utilized rivals, Verizon's Yahoo! and Microsoft's Bing, modern Americans would find it hard to function.

Google's search engine has undeniably made our lives easier. Finding the best local pizza parlor is helpful. Fetching directions at a moment's notice is very convenient. And resolving bar bets is a cinch. But the sweeping consequences of our collective addiction to search engines have only recently come into focus. By their nature, search engines aren't designed to tell us what's true. They're designed to direct us to potential answers to questions we'd like to resolve. They're designed to deliver results tailored to what we want to know, not necessarily what we need to know.

The rise of the search engine has severely restricted incidental discovery of information and led us to place our trust in algorithms that most of us don't understand. This shift puts tremendous power in the hands of algorithm creators, who retain vast influence over what we do and do not see online.

Although general information is available, the inner workings of Google's search engine algorithms are shrouded in secrecy. But users don't seem to mind. In fact, our trust in search engines is increasing. Some 64 percent of people said in 2017 that they trust search engines as a source for general news and information, marking the medium's fourth consecutive increase, according to global public relations firm Edelman's annual Trust Barometer survey. That's higher than the percentage of people who trust traditional news media, digital news media, and social media, according to the study.[7]

This means Google has profound influence over how we discern truth. Trust in the capability of search engines easily morphs into trust in the validity of the actual results. But while the search engine is amazingly proficient at spitting out information that matches up with the keywords entered into its toolbar, it cannot necessarily vouch for the believability of the pages it introduces to us.

"Some of them are accurate, some of them are inaccurate, some of them are completely wrong, and some of them are deliberately wrong," Rheingold said. "There's information, there's bad information, [and] there's disinformation. And therein lies the issue, which is if you can get vastly more information instantaneously but you don't have a guarantee of its veracity, it's up to you, the seeker of the information, to test it to figure out what the good information is."[8]

But assessing the legitimacy of online information is not a skill we're born with. Rather than using Google primarily as a vehicle for intellectual discovery, we regularly use it to selectively pinpoint information to confirm our preexisting notions about the world.

"We're very, very susceptible to confirmation bias," said Varol Kayhan, an associate professor of information systems and decision sciences at the University of South Florida St. Petersburg, who has studied Google. "Now add the search engine into the picture and it is just increasing the speed at which we access more confirming evidence. So it is not alleviating anything. If it is doing something, it is just increasing and exacerbating it tremendously. So we cannot deny the fact that search engines make the situation worse."[9]

This is particularly acute with conspiracy theories and misleading or blatantly distorted news and opinions that are easily findable through Google. The free extension of professional publishing platforms to ordinary internet users has lent the credibility of visible structure to rumor-propagators and liars, making it increasingly difficult for readers to differentiate between professional media and the crank next door. On Google, highly sensationalized or even fabricated headlines and memes created to mislead are often found alongside authentic news stories from legitimate outlets, allowing the deceptive items to build momentum from a respectable digital perch.

These include, for example, the hurtful and completely inaccurate theory that the 2012 slaughter of twenty-six Newtown, Connecticut, schoolchildren and staff members at Sandy Hook Elementary School was a hoax,[10] or the ridiculous assertion that Hillary Clinton and her campaign manager ran a child sex trafficking ring out of the basement of Washington, DC, pizza restaurant Comet Ping Pong.[11] The latter case turned violent in December 2016 when twenty-eight-year-old Edgar Maddison Welch of Salisbury, North Carolina, traveled to the restaurant to self-investigate the matter and opened fire.[12]

"Conspiracy theories aren't new, but the internet helps them circulate faster than ever before," said Brendan Nyhan, a Dartmouth political scientist who has studied people's perceptions of truth.[13] "The internet also aggregates viral misinformation more effectively than in the past. So in the past, there might have been a dispersed and disaggregated, slow-motion process where people were promoting various kinds of misinformation and conspiracy theories over months or years, haphazardly learning which ones resonated via word of mouth and print media.

"Now the internet lets you see which rumors and misinformation get traction in real time. And these stories can bubble up from the grassroots. There's a kind of Darwinian selection process for the most viral memes, and people like Alex Jones have learned how to harness, how to ride the tiger, and jump on these memes that are emerging from the grassroots," Nyhan said,[14] referring to the right-wing extremist leader of InfoWars who is known for inflaming rumors and mistruths, such as the Sandy Hook conspiracy theory.[15] "Rather than trying to determine themselves which ones are the most effective, often they're identifying and amplifying ones that are already proven to resonate."[16]

For anyone already inclined to believe misleading theories, finding information that seems to back them up is simple. Searchers are heavily biased in favor of results that answer "yes" to their questions, according to Microsoft researcher Ryen White, who has probed the interplay of search engines and people's biases. In White's study, people were two to four times more likely to click on self-affirming results than results that contradicted their preexisting beliefs about a particular topic.[17]

People find what they want to find. As searchers seek self-affirming information, search engines are very efficient at supplying the desired result. White concluded that "search engines strongly favor a particular, usually positive, perspective, irrespective of the truth," possibly because they are "learning from biased, aggregated user behavior."[18] In other words, the searchers' own confirmation biases, exhibited during previous pursuits of information, are driving the technology to deliver skewed results on future searches.

This counterproductive cycle portends serious consequences for users who rely upon search engine results to make life decisions. "Biases in the results provided by the search engine may lead users to incorrect answers; on average people were likely to find the wrong answer half of the time," White concluded.[19]

The disquieting reality is that most people don't seem to care because they're getting what they came for. "Although search results may not reflect the truth, they may reflect the dominant opinions of page authors or searchers, in which case, on average, people may well be satisfied with the answers provided, even if they are strictly inaccurate," White wrote.[20]

As we navigate the web in pursuit of information, we feel more informed and confident in our beliefs, diminishing our grasp of what we do and do not know. Search results that contradict our views are given little consideration. People "may read the disconfirming evidence that completely disagrees with what they are believing or thinking, and then they immediately discredit that. They're saying, 'Oh this is incorrect; I don't believe this. They are making this up,'" Kayhan said. "People immediately discredit what they read if it doesn't agree with their belief system."[21]

Another route by which searchers discard results they dislike is subtler. "People subconsciously ignore it because they know that it is going to challenge their initial beliefs, and they don't want to be cognitively bothered by that," Kayhan said. "They see it in the results, and they may not even click on it."[22]

In other words, we aren't necessarily ensconced in airtight echo chambers. We're simply choosing to deflect or skew information that makes us uncomfortable. This is human nature. We see what we want to see. With politics, it's even worse.

"In politics, you have initial beliefs, and you have your mind set already," Kayhan said. "When you do a search it is more likely that you're going to pick and choose. And then you're going to start blaming or discrediting the pages or links or sources that you think do not agree with you, saying, 'Oh, they're trying to make this person look bad. Oh, they don't know what they're talking about. Oh, this is a conspiracy theory. Oh, this doesn't make any sense.' Either way, it doesn't matter which political side you are. If it is against your beliefs, then you're more likely to selectively choose what you want to read. In your mind, you already know the truth."[23]

RANKING TRUTH

Amid this crisis of misplaced trust, the most sophisticated online actors are finding ways to capitalize by gaming the system, often through entirely legal strategies. This often involves using search engine optimization (SEO) to earn a higher ranking on the search engine results page. "All you have to do is fool Google—because if you can fool Google, you can fool everybody," said Wellesley College computer scientist Panagiotis Takis Metaxas, who has researched the spread of online rumors. "This effort to present themselves as the technology that will have the answer—and you don't have to worry about the way you figure it out—is very dangerous."[24]

Even legitimate sources, such as the mainstream news media, attempt to influence their standing in Google search results. I've done it myself. I've personally attended seminars at my past journalism employers where editors and reporters were given instructions on how to strategically construct headlines, keywords, metadata, photos, and story structure to appease Google's algorithms.

Common tips include using full names in headlines, putting keywords up front, using a certain number of words, deploying key phrases in link text, and linking to our own content. These are all acceptable strategies to Google. Nefarious online actors use more aggressive techniques that Google frowns upon and often seeks to punish, such as hidden text and excessive keywords.[25] But many figure out how to game the system or simply benefit from its shortcomings.

Either way, the upshot is that the more sophisticated you are, the more likely you can beat the system and get your site ranked highly on Google. But this is problematic because it means that sources without the wherewithal to invest in

SEO or other aggressive maneuvers are not able to break out of the clutter. They have little chance of making the first page of Google results.

The stakes are high because the first page matters most. In fact, only the top results on the first page draw much attention. Order dramatically influences engagement and perceived credibility. Only 7 percent of clicks are directed to listings below the fourth item in the average Google mobile results page, according to a study by Canadian digital marketing firm Mediative, which has been tracking search habits for more than a decade.[26]

Put another way, all items below the fourth result—which often number in the millions—collectively have a less than one-in-thirteen chance of getting clicked. This ordering effect is even worse in searches on smartphones, which are increasingly dominant. A world of information is sitting at their fingertips, but Google's mobile searchers click on the second page of results a pitiful one in four hundred times.[27]

"Whoever is ranked first gets the click," Kayhan said. "We know that for sure. But do you know how dangerous that it is? That means Google can set the agenda for us. We can search for something, and then Google decides on the order of the links, the ranking. And then eventually we click on what Google wants us to, and we make a decision accordingly because people do not go past the second or third link."[28]

Recognizing that people don't scroll far, and rarely look to the right side, Google announced in 2016 that it would reorient all of its lucrative text-based ads from the right to the top and bottom of each page.[29] As a result, users must now interact with up to four paid advertisements at the top of the page before reaching what industry observers call the "organic" results—that is, the sites that didn't pay for a higher ranking.[30] In an impatient world where people trust technology without thinking about it, marketers with money to burn are scooping up more traffic and gaining more credibility, while websites that don't pay are less likely to receive attention. It's a classic case of the rich getting richer, as the cliché goes.

When only one paid ad is present on a mobile search, it gets about 14 percent of clicks on the page. But when three paid ads are displayed, one of them gets a click 24 percent of the time. With three ads present, Google searchers will have to scroll to see anything that's not advertising.[31]

But on Google, scrolling is out. Clicking is in.

Americans are lingering on search engine pages less than ever, meaning paid results are receiving a greater share of searchers' attention. In 2006, the average person perused a search engine results page for 2.6 seconds before clicking something or closing the window. By 2016, that figure had dropped in half to 1.3 seconds.[32] So if you can't afford to pay for advertising space or savvy search engine techniques that ensure a high organic ranking on Google, your truth is likely to go unnoticed these days.

Using eye-tracking technology, Mediative also showed how, measured in the aggregate, searchers aren't reading the results page horizontally like they did a decade ago. Instead, our eyes dash down the page vertically, favoring the left side and thus raising the risk that we're absorbing only the first few words of each listing.[33]

One possible explanation for the increased speed is that searchers have become more adept at the process. Our digital muscles are stronger. We know what to look for. In addition, Google has become much better at fetching relevant pages for us, and website managers are placing more keywords at the beginning of their title pages to appease search algorithms.

But there's likely another factor at play: we have invited Google into our lives as a reliable source of memory and wisdom. We trust it to tell us everything from the trivial, such as directions, to the civically critical, such as information about candidates for public office.

Without giving it much thought, society has experienced "this incredible shift in the way we look and think about information," said Alison Head, executive director of Project Information Literacy, a nonprofit research institute, and a senior researcher at Harvard's metaLAB.[34] Yet without an intentional metamorphosis of mentality, we'll continue to seek, find, and circulate misinformation and lies that fit our preconceived notions about the world.

"We haven't made the shift in consciousness from print to digital," said Sam Wineburg, a professor and founder of the Stanford History Education Group, who has studied people's ability to authenticate material online. "We use a set of strategies that were adaptive and useful in one domain, and we import them into a domain in which they are harmful and maladaptive."[35]

That is, we interact with search engines as if trustworthy professionals have already vetted the results—much like journalists vetted information for us in the past. But the authoritative sources that we once relied upon to verify information on our behalf are greatly diminished, distracted, or disinterested.

And in some cases, they've disappeared.

CHAPTER 2

RULE BY METRICS

News is my passion. I've known it from a young age.

From the moment I first got my hands on a copy of *USA Today*'s sports section in middle school, I was hooked. I loved the idea of getting paid to tell other people about what was happening in the world. So I set my sights on a career as a journalist.

I didn't wait long to get started. A few years later, I joined the student newspaper, the *Golden Sting*, at my high school in Saline, Michigan. While still learning the basics of journalism under the tutelage of inspiring English teacher Mike Hill, I read newspapers voraciously. On a given day, it was not uncommon for me to buy print copies of the *New York Times*, *USA Today*, the *Detroit Free Press*, and the *Detroit News*, and read them during breaks at school and my free time. I was a newspaper nerd.

As my junior year was coming to an end in spring 2001, I landed a gig as a part-time staff writer for the community newspaper in my hometown, a city of about nine thousand residents just south of Ann Arbor. Tom Kirvan, the longtime editor of the weekly *Saline Reporter*, gave me the chance to cover high school sports, features, and local news for $7.50 per hour. Aside from me, there were about ten more experienced journalists assigned to write about the community and design the newspaper.

Among my regular assignments was to cover quaint nearby Lodi Township, with its mix of family farms and growing subdivisions. Every month until I graduated from Eastern Michigan University in 2006, I would cover the Lodi Board of Trustees meetings, sifting through a thick packet of government documents and monitoring the public proceedings for news. The trustees would often debate septic system requirements for new homes, zoning rules for the local gravel quarry, and public safety spending.

I had no idea what I was doing when I started. But I learned on the job, and I was proud of the civic duty I played in monitoring Lodi Township issues on behalf of the *Saline Reporter*'s loyal readers. Over time I developed a strong network of sources and came to those meetings well prepared, ready to sit there for hours in my role as a watchdog for residents. Afterward, I would summarize the news in succinct, no-nonsense stories and follow up with additional coverage if necessary.

I knew many residents of Lodi Township on a personal level, and they knew me. I'd like to think they even trusted me to keep an eye on the township for them—to ensure that their tax dollars were being spent appropriately. We had a relationship, even if solely through their recognition of my byline, and it fostered a degree of trust.

Today, the *Saline Reporter* is gone. It was shuttered several years ago, a casualty of local news media's implosion amid the rise of digital forces. No reporters attend those Lodi Township meetings anymore. I'm hoping there's no corruption there these days. There were good people in charge when I was there.

But how would I know there's no corruption? How would you know? There's no one there to keep watch on behalf of the community.

On a local level, the news industry's descent has been agonizingly steep. Coverage of small towns throughout the country has withered, even as journalism in New York and Washington has remained resilient by comparison.

In my home state, the entire news industry has suffered devastating cuts. The company that owned the *Reporter* also closed several other weekly newspapers in recent years, including the *Chelsea Standard*, the *Manchester Enterprise*, the *Dexter Leader*, and the *Milan News-Leader*. The major newspaper in my home county, the *Ann Arbor News*, went from daily print circulation to two papers per week in 2009, laying off dozens of reporters and editors and rebranding itself as *AnnArbor.com*. I worked at *AnnArbor.com* for nearly three years as a reporter and editor, but it, too, later suffered cuts and changed its name back to the *Ann Arbor News*.

Around the same time, owner Advance Publications slashed jobs and print frequency at its other Michigan daily newspapers: the *Grand Rapids Press*, the *Saginaw News*, the *Flint Journal*, the *Bay City Times*, the *Jackson Citizen Patriot*, the *Muskegon Chronicle*, and the *Kalamazoo Gazette*. Today, each of those publications has only a handful of reporters remaining, and much of their original news content is shared.

Consequently, many communities are essentially media-free zones.

"It's cryingly bad at the local level," said Fred Vultee, a journalism professor at Wayne State University in Detroit.[1]

Even Michigan's big-city publications have suffered. The state's two most influential daily newspapers—the *Free Press*, where I worked from 2012 to 2015, and the *Detroit News*—have slashed their print frequency and endured numerous rounds of newsroom cuts, including buyouts and layoffs, to compensate for lost revenue.

Taken together, these cuts are reflective of a crisis that's sweeping the nation. Local journalism faces the threat of extinction.

"IT'S UNTENABLE"

For generations, the news media played a vital role in providing Americans access to the truth about the world around them. In the several decades immediately preceding the internet, a mix of newspapers, magazines, trade publications, radio and television programs, and books supplied the preponderance of news for most people.

During this era, whether they thought about it like this or not, Americans implicitly trusted professional journalists to uncover, decipher, and circulate information on their behalf. News organizations sold the currency of their credibility to consumers who paid for the service of fact authentication and explanation. And advertisers paid for the audience that came with it.

But the internet has destroyed the traditional business model of print media and has gravely undermined the business model of broadcast media. Advertisers no longer need news publications for marketing. And the proliferation of free news online has terminated the need for consumers to fork over money for journalism.

From 2000 through 2015, inflation-adjusted newspaper industry revenue plunged about 64 percent to $29.2 billion, according to the Pew Research Center and News Media Alliance.[2] Nearly all but the finest reporting is now available online for free. Surging digital subscriptions at some of the most prestigious news institutions—including the *Wall Street Journal*, the *Washington Post*, and the *New York Times*—helped slow the pace of the industry's circulation revenue decline in 2016. But most organizations have no reprieve in sight as print revenue and readership plummet.

Total daily newspaper circulation hit a low in 2016 not seen since World War II, when the country was about two-fifths the size it is today.[3] During one particularly rough stretch from 2007 to 2010, which encompassed the Great Recession, nearly 250 US newspapers closed down or shuttered a print edition.[4]

"Parts of the country that used to get covered aren't getting covered, and if they do, it's often by people who don't know the community or the culture," said Nikki Usher, a journalism professor at George Washington University who has studied the media's coastal divide.[5]

Local news companies—and many larger news organizations—are flailing financially because they cannot offer the audience targeting and volume that Google and Facebook can provide by displaying advertisements based on a user's search terms or demographic profile. In 2017, research firm eMarketer projected that Google and Facebook would increase their collective US digital advertising market share to more than 60 percent.[6]

Before the internet pierced the business of news, "there was a model for having smaller publications because you're still trying to get through to a very clear audience," said Matt Hardigree, former executive editor of publishing partnerships at Gizmodo Media Group. "But on the internet there's just a drive to make the audience bigger and bigger and bigger."[7]

Online, the ad rates for content are "so low" that you need millions of unique visitors per month "to make enough money to keep the lights on," Hardigree said. "There's no way you're going to do that with a small, local paper. So what are you supposed to do? It's untenable."[8]

While the major TV networks and cable news companies continue to maintain editorial staff, they too are facing financial pressure that likely will result in their own retrenchment as Americans cancel live TV subscriptions and watch more on-demand content from web sources such as Netflix, Amazon, Hulu, and Google's YouTube.

The news industry's inevitable reaction to its revenue implosion has been to cut costs. From January 2001 through January 2016—the general period spanning the internet's ascent as a dominant force in the lives of ordinary Americans—newspapers slashed 56 percent of their jobs, according to the US Bureau of Labor Statistics. During the same time frame, periodical publishers cut 42 percent, book publishers axed 28 percent, and radio broadcasters eliminated 25 percent. Television fared better, despite a sharp drop in ratings, cutting only 4 percent of its workforce.[9] Virtually all areas of news coverage, with the possible exception of national politics and big-league sports, have been hit hard. Such critical issues as the environment, religion, immigration, business, and state and local politics have substantially fewer reporters covering them.[10]

"All we've been talking about for the last ten years is how our business model has been disrupted, which is tragic," said John Wihbey, who worked as a reporter at the *Star-Ledger* newspaper in Newark, New Jersey, and as a producer for a National Public Radio syndicated show during this period of decline before joining academia, where he now serves as a journalism professor at Northeastern University. "It's probably the case that it was the most rapid decline of any industry in American history, insofar as we lost half of the editorial labor force in about fifteen years. Even if you compare it to the steel industry, the steel industry declined massively, but it was over many decades."[11]

Although online start-ups offer a ray of hope in niche areas, they are typically staffed at much lower levels than traditional news organizations and are not usually focused on local issues. The Pew Research Center estimated in 2014 that the top 468 digital journalism companies in the United States—including Vice, Politico, BuzzFeed, *HuffPost*, Bleacher Report, Mashable, and Business Insider—collectively employed fewer than five thousand journalists.[12] By contrast, newspaper newsrooms had more than sixty-five thousand journalists as of 2008.[13]

Amid the industry's contraction and swift digital transition, readers who rely on print publications for connections to their communities have been left with a major void. In a survey of people whose local newspaper had circulation of fifteen thousand copies or fewer, 59 percent in 2008 said they relied on that publication as their primary source of news about their community. Only 18 percent said their primary source was the internet, friends, relatives, coworkers, word of mouth, or social media. But by fall 2013, the share of people who considered the local newspaper their primary source was down to 42 percent. And the share of people relying on those more informal outlets for community news had nearly doubled to 34 percent. We can only assume that those trends have since continued.[14]

Online-only local news outlets aren't filling the void. Of ninety-four local digital news organizations scattered throughout the country, more than half were losing money in 2014. Two-thirds reported revenue of $100,000 or less.[15] One of them is located in my hometown. In 2013, local journalist Tran Long-moore formed a digital start-up called the *Saline Post* to report on local news, crime, and sports. He has done an admirable job, surviving with a smattering of local advertising support and citizen donations.[16] But like most local digital news start-ups, his resources are limited. As a one-person shop, he can't do it all.

"Advertising, in the long run, isn't going to fund journalism," Longmoore said. "It's going to have to be readers of journalism, like it was in the old days when people subscribed to newspapers."[17]

The demise of local news has serious consequences for democracy. When no one is serving as a watchdog, the truth is easier to conceal or distort. Take Cincinnati, Ohio, as an example. The *Cincinnati Post* closed on December 31, 2007. The publication—owned by E. W. Scripps and run in a joint operating agreement with the more widely circulated *Cincinnati Enquirer*, which is owned by *USA Today* parent company Gannett—was known for highlighting challenges in the city's northern Kentucky suburbs. In fact, the *Post* accounted for 80 percent of the total coverage of those areas. Folks living in Boone, Campbell, and Kenton counties, as well as four other adjacent counties, were especially reliant on the *Post*'s reporting.[18]

In the Cincinnati area's Kentucky towns after the *Post*'s closure, "fewer people voted in elections for city council, city commission, and school board," according to one study. "Fewer candidates sought those seats," and "incumbents' chances of retaining office improved."[19] Although the study's leaders cautioned that they couldn't be certain the *Post*'s closure was to blame, they noted that other research has historically suggested that the presence of local newspapers increases voter turnout and lowers corruption.[20]

A separate analysis of how the decline of local news coverage affects members of Congress showed that citizens are "less likely to recall their representative's name and less able to describe and rate him or her." And members of

Congress "who are less covered by the local press work less for their constituencies," according to the study. They are less likely to show up for congressional hearings, and there's a greater chance they will vote with the party line.[21]

PARTISAN PRESS

The market forces that triggered the news industry's contraction have also prompted changes that have compromised its credibility in the eyes of the public, leading to deteriorating trust in journalists. As those binding molecules of trust are severed, people have gone bobbing for the truth somewhere else, often sinking in murky waters where the facts are abused.

One of the first places where readers and viewers have sought refuge is news with a partisan slant, where loyalty tends to be stronger than for nonpartisan outlets. The explosion of conservative talk radio, most notably through the launch of the right-wing *Rush Limbaugh Show* in the late 1980s, and the formation of media tycoon Rupert Murdoch's Fox News in the late 1990s, which appeals to conservative audiences, are among the most notable examples. Those broadcast sources have had a significant impact on how some people perceive the world. By 2014, 14 percent of Americans—and 47 percent of reliably conservative voters—cited Fox News as their main source of news about government and politics, according to the Pew Research Center.[22]

Meanwhile, the internet lowered the barrier to entry into publishing and broadcasting, paving the way for countless hyper-partisan voices to carve out their own digital niches by slinging ideologically slanted content that aligns with the preexisting worldviews of their target audiences. Willing to traverse territory that mainstream outlets have typically avoided, these biased sources have gained steam among certain politically wired Americans, many of whom believed their perspectives were not adequately represented in the popular press.

To nobody's surprise, "consistent conservatives" trust partisan outlets that repeatedly side with them, including right-wing sources Breitbart News Network, TheBlaze, and the Drudge Report, according to Pew's 2014 survey. Liberals are more likely to trust traditional outlets, such as the *New York Times*, CNN, and CBS, each of which is not trusted by consistent conservatives. But liberals, too, find refuge in online outlets that reliably align with their ideology, lending their trust to left-leaning sources like *Slate* and ThinkProgress.[23]

Unlike the mainstream news media, partisan outlets such as Breitbart—the powerful conservative outlet formerly led by anti-mainstream-media crusader and one-time Trump adviser Steve Bannon—have the luxury of promoting blatantly biased or downright misleading material that is more likely to score clicks and generate social media buzz than to give readers well-rounded perspective. They succeed because they provide much more than news. They provide reassuring access to a community of readers who think like each other, which nonpartisan news outlets don't provide.

But Fox News, Breitbart, and Limbaugh—often cited as the primary perpetrators of misleading right-wing content—are simply the most visible outlets in a vast sea of conservative organizations that are competing for people's attention and loyalty. No fewer than 187 partisan sites popped up during the 2016 presidential election, according to an analysis led by BuzzFeed's Craig Silverman. Most were conservative.[24]

These outlets certainly exert significant influence on how their viewers and readers perceive the world. But it would be a mistake to suggest that partisan media place news consumers in a bubble, or an echo chamber, that shields them from what the rest of the world believes.

When a trio of researchers led by R. Kelly Garrett at Ohio State University set out to study the impact of partisan outlets on people's perception of the facts in the 2012 presidential election, they reached a surprising conclusion. They found no proof that people who regularly peruse partisan online media sources are unaware of facts that contradict their beliefs. Those readers may actually be more aware of disconfirming evidence.[25]

Immersion in partisan media, it turns out, simply gives people the ammunition to portray disconfirming evidence in slanted ways. Consider, for example, one of the most common lies that abounded in conservative political circles for years: the assertion that President Barack Obama was not born in the United States. While ample evidence, including his birth certificate, proved that he was indeed born in the country and thus constitutionally eligible for the presidency,[26] the underhanded falsehood nonetheless reverberated in certain right-wing online sources. Periodic spurts of speculative rhetoric by the likes of Donald Trump and others amplified the lie's reach.

But contrary to conventional wisdom, the Garrett study found that people who had regularly used conservative sites were not less likely to know that mainstream experts had concluded Obama was born in the United States. They knew.[27] Nonetheless, they were much more likely to cling to their inaccurate belief, empowered by a reassuring online community of fellow believers.

Lest we assume this pandemic exclusively affects Republicans, consider an inaccurate belief that was common among Democrats during the 2012 campaign: the perception that GOP candidate Mitt Romney had outsourced jobs while he was working at Bain Capital. Heavy readers of liberal news sites were more likely than occasional readers to realize that fact-checkers had dubbed the Romney claim to be inaccurate. Yet they were more than three times as likely to discard that evidence and cling to their own belief that Romney had indeed outsourced jobs.[28]

Taken together, the study's results demonstrate that partisan media don't necessarily shield people from the facts. They simply give people the rhetorical tools to evade or skew the truth. "Citizens' beliefs can deviate from what they know about the evidence as reported in the media, and this deviation appears to be significantly impacted by their use of ideological websites," the researchers concluded.[29]

THE DRIVE FOR TRAFFIC

As paid circulation and print advertising have imploded and partisan outlets have gained steam, traditional outlets have been desperate to build online audiences to make up for the lost revenue. The rise of 24/7 news culture has challenged the industry's commitment to sober headlines, polished prose, and coverage of mundane issues, while increasing the incentives to choose sensationalism over nuance and immediacy over substance.

Although many professional journalists recognize that the need to constantly feed their news websites and social media accounts with fresh content undermines overall quality, they often feel handcuffed by the demand for new posts as the business thirsts for digital revenue. But the effect of these hasty pursuits on their collective relationship with the reader cannot be ignored.

"The culture of speed is a real problem because it ultimately diminishes the things that really matter for a lot of news organizations—the first being trust," said Usher, the George Washington University journalism professor. "A lot of reporting takes place first and is dispensed over Twitter, which is exactly what journalists have been trained to do for the past [several] years. You get something, you write it up on Twitter, then you write a blog post or write a brief, [and] then you write a longer story. It's tweet first, then think, almost. I think journalists would say, 'We know what we know when we know it, and we're doing it as right as possible at that moment.' And I respect that. But there's a question of, are you moving too fast in a way that discredits the trust you have with people?"[30]

From a practical perspective, the drive for speed and hyperbole comes in part from the rise of new digital metrics tools that have given newsrooms the ability to measure readership instantaneously and tailor content for maximum appeal. One measurement tool that has spread rapidly throughout the industry, invading newsrooms and reorienting coverage decisions, is a service called Chartbeat. Chartbeat, which can be installed on a desktop browser and downloaded to a smartphone, delivers eye-opening real-time readership data.

Journalists can see exact figures detailing how many people are consuming a story at any given moment and how long they are spending on the page. This allows editors to constantly tweak headlines to bolster readership, strategically reposition content to maximize impact, and select specific photos and videos to garner people's attention. As of spring 2017, Chartbeat was in use on more than fifty thousand sites in more than sixty-five countries, including 80 percent of the top news websites in the United States.[31]

"What it's done more than anything is just given journalists and editors data fluency and also enabled them to see graphically the people on the other end of the screen," said John Saroff, CEO of Chartbeat. "In the old days, you wrote an article, you put it up or you put in the paper, and you didn't actually know what people thought of it. And now you know some version of what people thought of it based on Chartbeat."[32]

Journalists can see how long visitors are reading a story before closing the page. Chartbeat calls this scroll depth. The service also tracks the rate at which people click onto another story versus how often they lose interest and venture to a different site. Chartbeat calls this recirculation. And perhaps most importantly, a constantly updated list shows what stories are most popular at any given time.

In general, Chartbeat illustrates how fleetingly people engage with digital content. Readers graze and click but rarely stay for long. Altogether, they spend only twenty-eight seconds consuming an average piece of content across Chartbeat's clients. But 55 percent of pages are viewed for only fifteen seconds or less.[33] That's enough to read a few sentences, at most.

Although the numbers are depressing for newsrooms to absorb, Saroff said Chartbeat can play a productive role in helping journalists better connect with readers. "We still think for writers, editors, and publishers, the reason they got into the business and the reason they wrote their article is to get it read," he explained. "So we think that editorial analytics have a really important part to play. We think they should be at the center of any newsroom's decision-making."[34]

Where this becomes problematic, however, is when access to real-time data motivates journalists to stretch headlines to generate more interest, snuff out the visibility of legitimate content that people should see, or choose not to pursue important stories at all because perceived interest is limited. All of these missteps are common in the industry today.

"There are all sorts of different ways that people use Chartbeat. In some newsrooms, literally our data is the pulse of the whole outfit. And in some places, there still is much, much more old-fashioned intuition—and we're supportive of both," Saroff said. "Ultimately you as the journalist or editor or audience-development executive have to make the decision about what you're going to do with the data. We don't move a story from one place or another on a site. The editor has to do that because we believe that the interaction between humans and technology is absolutely essential to journalism and media being successful. The editors and creators of the content know the users better than we do. We know what the users are doing right now, and we can report that back. But every editor in chief, every CEO, every journalist has someone they're trying to reach, and we try to supplement that judgment rather than replace that judgment."[35]

Cultivating a lasting relationship with readers should be the priority. "To us, the whole publishing business is in some way about loyalty," Saroff said. "When a reader is loyal and they're likely to come back, you don't have to go out and win them again and again and again. Once you've won them, they're more likely to subscribe."[36]

Access to real-time readership data is captivating. I've had access to Chartbeat through my roles as a business reporter at the *Detroit Free Press* and *USA Today*. It's exhilarating to see your stories taking off. But it's also disheartening to see a long-form piece of investigative journalism flop despite thoughtful attention to detail, while some frivolous bit of celebrity news flourishes.

As professional journalists, many of us were trained on news judgment. We were historically taught to give readers a balanced mix of what they need to see and what they want to see. Headlines should accurately capture the essence of the story and not mislead, we were instructed. Stories of little substance should generally be ignored, and stories of greater heft should be pursued—with only a few exceptions. But the industry's financial collapse and the rise of digital metrics have challenged these values.

"These tensions have been there. It's just been easy to ignore them," said Caitlin Petre, a Rutgers University journalism professor who studied newsrooms' handling of traffic data while serving as a research fellow at Columbia University's Tow Center for Digital Journalism. "Now we can't really ignore them anymore."[37]

When given access to raw readership data, journalists cannot look away. We've been told that increasing web traffic is key to our industry's survival. But it's also just human nature to seek an audience. No one wants to be ignored.

"Once you have the metrics to see how many people are reading your story and how long they're reading it for, it's impossible to turn it off and ignore it," said Hardigree, who served as editor in chief of automobile blog *Jalopnik* when it was owned by the now defunct Gawker Media. "Some people say they do. They're lying. Once you taste the apple, there's no turning back. You download Chartbeat to your phone, and that's the end of it."[38]

Hardigree recalled a defining moment in 2013 while leading *Jalopnik*. He was walking the streets of New York, searching for an apartment, and periodically checking Chartbeat to see how the auto blog was performing. At any given moment on a typical day, the site would average about one thousand to two thousand concurrent visitors during his tenure.[39]

"I'm out, and I look down, and there's twelve thousand concurrents— twelve thousand people at any given second reading this one post that was just a video, a YouTube video, with a few paragraphs about these Swedish people developing an invisible bike helmet that you wear with a collar around your neck. If it thinks you're going to crash, it'll inflate a bag so your own personal airbag comes up to protect your head, so you don't have to wear a helmet," Hardigree said.[40]

He quickly consulted with his staff to assess the source of the traffic on the goofy item. Almost all of it was coming from Facebook, where the item had gone viral for some reason. "Then it goes up to fifteen [thousand] and sixteen [thousand] and seventeen thousand concurrents," he said. "This was the most I'd ever seen on a *Jalopnik* post." Ultimately, the item racked up more than six million views, the highest ever on the site to that point. "It made me feel great," Hardigree said.[41]

The challenge that journalists must grapple with is how to responsibly handle access to dynamic readership data. Metrics have clearly demonstrated that emotionally resonant content performs the best. Stories that make people scream are particularly successful. Regrettably, this realization pairs with a bias toward conflict that's already deeply rooted in the traditional news media. Fights sell. Compromise is boring. And good government is less interesting than dysfunction.

Easy access to metrics—including other tools such as Google Analytics, Omniture, and CrowdTangle—has caused many prominent news organizations to embrace emotionally provocative headlines and angles, compromising their credibility and blurring the divide between fact and fiction. Editors and reporters who favor traffic and social engagement over substance are expanding their use of superlatives, hyperbole, and exaggeration.

A 2017 review of one hundred million items posted to Facebook found that the top twelve most common three-word phrases in headlines included "are freaking out," "tears of joy," "make you cry," "give you goosebumps," and "shocked to see."[42]

"It used to fall to the copy desk to say, 'Let's be boring.' There was a lot of institutional pushback against making something seem more exciting than it was. The odds were higher that it was going to be a headline that somebody wrote toward, 'What's the real point?' and with an eye toward being fair," said Vultee, the Wayne State University journalism professor. Naturally, though, following the decline of local journalism and the rise of metrics, "there's less professionalism when there are less professionals."[43]

To be sure, the effect of metrics on news culture is not evenly spread among the entire industry. Like anything, there are responsible actors and bad actors. "You can't look at tools like Google Analytics and Chartbeat and infer just from the tool what the effect in the newsroom is going to be because the same tool can have a really different effect based on the distinct organizational structure and newsroom culture," Petre said. "So in other words, what particular organizations decide to do with metrics depends on factors that are not inherently in the data themselves."[44]

But what many journalists fail to grasp is that not all page views are made alike. A click on a story about the latest Kim Kardashian gossip is less valuable than a click on an enterprise report on the nation's opioid crisis, for example. Credibility matters online.

That's actually good news for anyone who believes journalism is an important element of a healthy democracy. An emphasis on traffic data can coexist with and even boost great journalism, particularly when newsrooms prioritize loyalty and depth. After all, those are the metrics that advertisers prize.

I've personally experienced how in-depth, responsible journalism often thrives online. After three months of reporting, writing, and editing in 2013, my *Free Press* colleague John Gallagher and I published an investigation on Detroit's financial collapse. The special report included gritty historical data and extensive analysis on arcane issues such as pensions, bonds, and healthcare. It was not the type of subject that typically takes off. But the response from readers was incredible.

The story, titled "How Detroit Went Broke," went viral, racking up more than five hundred thousand visitors and setting records for average time spent on a single article.[45] That piece added significantly more value to the news organization than five hundred articles with one thousand views apiece could ever contribute because it bolstered our credibility in the chaotic digital universe, built trust with readers who were craving insight, and established the *Free Press* as the go-to place for coverage of the city's historic bankruptcy.

"We really, really coach our clients to focus on those quality metrics because we think they are key indicators—and oftentimes leading indicators—of how your business model is doing," Saroff said.[46] Unfortunately, this is easy to do in theory but much harder in practice. For starters, with substantially less revenue, there simply isn't enough time or money for many organizations—especially local outlets—to regularly deliver substantive enterprise journalism. But also, as servants to metrics, many news organizations are obsessed with the pursuit of quick hits.

Petre, who personally observed reporters and editors analyzing metrics for her Tow Center report, said it's difficult for journalists to navigate this "emotional roller coaster" of data. "There's these moments of feeling really high . . . where you write something that just is through the roof traffic-wise," she said. "That was, in my research, a very, very powerful experience for people—an addictive high that people wanted to experience as much as they could."[47]

That experience mimics "certain types of addictive games," Petre said. With Chartbeat, "you're actually seeing this dial literally go up and down . . . based [on] how many people are coming to look at your content that exact second," she said. "I think that's one of the reasons Chartbeat has been so successful. They're able to create these features that draw people in and make them feel like they can't look away."[48]

HOW TRUMP RODE THE WAVE

The weakening of local news media, the pervasive spread of partisanship in online sources, the rise of headline culture, and an obsessive focus on socially viral content formed the journalistic foundation for Donald Trump's campaign media strategy.

To be sure, Trump exemplified the qualities that have always left journalists salivating. He generated wild headlines. He delivered consistent conflict. And he provided access to power. That's a proven recipe for coverage—it always has been. There's ample evidence that Trump grasped this long before the internet and 24/7 cable TV news.

"One thing I've learned about the press is that they're always hungry for a good story, and the more sensational, the better. It's in the nature of the job, and I understand that," he wrote in *Trump: The Art of the Deal* in 1987. "The point is that if you are a little different, or a little outrageous, or if you do things that are bold or controversial, the press is going to write about you."[49]

The dawn of the metrics age simply exacerbated the news industry's worst instincts—and Trump capitalized. For years, politicians complained about how journalists were obsessed with incremental news and flashy stories lacking substance. Now it's worse because an obsessive focus on ratings and web traffic shows that people love the frivolous stuff more than we ever realized before.

But Trump didn't fight it. He constantly fed the beast, realizing the tremendous publicity value in spontaneity and drama.

"Their ratings are through the roof," Trump, the former host of NBC reality show *The Apprentice*, declared during an early campaign event in Dallas in a comment that also applies to web metrics. "If they weren't, they wouldn't put me on. I'll be honest with you. It's a simple formula in entertainment and television. If you get good ratings—if you get good ratings, and these aren't good, these are monster—then you'll be on all the time, even if you have nothing to say. If you come up with a cure for a major, major, horrendous disease and if you don't get ratings, they won't bother even reporting it. It's very simple business."[50]

Through early March 2016, which was well into the primary campaign, Trump had garnered the equivalent of $1.898 billion in free media publicity, or more than six times his closest Republican opponent, Senator Ted Cruz of Texas, at $313 million, according to news coverage tracking firm mediaQuant. For the entire campaign, including the general election, Trump received $4.96 billion in free publicity, about 53 percent more than Hillary Clinton's $3.24 billion. In historic terms, the totality of Trump's media coverage was astonishing. He received more than five times as much free publicity as President Obama during his reelection campaign in 2012 and more than seven times the amount that Republican candidate Mitt Romney received in that contest.[51]

"This media firestorm took off almost immediately," said Paul Senatori, chief analytics officer of mediaQuant. "We started to see the number shoot beyond any brand, athlete, or celebrity we had ever tracked for the last four years. We started to see media volume across the board, not just in Twitter, not just in the online segments, but broadcast and global newspapers, US newspapers, regional publications."[52]

Even overseas. "We saw that there was tremendous interest overseas in the Asia-Pacific segment that we track and also all over Europe," Senatori said. "There was no variation on the question of, 'Is this phenomenon hitting all markets?

Is it a phenomenon across the entire media landscape?' And it was. There was no ebb. There was nowhere to hide. Industry trades, wire stories, broadcast, the niche segment. It was all being picked up."[53]

The coverage was unique, as well, because it was often narrowly focused on Trump's latest tweet, his antics at a rally, or the latest bout of drama he had injected on the traditionally predictable campaign trail. Other candidates were not able to ride the wave.

"His coverage tended to be singularly focused on the Trump brand and the person, versus it being about one candidate versus the next, or about issues, which would have rolled in more candidates," Senatori said. "So nobody else could draft off of his coverage, which is unusual. Usually the drafting is a big part of PR and media planning. Find somebody who is driving the headwinds and get behind them, and you can follow on the coverage. That didn't happen. Nobody could jump on the train."[54]

Trump's willingness to grant sweeping access to the media, whether through live TV or phone calls with print reporters, also set him apart from the traditional candidates. He took advantage of one basic tenet of journalism: we can't turn down direct access to elites—especially not elites who are flinging inflammatory rhetoric in a charismatic manner while running for president. In this respect, Trump's freewheeling media strategy paired naturally with the metrics age and contrasted sharply with Clinton's conservative approach of withholding access from the media and avoiding headlines.

Through tweets in which he would constantly misstate the facts, boast inaccurately about his performance, skewer journalists, and deride his opponents, Trump seized on the news media's obsession with anyone who breaks sharply from tradition. After years of reporters complaining about scripted press conferences, boring interviews, and well-choreographed campaign events, Trump delivered jaw-dropping tweets, stunning quotes, and spontaneous theater. His campaign was a political form of improv. And he delivered the goods in digestible, bite-sized portions.

It was a recipe for buzz in the age of metrics.

NO SUCH THING AS BAD PUBLICITY

That penchant for surprise also allowed Trump to capitalize on a more traditional element of the campaign trail—repetition—because the news media, and news consumers, couldn't look away. Despite the many surprises he delivered, Trump was actually consistent in simple ways that resonate online, where it's hard to break through the clutter.

"Strong and wrong beats weak and right," said Aaron Pickrell, a Remington Road Group political consultant who served as a senior adviser to Clinton's campaign in Ohio. "Our campaign didn't operate in that sort of definitive fashion. Secretary Clinton, she was putting forth thought-out policy prescriptions that were more nuanced."[55]

Trump, in contrast, showed how to "find a couple of really potent snippets and constantly beat the drum on those snippets," Pickrell said. "And then you build the narrative around those snippets. It's instructive what the president did. Build the wall, 'make America great again,' repeal NAFTA, bring back manufacturing, bring back coal. Those were the things that he just kept saying over and over. And there wasn't even really any policy built around it."[56]

Repetition, in fact, is a scientifically proven route to building influence, irrespective of accuracy. In a 2011 study, cognitive psychologists Linda Henkel of Fairfield University and Mark Mattson of Fordham University set out to assess the "truth effect"—the theory that people are more likely to believe something is true over time even if they initially understood it to be false. They asked their test subjects to review a set of statements from two different sources, one reliable and the other unreliable. In each source, twenty different statements were listed once, while another twenty statements were repeated three times apiece. In a series of tests, the subjects were later asked to assess the accuracy of the same statements. Across several variations of the same experiment, participants consistently dubbed the repeated statements from the unreliable source to be valid.[57]

"If you repeat something enough, it feels more true," Henkel said. "It increases how easily the information is processed. Cognitive psychologists talk about this processing fluency—when things come to mind easily and readily, they tend to be thought of as being true."[58]

Processing fluency is simply magnified in the headline culture that now characterizes news consumption. With metrics demonstrating that readers obsessively scan headlines and rarely dive deeply into stories, people's capacity to internalize truth and decipher fact from fiction has been severely compromised. In these surface-deep conditions, policy expertise and depth take a back seat to assertiveness, sound bites, and repetition. That's why there is a considerable amount of truth to the old adage that there's no such thing as bad publicity.

In fact, subjects that endure negative publicity often end up benefitting from it. "We've got countless examples of brands that get negative—or what some people consider to be negative—coverage, and they're able to either spin it directly or they don't even need to spin it at all. It puts them in a whole other stratosphere of media awareness that they would not have gotten through classic marketing programs and messaging and outreach," said Senatori, the media-Quant analyst.[59]

Consider the case of retailer Lululemon Athletica. After an embarrassing controversy in which some of its yoga pants were revealed to be see-through, brand awareness of Lululemon skyrocketed. The company had a mediaQuant awareness rating in the thirties, out of a maximum of one hundred, before the controversy. Then "it gets posted on Twitter and goes out on blogs and Facebook," and buzz about Lululemon erupted, Senatori said. That effectively publicized the brand to many shoppers who had never heard about it and reminded others to stop by.[60] Consumer awareness more than doubled into the mid to high seventies on mediaQuant's ranking. "They rode that media exposure for four years," Senatori said.[61]

Although the news coverage might've been unflattering, most people who encountered Lululemon stories didn't dive into the details. In our feverish 24/7 news environment, the actual content of a story is less relevant than the keywords in the headline and the corresponding social media buzz.

"Often the headline is all people are reading, which does make the problem with sensationalism that much worse," said David Berkowitz, chief strategy officer of social media analytics firm Sysomos. "For even a lot of established outlets that try to resort to clickbait tactics, they're not even getting the clicks from it. They're getting the retweet or the like, so more people are going to see it. But if the headline doesn't represent the article, all people are going to see is that headline."[62] Under these conditions, substance is nearly irrelevant. So authority figures can promulgate misleading agendas and draw attention to themselves without paying the consequences of deception and offensiveness—because the system effectively rewards controversial decisions and rhetoric.

During his campaign, Trump repeatedly took advantage of this formula to keep his name in the headlines and drown out substantive discussions of his policy plans or credentials. For instance, he famously and crudely suggested that Fox News debate moderator Megyn Kelly had "blood coming out of her wherever"; alluded to the size of his genitals; argued that a federal judge could not be impartial because of his ethnicity; suggested that Vietnam War veteran, former prisoner of war, and US senator John McCain was not a hero; hinted erroneously that Senator Cruz's father was connected to the assassination of President Kennedy; and labeled Mexican immigrants as "rapists" and criminals.[63]

Trump, whose White House press team did not respond to a request for an interview for this book, has always understood the inherent value of bad publicity. "The funny thing is that even a critical story, which may be hurtful personally, can be very valuable to your business," he wrote in 1987.[64]

Any one of Trump's above statements probably would have been enough to disqualify him from contention in an earlier age. But in the post-fact era, espousing baseless rhetoric allows you to assemble influence and attract an audience, capitalizing on the news media's bias for negativity, ratings, and clicks.

Of the major outlets that covered the nominated candidates in 2016, 71 percent of their output had a negative tone, marking the eighth consecutive presidential contest in which the majority of the coverage was negative, according to an analysis conducted by Thomas E. Patterson of the Harvard Kennedy School's Shorenstein Center on Media, Politics, and Public Policy. During the general election, 77 percent of Trump's coverage was negative, while 64 percent of Clinton's coverage was negative. What's more, the media largely ignored policy issues during the campaign—the type of content that does not generate many hits. Stories focused purely on what side was winning represented 42 percent of the coverage. Coverage of policy issues took up a paltry 10 percent, while stories focused on leadership and experience accounted for only 3 percent.[65]

"In politics, it's the horse race frame—who's up, who's down, who's insulted whom. It's not necessarily about policy. The press in that approach doesn't do itself any favors," said Wihbey, the former journalist turned Northeastern University professor. "What ends up happening is the public becomes more cynical about politics and public affairs."[66]

On political issues aside from elections, the press skews heavily negative, as well. From 2010 through 2016, 87 percent of coverage of Islamic issues, 84 percent of coverage of immigration, 71 percent of coverage of health policy, and 70 percent of coverage of the economy was negative.[67]

"When everything and everybody is portrayed as deeply flawed, there's no sense making distinctions on that score, which works to the advantage of those who are more deeply flawed," Harvard's Patterson wrote. "Civility and sound proposals are no longer the stuff of headlines, which instead give voice to those who are skilled in the art of destruction. The car wreck that was the 2016 election had many drivers. Journalists were not alone in the car, but their fingerprints were all over the wheel."[68]

Still, while it's easy to blame the press for the emphasis on negative content, the harsh reality is that readers want it. Metrics prove it. When *New York* magazine recently used content optimization tool Naytev to test two versions of a headline on the same topic, the results were clear. People were three times more likely to click the negative one than the positive one.[69]

DISTRUSTED

The relationship between metrics-driven journalism and negativity has directly contributed to Americans' declining trust and confidence in the news media. The share of US citizens who trust the media hit an all-time low of 32 percent in 2016, according to Gallup. That was down from 53 percent in 1997, about the time the internet started to make headway in American households.[70]

Another obvious reason for the loss of trust is the demonization of the media by the political class, including Republicans and Democrats at various times and for various reasons. Certainly Trump has taken this strategy to new heights by repeatedly excoriating reporters and questioning their integrity. But efforts to delegitimize media coverage have been commonplace for as long as news has existed. To place all of the blame for the industry's reputational crisis on political criticism ignores the depth of the problem. Also, that type of rhetoric is not going away. So the news industry would benefit from focusing on changing things it can control to counteract the criticism.

One factor that deserves greater attention is the industry's lack of diversity. If the press doesn't reflect the country that it covers, Americans will naturally hesitate to trust the media. In recent years, the industry's contraction has consolidated influence with isolated, white, male, coastal journalists, like myself, whose comprehension of the challenges facing ordinary folks in the heartland—such as police brutality in Ferguson, Missouri, and extreme poverty in rural Appalachia—will never compare with the grasp of local reporters embedded in their communities.

Minorities represented only 17 percent of US newsroom employment in 2016, and women made up only one-third, according to the American Society of News Editors.[71] Although the number of minorities has increased in recent years, it has trailed the pace of diversity growth in the United States.[72] We're falling further behind.

Political diversity is also lacking. In 2008, which culminated in Obama's ascent to the White House, 61 percent of journalism jobs were located in counties Obama won, with 32 percent located in counties where he won by at least 30 points. But by 2016, 72 percent of newspaper and online publishing jobs were located in counties won by Clinton, and 51 percent were located in counties where she won by at least 30 points.[73] In other words, journalism jobs are highly concentrated in America's most liberal areas.

"The criticism that might be valid is whether the media understood the circumstances that caused so many Americans to vote for Donald Trump," *New York Times* editor Dean Baquet told *New York* magazine after the election. "It's always hard to have your finger on the pulse of the country. It's one of those things that we're always beating ourselves up for. We probably didn't quite understand the deep economic fallout after the financial crisis a few years ago. There were fewer national correspondents out in the country, and we're one of the last institutions to have a big national staff. That's probably part of it."[74]

Still, as metrics gain greater sway over news decisions, editors and reporters will find it increasingly difficult to justify covering issues affecting small towns and minority groups—topics that, by definition, often have limited appeal. And if our industry remains captive to the whims of social media, we will fail to reestablish trust with the public, no matter whom we hire or how much revenue we generate.

"It's so hard to sift through and find high-quality content," said Elizabeth Stoycheff, a Wayne State University journalism professor. "There is good reporting that is happening. There are really, really good stories, but they're getting drowned out, unfortunately. Media are no longer serving as the gatekeepers, as the filters of information. We're now getting tweets from Donald Trump himself that are immediately picked up by basically every outlet. So he gets to have his message exactly the way he wants it, without any sort of editing or filtering."[75]

As journalists, we don't even have to actively monitor Twitter to let tweets influence our news coverage. Through a rapidly growing tool called Dataminr, more than 250 news companies receive email and app alerts on viral, newsworthy tweets—often within minutes after they're posted. The company says it "uses proprietary algorithms to instantly analyze" all five hundred million public tweets per day, delivering "the earliest tips to breaking news and pre-trending stories."[76]

Backed by $180 million in capital from blue-chip investors such as Goldman Sachs, Fidelity, and Credit Suisse, Dataminr has clients in many industries, including corporate security, government, and finance. But the company's artificial intelligence has already reshaped how national and international stories are reported.[77]

When I describe Dataminr to people who don't know about it, I give a simple example: if a car bomb goes off in the street outside the café where you're lunching halfway around the world and you proceed to tweet about it, I'll get an email within minutes about your post, even if I've never met you and don't follow you on Twitter. It doesn't matter who you are or how many followers you have. Dataminr's algorithms likely will catch it, presumably by assessing your word choice and how quickly your post is retweeted or liked.

That's incredibly helpful to journalists, and it speeds the flow of information. But it's problematic when newsrooms let viral tweets that generate alerts take the place of their editorial judgment.

As you might have suspected, Donald Trump's provocative tweets almost always generate alerts.

CHAPTER 3

DIGITAL MANIPULATION

For Veerender Jubbal, reliving the November 2015 night that his image was transformed into anti-terrorist propaganda is still traumatizing.

More than a year earlier, the Toronto resident had garnered a sizable following on social media through his role as a grassroots digital activist opposing racism and misogyny in video gaming. Known on social media as GamerGate, the global internet culture war over exclusionary, insensitive, and offensive games and players had been raging for months when Jubbal created a Twitter hashtag to catalyze a movement: #StopGamerGate2014. He was nineteen years old at the time.[1]

"I called out the author of a video game, which was very racist, and I tweeted it out at the publisher specifically—and that's when I definitely started getting an immense amount of death threats and racist comments and harassment," Jubbal said. "I would come home from work, and they would just pile up more and more. That happened for about ten days straight."[2]

Soft-spoken and unassuming, Jubbal exudes a spirit of respectfulness and kindness as a proud member of the Sikh religion, which traces its roots to northern India and emphasizes love of God through peace, racial harmony, generosity, equality, and service. He refers to himself in his Twitter profile as "cute as gosh." His gentle demeanor was even evident in his approach to challenging the creator of the insensitive video game.

"I thought I did it in a very kind and concerted manner," he said. "I just said, 'Hey, hope you're doing well. This box art is racist.' I think I put, 'Have a great day,' as well. But then I had numerous, numerous gamers continually harassing me."[3]

After the mainstream press started to take note of the GamerGate controversy, including a *New York Times* story that mentioned Jubbal's hashtag, the digital harassment directed at him intensified.[4] Although at one point he took a two-month break from social media to let the firestorm subside, he soon continued to engage in the online debate over video game culture because he believed he could make a difference.

"I wanted to do something to be supportive and to try to have some sort of dialogue going with people who were being affected by it. It was women, trans folk, queer folk—POC, in general, such as myself," he said, using an acronym for people of color. "So the hashtag blew up and gave me an audience for that."[5]

In the most wretched moments, Jubbal faced animosity aimed at his religion and ethnicity. But on the November 2015 day that terrorists attacked Paris, using explosives and assault weapons to slaughter innocent people in the name of the violently radicalized Islamic State, the animosity against Jubbal went viral. He was asleep when it started. "I was not feeling well. Sometimes sleep is good for that," he recalled.[6]

With misinformation swirling online about the nature of the Paris attacks, Jubbal woke up around 3:00 a.m. and glanced at his phone. He had received message after message from friends flagging a doctored photo of him that was spreading on social media. He clicked, apprehensively, to see the image. "I knew right then and there it was going to blow up," he said. "I don't know what made me think that so strongly or suddenly."[7]

Using photo-editing software, someone had altered a selfie Jubbal had posted about three months earlier. In the authentic image, he is seen using an iPad to snap a mundane shot of himself smiling innocently at a mirror with a bathtub in the background. But the doctored photo added a suicide bomber's vest to his chest, made his eyebrows sharper, changed the iPad to a Koran, made his head slightly larger, increased the size of his beard, and added a dildo on the ledge of the tub. When Jubbal looked at the photo recently for the first time in many months, he paused briefly as traumatic emotions came flooding back. "It tried to make me into the angry, brown person," he said, "especially because I have a turban."[8]

Although a close look at the photo would have revealed that it was likely altered, the image nonetheless flourished on social media, as users proclaimed without a shred of evidence that it showed one of the Paris terrorist bombers. Within hours, it had spread around the world, as users showered Jubbal with hate through Twitter, Facebook, and other outlets. Jubbal immediately asked his friends to report the accounts that were spreading the false image, and he posted a detailed Twitter thread telling people that the photo was inaccurate.[9] He had never even visited France and wasn't Muslim, let alone an extremist or a terrorist.

"I had family calling in from India that they see this in the news," he said. "Millions and millions of people either saw the picture or they read my name. And even though there were journalists and writers who wrote articles like, 'Hey this is a Photoshop,' even saying this is a Photoshop and being very evident that it is, it still gathered eyes and views."[10]

For weeks afterward, the hoax continued to reverberate online. Then, on Christmas Eve 2015, an anonymous Twitter user threatened to kill Jubbal. "I'm hitting @Veeren_Jubbal," the user said in a since deleted tweet that spelled out Jubbal's exact address in Toronto and included a photo of an assault weapon. "Who's with me?"[11]

Local officers responded by visiting the freelance journalist's home but said there was little they could do to track down the anonymous threat. "The police told me to leave Twitter," he said. So he did for a few weeks. Then he rejoined, hoping to continue his anti-GamerGate campaign.[12] But when terrorists struck Brussels in March 2016,[13] the doctored photo began circulating online again. Jubbal decided he had to move. And this time he indefinitely stopped using Twitter. As of summer 2017, he hadn't reengaged.

"It took me an immense amount of therapy in general just to be able to leave the house," he said. "And whenever I did, I was too recognizable. My face was everywhere."[14]

GET WHAT YOU WANT, NOT WHAT YOU NEED

Before the internet—at least in the post–Vietnam War period—professional journalists were able to shield the public from easy access to misinformation. Rumors such as the doctored photo of Jubbal were typically vetted before being presented to members of the public, who had limited means to rapidly authenticate or circulate misinformation on their own. The tools simply didn't exist.

The pursuit of the truth was placed squarely at the center of any responsible editorial organization's culture. The reader's personal interests were always considered but were not necessarily at the forefront of the decision-making process. To be sure, this old-fashioned culture was not without its flaws, including a lack of diversity that caused news organizations to overlook the plight of women and people of color, for example. But the standard newsroom ethos, for however many times it faltered, was clear: the facts were paramount.

The values underpinning this culture were so central to the core of traditional journalism that they were literally carved into the building that housed the competing *Detroit Free Press*, where I worked from 2012 through 2015, and *Detroit News*. Chiseled into stone panels at the top of the stately structure, which architect Albert Kahn designed for the *News* in 1917, the guiding principles of journalism served as a reminder of our daily purpose: "Mirror of the public mind. Interpreter of the public intent. Troubler of the public conscience. Reflector of every human interest. Friend of every righteous cause. Encourager of every generous act. Bearer of intelligence. Dispeller of ignorance and prejudice. A light shining into all dark places. Promoter of civic welfare and civic pride. Bond of civic unity. Protector of civil rights. Scourge of evil doers. Exposer of secret iniquities. Unrelenting foe of privilege and corruption."[15]

In the age of algorithms, however, the basic journalism principle of putting the truth first has been replaced by a digital doctrine that puts the user experience first. What users want to see takes precedence over what they need to see. This cultural mind-set is pervasive in Silicon Valley, and it's embedded in the algorithms that drive social media such as Facebook and the company's Instagram app.

Two former Facebook executives said this mentality has always guided the social media giant's steps. "It was very, very much driven from the executive team, as well as just part of the culture," said one of the former Facebook executives, both of whom agreed to speak confidentially for this book to openly discuss secret, internal decision-making. The company's attitude was that "we don't want to be playing sides. We always want to lean on what users want to see. It comes from a perspective of wanting to put the users first. We let them dictate their own environment. We don't even call them 'users'—we call them 'people' because we think 'users' implies that they're less personal. The idea that everything is driven off the feedback or the engagement of the user is really central to the company."[16]

Facebook, this person said, was always highly sensitive to any suggestion that it was squelching free speech or "playing big brother." "You've got to remember this is an algorithm that's based on showing people stuff that's engaging," the executive said. "It's simply a company that built a business that's helping people find stuff they care about and surfacing things that are engaging based off the people in their network that they interact with. That's always been the value of the company."[17]

The second former Facebook executive independently echoed this description, saying that a tight embrace of political neutrality is what has historically prevented Facebook from taking proactive steps to block dubious content. "Ultimately the fact that they come back to the user, the user, the user, stymies them from making a call," this person said. "They never say, 'We can decide what is truth or not,' which I actually think is false. We can all decide what is true or not. But they don't want that responsibility, and it's because of the user. They never want to get in between the user and what the user wants. And I think that might be why a lot of the efforts they're making now might not ultimately work."[18]

What users want, Facebook concluded long ago, is to see content that their friends are consuming and sharing. The company's News Feed displays an endless stream of text posts, photos, videos, articles, and other links posted by friends, celebrities, and organizations each user follows. All of this is curated by opaque algorithms that pick out certain items to highlight and other items to downplay. Facebook also injects advertisements, called sponsored posts, into the stream.

"Right now, the way that we rank News Feed for people is we look at what your friends are posting and the pages that you follow, what they're posting, and how many people have engaged with those posts, and try to figure out what are going to be the most interesting things and show those to you first," Facebook CEO and cofounder Mark Zuckerberg told investors in June 2016.[19]

As posts accumulate comments, likes, shares, or other emotional reactions, they're more likely to stand out. So when it comes to news content, friends and family effectively control much of what we see. In this way, the News Feed is one of the most influential services in technology because it exerts sweeping but subtle influence on how we perceive the world around us.

"My sense—and certainly my point of view while I was in it—was, 'Wow, this was a good thing. We're helping people discover more of what they want and interact with it and helping people organize with other people who are like them,'" the first of the former Facebook executives said. "The dark side of that power is it's so powerful that people feel like they found their community and they stay in it. And it's pretty infinite, right? 'I like this stuff more than I like others; therefore, I get one point of view and not others.'"[20]

But Donald Trump's ascent to the White House revealed that even Facebook executives didn't fully grasp the breadth of the company's impact on the world. "I think there are very few people in the entire company who totally understand exactly how the News Feed works at any given moment," the second Facebook executive said. "I call it an ecosystem rather than one algorithm. They have built a little planet, and we and all the other billions of people are growing in it. They make some changes. They have some guesses on how those changes are going to affect the ecosystem, but until it actually happens, they're not entirely sure. Sometimes they'll pull them back right away. Other times they'll pull them back after a while. Other times they'll let them grow because they think it's positive, and they'll have other consequences that come up like three years later. It's extraordinarily complex but really hugely impressive. The scale is immense."[21]

MONETIZING MISINFORMATION

About a decade ago, when social media was still in its infancy and wasn't being actively used to circulate news stories, Filippo Menczer tried his hand at circulating fabricated news stories online. Since Google and Yahoo! were already giving amateur website operators the chance to earn revenue by placing text ads on their pages, the Indiana University computer scientist and informatics professor posited that the financial incentive for fabricating content was in place.[22]

"To show that this would be one form of abuse that could be financially rewarding, I just created a fake website that had some fake news," he said. "These were automatically created with just a natural-language generation tool. You would visit this website, and it would create some fake news, using names of celebrities. Or if you searched for a fake name, it would create fake news using that name."[23]

His experimental site would manufacture "silly reports" like rumors that the subject had been "arrested for drunk driving in Hollywood," Menczer said. "So it was very rudimentary. It was just something as a toy done quickly, and we put some ads there," he recalled. "And then I got a check in the mail."[24]

He had earned an immaterial amount of compensation for deceiving online visitors—an early form of what people, more than a decade later, would call fake news. "So that was proof," Menczer said. "You could monetize misinformation online."[25]

The content creator could glean revenue. But so could the advertising platform—in most cases Google. "The advertiser is winning because they get traffic. The intermediary, Google or the ad network, is getting a cut. There are a lot of people who are gaining in this. So who's losing?" Menczer said. "Everybody else. The public. Their online environment, the web, was being polluted with junk, so it would be harder to find whatever quality information they were looking for because it was now mixed with so much junk. People's time, people's attention would be wasted looking at low-quality content."[26] Worse, they could be deceived into a false frame of mind or even inspired to take misguided action.

But the principles of capitalism are straightforward: if there's money to be made, someone will find a way to make it. That partially explains why misinformation flourished online during the 2016 presidential campaign. The avalanche of attention paid to the election created a fortuitous opportunity for anyone willing to bend the truth to make a buck.

"Google and Facebook enabled and weaponized fake news," said Dartmouth professor Brendan Nyhan, who has researched people's misperceptions. "They created an economic incentive for entrepreneurs to enter that market and mislead people."[27]

In perhaps the highest-profile example, teenagers in Macedonia profited by propagating fake-news stories on sites that were often designed to look like American political news pages. BuzzFeed estimated that people in the Macedonian town of Veles had created at least 140 sites, such as Trump Vision 365 and USA Daily Politics. The sites circulated fake headlines such as "Hillary Clinton in 2013: 'I Would Like to See People Like Donald Trump Run for Office; They're Honest and Can't Be Bought.'" The deceitful ventures generated traffic by distributing headlines through social media posts that occasionally gained momentum or even went viral, hurdling the Facebook algorithm's bar for display in the News Feed. From there, unsuspecting users would click on the links and see advertising that earned some site creators thousands of dollars in compensation.[28]

The Macedonian anecdote, although eye-opening, could incidentally create the false impression that purveyors of fake news are always distant foreign entities. This is wrong. In one case after Trump had taken office, a single Miami-based company, American News LLC, was identified as the owner of left-wing and right-wing sites that distributed bogus headlines on the exact same topics in some cases. "White House FINALLY Gives Kellyanne Conway the Boot, Are You Glad?" the Liberal Society blared in a bogus story about the Trump adviser. "White House Just Gave Conway the Boot, Prepare to Be Infuriated," sister site Conservative 101 declared. Both stories were total falsehoods. But they rang true to many of the seven million fans the two sites had collectively piled up on Facebook by February 2017.[29]

Maryland Republican and Trump voter Cameron Harris was another example of an American slinging fabricated content to cash in. In the weeks leading up to the election, Harris strategically concocted fake stories through a site he created called ChristianTimesNewspaper.com. Harris published headlines such as "BREAKING: 'Tens of Thousands' of Fraudulent Clinton Votes Found in Ohio Warehouse," which quickly went viral along with a photo of a man posing with a ballot box that, Harris falsely wrote, depicted the material's dubious discovery by "a Columbus-area electrical worker." The false story, complete with analysis and fabricated quotes, earned Harris about $5,000 in advertising dividends within a few days. It had taken him fifteen minutes to compose the item, which contributed by the end of the campaign to a total haul of $22,000 from Google ads for his efforts. He used the cash to help pay off loans and rent.[30]

Both Facebook and Google announced after the elections that they would crack down on people's ability to profit from falsified stories by cutting off access to their respective platforms. But Paul Horner, who claimed to be making $10,000 per month on anti-Trump fake news through Google's advertising platform, sounded a skeptical note about whether the sites could actually make headway. "I know ways of getting hooked up under different names and sites," he said after the election. "So probably if they cracked down, I would try different things. I have at least ten sites right now. If they crack down on a couple, I'll just use others."[31]

As long as the possibility for financial gain remains, fabricated content will live on. But it would be a fallacy to suggest that fake news exists exclusively because it can be profitable or that it can be stamped out by squashing its moneymaking potential. Rather, an intent to deceive, persuade, inspire, confuse, divide, or enrage is the key driver for many propagators of bogus content.

PROPAGANDA IN THE DIGITAL AGE

While serving as a communications professor at Elon University, media analytics expert Jonathan Albright conducted a forensic audit of fabricated or highly biased content on 117 hyper-partisan sites that were active during the presidential campaign. Albright, who later became a research director at the Tow Center for Digital Journalism at Columbia, coined the term "micro-propaganda machine" to describe sites that often look alike and regularly spit out versions of the same false information or extremely biased material, generating viral hoaxes and strong emotional reactions. "It's different than mass propaganda," Albright said. "This is a new era of hyper-customization."[32]

In the weeks following the election, he analyzed more than eighty thousand different links from offending sites that specialized in hoaxes, conspiracies, pseudoscience, and outright lies.[33] Some of the sites—all of which had been identified by nonpartisan, third-party sources as perpetuating untrustworthy content—imitated the domain names of traditional news brands. USAPoliticsToday.com sounds like USAToday.com. CNSNews.com is close to CBSNews.com. MSNBC.com.com resembles MSNBC.com. And ABCNews.com.co looks like ABCNews.com.[34]

Albright estimated that 60 percent of the traffic to sites he analyzed came from Facebook or Twitter—and he's skeptical that it can be stopped. "It's a good thing to take away their ability to monetize, but from the get-go for a lot of these sites I don't think that's part of the equation. They're not out to monetize. They're out to actually persuade," he said.[35]

Indeed, the explosion of automated social media activity during the 2016 presidential election points to the likelihood of surreptitious political motivations behind many of these online actors. Automated bots were widely used throughout the campaign to post content in rapid-fire fashion, including targeted political messages, hashtags, links, photos, harassment, and spam.[36]

"Political actors and governments worldwide have begun using bots to manipulate public opinion, choke off debate, and muddy political issues," according to a study of automated social media content during the election by researchers at the Project on Computational Propaganda. "Political bots tend to be developed and deployed in sensitive political moments when public opinion is polarized."[37]

The researchers—Bence Kollanyi of Corvinus University, Philip Howard of Oxford University, and Samuel Woolley of the University of Washington—analyzed about nineteen million tweets with hashtags referencing Trump or Hillary Clinton in the final days leading up to the election. By Election Day, 82 percent of "highly automated" content posted to Twitter was favoring Trump, according to the study. On the whole, this contributed to an overall tilt toward Trump on the social media platform. About 55 percent of election tweets with hashtags favored Trump, compared with 19 percent that favored Clinton. The researchers also found that automated Twitter traffic spiked during key moments in the campaign, such as the debates.[38]

US intelligence officials have blamed a significant portion of these automated posts on Russian efforts to exert influence on and interfere with American politics, including the country's attempt to help Trump get elected. Russia has revived the Soviet Union's tactic of "active measures," a form of political warfare in which disinformation is used to disrupt foreign adversaries, and has given it a digital flair. Former Federal Bureau of Intelligence agent Clint Watts, a fellow at the Foreign Policy Research Institute and George Washington University's Center for Cyber and Homeland Security, said the shift was shrewd and strategic.[39]

"As compared to the analog information wars of the first Cold War, the internet and social media provide Russia cheap, efficient, and highly effective access to foreign audiences with plausible deniability of their influence," he told the US Senate Intelligence Committee in March 2017.[40]

The overhauled Russian disinformation scheme had already taken root by late 2014—long before Trump's campaign—seeking to provoke confusion, dissension, and upheaval. Russian forces spread many rumors, including that the US military had enacted martial law through Jade Helm exercises, that internal chaos had erupted among Black Lives Matter protesters, and that tensions had spiked during a ranch standoff in Oregon. The disrupters "churned out manipulated truths, false news stories, and conspiracies" aimed at tarnishing elected officials, weakening confidence in the US economy and companies, increasing division among individuals, and spreading fears about global crises, according to Watts.[41]

"From these overt Russian propaganda outlets, a wide range of English language conspiratorial websites, some of which mysteriously operate from Eastern Europe and are curiously led by pro-Russian editors of unknown financing, sensationalize conspiracies, and fake news published by white outlets, further amplifying their reach in American audiences," Watts said several months before politicos in Washington started airing grievances over Russia's infiltration of social media to influence the campaign. "American-looking social media accounts . . . and hackers . . . working alongside automated bots further amplify and disseminate Russian propaganda amongst unwitting Westerners. These covert, 'black' operations influence target-audience opinions with regards to Russia and undermine confidence in Western elected leaders, public officials, mainstream-media personalities, academic experts, and democracy itself."[42]

By late 2015, Russian digital forces had focused their attention on the election, seeking to stir opposition to or support for Republican and Democratic candidates based on their positions toward Russia. In some cases, there appeared to be coordination between Russian news media and social media bots. On July 30, 2016, for example, Russian news outlets RT and Sputnik News "simultaneously launched false stories of the US airbase at Incirlik being overrun by terrorists" and "within minutes, pro-Russian social media aggregators and automated bots amplified this false news story and expanded conspiracies asserting American nuclear missiles at the base would be lost to extremists," Watts said. Within fewer than eighty minutes, automated Twitter accounts that the FBI had identified as known proponents of Russian propaganda posted more than four thousand tweets circulating the fake news about the Turkish base, using hashtags such as #Nuclear, #Media, #Trump, and #Benghazi. Many of their user profiles contained keywords such as "God," "military," "Trump," "family," "country," "conservative," "Christian," "America," and "Constitution."[43]

"This pattern of Russian falsehoods and social media manipulation of the American electorate continued through Election Day and persists today," Watts said. And the Russians' targets have transcended partisan boundaries. In March 2017, Russian accounts took aim at US Republican Speaker of the House Paul Ryan, "hoping to foment further unrest amongst US democratic institutions, their leaders, and their constituents."[44]

At Facebook, the trending-news curators, who were eventually fired and replaced by poor-performing algorithms, had a close-up view of suspicious activity on the platform. "There were so many people gaming the system, especially internationally. If you worked the US, around 2:00 or 3:00 a.m. almost every night there would be this bombardment," said Benjamin Fearnow, one of the former curators. "And then you'd go into the tool and see they had gamed it. There were so many groups with fake bots that had just shared . . . the story that it would show up to us because it had enough pulse."[45]

Foreign forces—namely, the subversive Russian actors—sowed distrust on Facebook using several techniques. Their strategies ranged widely but relied heavily on the creation of bogus accounts they used to pepper the site with seemingly authentic content. That gave the appearance of a grassroots uprising, a plot known as astroturfing.[46]

"So you create some fake accounts, and you create a page on Facebook in which you claim whatever you want to claim or want to promote," said computer scientist Panagiotis Takis Metaxas, the Wellesley College professor and expert on how fabricated content spreads on social media. "Then you have these accounts penetrate a particular community and befriend, let's say, people who are supporting Bernie against Hillary or people who are supporting Trump or the other Republican candidates. In the beginning, they have these accounts be part of the conversation. Once you find yourself in this environment, then you start posting your fake rumors and you just relax and watch people as they get upset and they start sharing what you had just said."[47]

The rumors don't even have to be fake. One practical example of how Russian forces stirred dissension was their apparent role in a digital campaign dubbed Don't Shoot Us. The Russians ran Facebook, YouTube, Twitter, Tumblr, and Instagram accounts under the premise of Don't Shoot Us, posting videos and messages about police brutality to promote disunity, according to a CNN investigation.[48] In doing so, they successfully divided Americans by leveraging the ricochet effect of viral videos, messages, and photos on social media.

"All you need to do, essentially, is find a community that has upset members, angry members who would be willing to agree with your message. And then once you become part of this community, you just spread fake news, and then you let them do the work. You let the community get even more angry in their own echo chamber," Metaxas said.[49]

Facebook publicly admitted in an April 2017 report that "malicious actors" had created "inauthentic accounts" during the presidential campaign to spread false rumors, distorted material, and fabricated news, though the company denied that automated accounts had played a significant role in the outcome of the election.[50] "We have observed that most false amplification in the context of information operations is not driven by automated processes, but by coordinated people who are dedicated to operating inauthentic accounts," the company said in the report, acknowledging that it had been used to spread distrust. "We have observed many actions by fake-account operators that could only be performed by people with language skills and a basic knowledge of the political situation in the target countries, suggesting a higher level of coordination and forethought. Some of the lower-skilled actors may even provide content guidance and outlines to their false amplifiers, which can give the impression of automation."[51]

The company downplayed the impact of foreign operations as "statistically small," saying the "reach of the content shared by false amplifiers was marginal compared to the overall volume of civic content shared during the US election." But it admitted in the April 2017 report that "our data does not contradict"[52] the US intelligence community's conclusion that Russia had used social media—including paid "professional trolls"—to promote Trump during the presidential election.[53]

Several months later, Facebook was forced to admit that Russia's disinformation campaign on its platform was actually much broader than it had previously disclosed. The company estimated in early November 2017 that 146 million American users on Facebook and its Instagram app had been exposed to the influence campaign linked to the Kremlin.[54]

In addition to the organic, or free, posts that the Russians generated surreptitiously, Russian actors also purchased US political ads on the sites, reaching millions of Americans with divisive messages on topics such as LGBTQ rights, race, immigration, and guns.[55] Instead of a pay to play scheme, it was pay to deceive. And Facebook said it had no clue about the ads at the time—in part because not a single ad was purchased by actually talking to one of the company's employees. Instead, the Russians circumvented human oversight by placing their ad orders through Facebook's "self-service" platform.

The Russian meddling forced Facebook to acknowledge that its "ad targeting can be abused," and the company pledged to "aim to prevent abusive ads from running on our platform" by "tightening restrictions on advertiser content."[56] The company announced that it would publicly disclose the Facebook pages of ad buyers, require US election ad buyers to submit "more thorough documentation," and "confirm the business or organization they represent before they can buy ads."[57]

Mark Zuckerberg pledged to add ten thousand employees by late 2018 "to better enforce our community standards and review ads" as the company at least doubles its engineering spending on security. "I am dead serious about this," he told investors in early November 2017, even saying that the moves would "significantly impact our profitability going forward."[58]

Those measures will help. But with revenue of nearly $27 billion in 2016—and rising quickly—there are simply too many ads for humans or automation to catch everything, according to experts.[59]

Facebook also has a significant incentive to let most political ads continue flowing. It's big business. The company has long understood this, even bragging to its investors about the political spending on the site. "We are pleased by what's happened on Facebook for the elections—for the election cycle, not just on the pay side but actually on the organic side as well," Sheryl Sandberg, Facebook's chief operating officer, told investors in July 2016, about four months before Trump won. "We really see Facebook being embraced by politicians all over the world to get in touch with their constituents."[60]

Those comments were made before the company came under fire for fake news and Russian interference. But even after those disclosures and the changes it promised to make, Facebook still refused to completely stop foreign actors from placing US political ads, including certain nonprofits with global interests.[61] Consequently, it is not difficult to imagine the Russians using seemingly reputable, third-party groups to continue advertising on Facebook in the future to dodge the company's new, more restrictive parameters.

"The right to speak out on global issues that cross borders is an important principle," Elliot Schrage, Facebook's vice president of policy and communications, said in a blog post. "While we may not always agree with the positions of those who would speak on issues here, we believe in their right to do so—just as we believe in the right of Americans to express opinions on issues in other countries."[62]

"THIS IS BIG, BIG MONEY"

It makes sense that foreign actors seeking to sow chaos targeted Facebook because the platform's design and fundamental digital character are fertile ground for the cultivation of deceit.

"On Facebook, whenever you write something, it gets some prime real estate," Metaxas said. "It gets a big box, it gets a picture, [and] it gets some larger text as a title. It gets some subtext underneath that. Anybody who looks at this and wants to disagree can only write a comment, and the comment will be smaller font underneath. And the moment somebody else writes a comment, and somebody else writes a comment, it's been buried. So the interface of Facebook is such that essentially any debunking or any disagreement of any claim is disappearing."[63]

It's good that Facebook is trying to crack down on bogus and disreputable content. But the company's addictive appeal and financial success remains predicated on putting friends in charge of their friends' content consumption via faceless algorithms. So if your friends want to share terribly skewed perspectives on the news, that's what you'll see in your feed. The only way this will change is if Facebook revises its algorithms to largely prevent users from seeing what their friends have shared or drastically limits the sources of content that can be posted to the site—both of which are highly unlikely.

"This is big, big money, and it's tied into their business model," Albright said. "You have to realize that the internet is monetized on attention, and the more engagement they get, the more their company is worth."[64]

That reliance on engagement for profits is savvy because it capitalizes on a phenomenon that sociologists have historically called homophily, which describes the tendency of people to congregate with others who are like them. This concept was developed to describe our offline lives, but it's also applicable to our online circles.

In our social lives before the internet, sharing a political news story was possible only by physically clipping it and sending it to someone or verbally discussing it with a few people. But today we can instantly share content with hundreds or thousands of friends, family, and strangers.

"People are more likely to be exposed to information that is homogenous, that is not so diverse—or at least information that comes from sources that are not as diverse," Menczer said. "All platforms have this kind of bias. And they also have a popularity bias where you're more likely to be exposed to things that other people like a lot."[65]

The more we like it, the more we share it. The more we share it, the more it shows up in other people's feeds. As this cycle continues, we spend more and more time on the platform, which racks up more profits for the host.

"That's how they make money," Menczer said. "All the algorithms that are used to decide what you see and what you don't are carefully trained and constantly optimized to maximize the time that you stay online, the number of things you click, that you like, that you retweet, that you share. Those are all metrics of engagement."[66] Engagement is a function of our own likes and the interests of the people we like, regardless of whether those interests align with what we really need to know about the world.

"That role that used to be played by editors in making that decision—now that role is being taken by your friends who share something. They don't share it because they think this is important news you should see. They share it because they think it's engaging and interesting and fun. So we are substituting engagement for accuracy," Menczer said.[67]

To test how social media exacerbates the effects of homophily, Menczer created a digital model that simulates networking dynamics. The model assumes that people will occasionally encounter information on social media that they don't like and that once in a while they will unfriend the person who posted the offending material. Over time, the user's circle of friends narrows into a community of people who are more like them, according to Menczer's model. "The outcome is always the same," he said. "Our model predicts it, and it is inescapable. These are the basic ingredients of every social media system out there."[68]

When fabricated, highly distorted, or sensationalized political content enters the mix, it accelerates the disintegration of social bonds between people who previously had some common ground and distances them from people they disagree with. Yet divisive content is almost guaranteed to thrive on social media, despite the dissension it inexorably stirs up, because it is specifically tailored to be engaging. Menczer said,

> If I'm generating content and I want it to go viral, then I can design it in such a way that it's more likely to be viral. If I already know that there is a population of people out there who are super conservative, and they hate Obama, and they are angry about Obama, then I can just make something up about Obama that depicts him in a negative light, and people will believe it and get angry. Likewise, if I know there are a bunch of people who hate Trump, and they are upset and angry and worried and concerned, then I can say just about anything about Trump and they will believe it as long as it depicts him in a bad light. So given that we know that these populations exist, it is not difficult to design, to engineer a message that leverages those preexisting ideas.[69]

This was clearly on display during the election. Still, to lay the responsibility for bogus content's proliferation solely at the feet of social media would ignore its broad footprint. In fact, one old-fashioned tool that was largely overlooked in the post-election coverage of fake news was email. The influence of email newsletters run by fake or hyper-partisan sites remains significant.

Albright concluded that about 40 percent of the traffic to those sites during the election came through direct links, which included newsletters, text or instant messaging, and direct site visits. Many of the sites he analyzed pushed email newsletters through aggressive measures, such as pop-up boxes that forced the user into action. "Email still works. People use email, and you can see this through some of the referrals of traffic to these sites," Albright said. "It's important not to overlook these types of connections that people are making to targeted audiences. In some workplaces, Facebook is not okay, but email's a different story. It's still important."[70]

SWAYING THE ELECTION

Whether fabricated, distorted, or sensationalized content swayed the outcome of the election is impossible to say conclusively. But Menczer said the financial gains for the purveyors of bogus content and the emotional responses provoked by foreign actors collectively point to a substantive impact:

> Given how close our elections have been recently, decided by just a small number of states with a relatively small margin, you don't really have to influence millions of people to affect an election. You just have to get a few thousand people more to vote on one side or a few thousand people less to vote on the other side, and that's it. Given the fact that there are hundreds of millions of people who literally access their media mainly through social networks like Facebook, then there is a very large population of people who are exposed to this stuff.... I think we cannot rule out that there might have been an influence on the election.[71]

Shortly after the election, if not before, many social media users began to realize there was a problem. In a Pew Research Center survey in December 2016, 14 percent of Americans admitted to sharing a story they knew was fake, while another 16 percent acknowledged sharing a story they had later discovered was false. Nearly nine in ten Americans agreed that fabricated content had caused "a great deal of" or "some" confusion.[72]

Although he later figured it out, Mark Zuckerberg was originally not among them. "To think it influenced the election in any way is a pretty crazy idea," Zuckerberg said two days after the election, adding, "I do think there is a certain profound lack of empathy in asserting that the only reason someone could have voted the way they did is they saw some fake news. If you believe that, then I don't think you have internalized the message the Trump supporters are trying to send in this election."[73]

It should not come as a surprise that Zuckerberg's immediate reaction after the election was dismissive of the possibility that his platform had inadvertently stoked political chaos through misinformation, posing serious consequences for democracy. In fact, whenever they were challenged on this issue during the presidential campaign, Facebook executives would often cite an internal study that they believed proved the platform actually exerted a productive effect on people's perceptions about ideological issues. In 2015, one of the tech giant's own researchers had led a study on the site's effect on people's exposure to views they reject. While the study concluded that Facebook did slightly reduce the amount of "cross-cutting" information people were exposed to, it laid the responsibility primarily on the user, not its own algorithms.[74]

"We conclusively establish that on average in the context of Facebook, individual choices more than algorithms limit exposure to attitude-challenging content," the researchers concluded. "Despite the differences in what individuals consume across ideological lines, our work suggests that individuals are exposed to more cross-cutting discourse in social media [than] they would be under the digital reality envisioned by some. Rather than people browsing only ideologically aligned news sources or opting out of hard news altogether, our work shows that social media exposes individuals to at least some ideologically cross-cutting viewpoints."[75]

That study provided the basis for Facebook's defensive stance on the role it plays—or doesn't play—in exposing users to alternative perspectives for the sake of a healthy democracy. The company's top executives clung tightly to its findings.

"This is something we care a great deal about, and what happens is that Facebook actually, in many ways, broadens the kind of news you hear," Facebook's Sandberg told shareholders in a conference call in June 2016. "What Facebook does is let us hear from more people on a daily basis. What you might call your weaker ties, the people you went to school with, the people not in your current company but your last job, the people who used to be in your hometown. And so what you get are just more ability to keep in touch with more people. And over time, we believe more diverse viewpoints."[76]

But the Facebook study seemingly backing up Sandberg's assertion had come under fire in the days following its publication. One critic called it "Facebook's 'It's Not Our Fault' Study," assailing the attempt to imply that users can escape the effects of Facebook's algorithm at all.[77] Several critics impugned the legitimacy of the results by pointing out that the study relied upon a sample of Facebook users who specifically identified their political ideology in clear terms on their accounts. That cohort represented only about 4 percent of the entire user base.[78]

Another critic said the study was emblematic of Facebook's tendency to hide its head in the sand. "To ignore these ways the site is structured and to instead be seen as a neutral platform means to not have responsibility, to offload the blame for what users see or don't see [onto] the users," wrote Nathan Jurgenson, a sociologist for Facebook rival Snapchat.[79]

As Jurgenson suggested, Facebook's decision to hand the keys of its News Feed over to human-designed algorithms that champion engagement over substance, depth, and truth was a choice. And that choice padded the bottom line. But in making that choice, the company failed to recognize the human tendency to fall prey to deception—a tendency embedded in the fundamental elasticity of our memory.

THE SLEEPER EFFECT

In a 1950s study, Yale psychologist Carl Hovland showed how people consistently fall for false information. Even when his study participants initially understood material they encountered to be inaccurate, they later forgot that they had once rejected the information in the first place. "The subjects tended to disassociate the content and the source with the result that the original scepticism faded and the 'untrustworthy' material was accepted," the researchers concluded.[80]

This tendency to forget the initial source but remember the actual information is what psychologists call the sleeper effect. False information has a way of staking a claim to our memory, even when we want to forget it. We'll remember that we heard something but not where we heard it.

"People don't pay that much attention to the source, and even when they do, our memory system doesn't work so that we typically retain information about the source," said Fairfield University cognitive psychologist Linda Henkel, who has studied memory issues. "Things that are very fluent, that are easy, that come to mind—we just think they're true."[81]

Although social media users may initially discount a doctored photo of Veerender Jubbal as unreliable, over time they are more likely to believe it was authentic all along. And they may even share it with their friends, where it will inevitably take off because it provokes the type of emotional response that social media favors.

"Lies, in fact," Hovland concluded, seem "to be remembered better than truths."[82]

PART 2

DISCONNECTED

CHAPTER 4

DIVIDING AND DENYING

The science was irrelevant to Bob Inglis.

When the Republican politician was serving his first stint in Congress in the middle to late 1990s, he didn't lend any credence to the widespread scientific consensus that greenhouse gas emissions were warming the earth, contributing to extreme weather, and threatening to flood coastal areas, undermine biodiversity, and jeopardize crops.

"I said that climate change was nonsense for my first six years in Congress," the lifelong conservative and devout Christian recalled. "I didn't know anything except that Al Gore was [active on] it—and that was enough because I represented the reddest district in the reddest state in the nation: Greenville–Spartanburg, South Carolina. I mean, there may be somebody in Idaho or Texas that could fight me for that distinction, but Greenville–Spartanburg is a pretty conservative place."[1]

Inglis served three terms, dutifully casting vote after vote along party lines to validate his ideological credentials before relinquishing his post following an unsuccessful bid for the Senate in 1998. Then before he recaptured his congressional seat in the 2004 election, the oldest of his five children, his then eighteen-year-old son, came to him with a concern. "Dad," his son told him, "I'll vote for you, but you're going to clean up your act on the environment."[2]

That conversation began to stir Inglis to change. Then, during a trip to Antarctica with a House committee, he witnessed first-hand evidence of climate change causing polar ice to melt. It was getting increasingly difficult for him to deny the facts. But it wasn't until a committee trip to Australia, where he snorkeled at the Great Barrier Reef with Aussie climate scientist and fellow Christian Scott Heron, that his perspective went through a transformation.

"I could tell, as he was showing me the wonders of the reef, that he was worshipping God and that we shared a worldview without any words being spoken," Inglis said. "I could see it in his eyes, I could hear it in his voice, [and] I could see it all over his face that he was excited about God's creation and was sharing it with me in a worshipful way."[3]

Later, Heron told Inglis about how he lived out his faith. "He told me about conservation changes that he was making in his life in order to love God and love people. He rides his bike to work, he hangs his family's clothes out on the clothesline, he tries not to use the dryer, [and] he tries to do without air-conditioning in Townsville, Australia, which is a pretty hard thing to do," Inglis said, marveling at Heron's personal sacrifice in blistering heat to lower his carbon footprint. "He does all of these things in order to consciously love people who come after us. So I got really inspired by that. I wanted to be like Scott, loving God and loving people."[4]

Inglis was finally convinced that climate change was real and had to be stopped. So when he returned to Washington, DC, after the trip to Australia, Inglis introduced the Raise Wages, Cut Carbon Act of 2009, a proposal to lower Social Security payroll taxes and implement a new tax on carbon emissions. It was a revenue-neutral plan designed to appeal to both political parties.[5] But it fell on deaf ears.

"My timing wasn't really good in terms of politics," Inglis said. "With the Great Recession coming on and the Tea Party happening, it didn't go well for me."[6]

Fellow Republicans—most importantly, conservatives in his home district—were outraged. "I committed some other heresies, too," Inglis acknowledged. He had backed immigration reform, voted for the bank bailout package, and opposed President George W. Bush's troop surge in Iraq. One day, not long after President Obama took office, Inglis faced a loyalty test before his constituents at a campaign breakfast event in South Carolina.[7]

"A guy stands up. He's so angry. He says to me, 'The president is so unpatriotic [that] he doesn't put his hand over his heart when the Pledge of Allegiance is recited or the national anthem is played.' Then he just sat down in total disgust," Inglis recalled.[8]

Until that point, the Republican congressman had refused to join the chorus of personal animosity directed at the nation's first black president, much of it tinged with racial overtones. As he calculated an appropriate response, Inglis realized he had an opportunity to take the politically expedient route. "'What do you expect from a secret Muslim, non-American socialist?' would have done just fine at that moment. The whole crowd would have been reassured 'Bob's with us,'" he said. "But I'm standing there thinking, 'Can't do it. Won't do it.'"[9]

Instead, he defended Obama. "You know, I've been with the president," Inglis told the disgusted voter. "I have seen him put his hand over his heart. What you've just said is simply not true. The president is a loyal, patriotic American who loves his country, loves his wife, loves his kids. I just disagree with him on most everything."[10]

Even that offense might have been pardonable in the eyes of his supporters. "But my most enduring heresy was saying that climate change is real and let's do something about it," he said. "It appeared to the wonderful conservatives that I represented that I had left the tribe, that I had been untrue to the tribe, that I had gone over and started marching with Al Gore and people like that—that I was no longer to be trusted."[11]

Inglis was voted out of office in the next Republican primary.

THE POLARIZATION OF SCIENCE

During the Cold War, Americans viewed science as crucial to combating the Soviet Union. Trust in science in its many forms propelled Americans to the moon, enabled transformative medical treatments, and led to the creation of the internet. Fueled by the government and the private sector, these types of advancements strengthened the country's economy, military, and culture. Quality of life soared.

Without trust in the capabilities of science, the United States could have fallen behind the Soviets. This was widely understood during the Cold War.

Trust in science even transcended political boundaries during that period. In 1974, conservatives, in fact, were slightly more likely than liberals to trust in science, according to national survey data analyzed by University of North Carolina at Chapel Hill sociologist Gordon Gauchat in a widely cited study on the evolution of attitudes toward science from 1974 through 2010.[12]

The general consensus on the necessary role of science in public affairs extended to political opinions on the need to protect the environment. From 1974 through 1991, the period leading up to the Soviet Union's collapse, there was "no partisan or ideological polarization or increasing divergence over time" in Americans' opinions on government spending to protect the environment, according to a separate analysis led by Michigan State University sociologist Aaron McCright.[13]

This began to change around the time that Soviet communism imploded. From 1993 to 2012, views on the environment split along political boundaries, as conservatives became more likely to deny that climate change was occurring, while liberals became more committed to environmental protection policies. That finding aligns with a "clear pattern of political polarization on a range of social, economic, and cultural issues" that developed during this time period, McCright and his fellow researchers found.[14]

McCright does not believe that the timing of increasing polarization on scientific issues following the Cold War's conclusion is coincidental. "You have this huge vacuum, where there's no more boogeyman," he said. "There's no more enemy, no more evil empire."[15] It was around this time that certain conservative think tanks, partisan media, Republican politicians, energy companies, and right-wing public relations professionals began impugning the political motives of governmental regulators who championed scientific solutions to public problems.

That anti-climate sentiment was widely visible in conservative materials, including publications such as the *National Review*, that were popular among influential Republicans during the 1990s, said McCright, who conducted a content analysis of "movement magazines" from a period of several decades.[16] Seeking to divide, conservative leaders would label climate activists with communist rhetoric.

"They started calling them 'watermelons—green on the outside, but they're really red on the inside,'" he said. "It's largely because they see this threat of global environmental concern as leading to major international regulations that will usurp US sovereignty and cause our economy to be controlled by extra-state actors who are telling us what sort of fuels we can use, what sort of cars we can drive. So it was sort of pre-ordained that the conservative movement would look at environmentalism, especially these new global environmental problems, as the next big boogeyman."[17] This newly oppositional attitude built upon President Ronald Reagan's anti-government policies and rhetoric, which undermined the public's general consensus that the Environmental Protection Agency, created a decade earlier by Republican president Richard Nixon, should play a proactive role in shielding Americans from pollution and other environmental threats.

As conservative ideology crystallized around the Reagan philosophy during the polarizing two-term administrations of Democratic president Bill Clinton and Republican president George W. Bush, a form of anti-regulatory religion came to define the conservative platform, particularly on energy and environmental issues. When Gore, following his defeat in the 2000 presidential election, took up the mantle of fighting for action on climate change, culminating in his 2006 documentary An Inconvenient Truth, views on the matter hardened further along ideological lines. By the time Obama tried to fight climate change by cracking down on emissions from coal-fired power plants and backing a global accord in Paris on carbon reductions, Republican opposition was already entrenched.

Indeed, the transfer of political philosophy on environmental regulation from the nonpartisan column into a rigidly ideological category was swift from a historical perspective. In 1997, party beliefs on climate change were barely distinguishable, with 52 percent of Democrats and 48 percent of Republicans agreeing that global warming had exerted effects on the environment.[18] Just ten years later, however, that gap had ballooned. Some 70 percent of Democrats agreed, while only 46 percent of Republicans said the same, even though climate change had actually worsened during that period.[19]

On the question of whether most scientists believe global warming is happening, 82 percent of Democrats agreed in 2016, while only 47 percent of Republicans responded affirmatively.[20] What's more, Republicans were about five times more likely to say that the gravity of the threat was exaggerated in news reports.[21]

One explanation for the suddenly ideological nature of climate change is the willingness of many Republican politicians, talk show hosts, and writers to openly question the widely accepted scientific consensus on climate change.

Their strategy has typically involved highlighting fringe studies that appear to cast doubt on the consensus among 97 percent of climate scientists that humans are, in fact, causing climate change.[22]

"The Earth is no longer warming and has not. For about the past thirteen years, it has begun to cool," Representative Marsha Blackburn, a Republican from Tennessee, said in 2016, in one of many similarly incorrect claims by climate-change-denying conservatives. "It's not a settled science. There's a debate in that arena. There are those who say, 'It has cooled, it has leveled off,'" while others say, "'It's still warming.' The point being, there again it's not something that you'd say is a settled science."[23]

Activist groups and energy companies—often working in concert—have also played a key role in sowing doubt, promoting lies, and fighting action on climate change. For example, the Heartland Institute in 2017 sent a book dubiously titled *Why Scientists Disagree about Global Warming* to teachers throughout the country. "I am writing to ask you to consider the possibility that the science in fact is not 'settled,'" Heartland Institute Center for Transforming Education manager Lennie Jarratt wrote in a letter accompanying the materials. "If that's the case, then students would be better served by letting them know a vibrant debate is taking place among scientists on how big the human impact on climate is, and whether or not we should be worried about it."[24]

Certain fossil-fuel companies for years quietly backed groups that publicly challenged the scientific consensus. Exxon Mobil, for example, funded the Heartland Institute and other groups that long questioned climate change before publicly proclaiming in 2009 that it would sever all such remaining ties.[25]

The Union of Concerned Scientists compared Exxon's campaign to thwart a public consensus on climate change science and policy to the tobacco industry's decades-long effort to mislead the public about smoking's damaging health effects. "The two disinformation campaigns are strikingly similar," the liberal organization said in a 2007 report, describing Exxon as having challenged scientific findings on the effects of fossil fuels, funded "front organizations" to distribute bogus information, backed misleading characterizations of peer-reviewed studies, and leveraged political connections to block climate change action policies.[26]

By 2017, 66 percent of Democrats were worried "a great deal" about climate change, while only 18 percent of Republicans felt the same way, according to

Gallup.[27] Considered in sum, these trends show how one's belief or disbelief in the science of climate change has morphed into a test of ideological purity. But that's a big change. Gauchat, whose study tracked trust in science from 1974 through 2010, concluded that conservatives "begin the period with the highest levels of trust and end with the lowest."[28]

THE THREAT OF MOTIVATED REASONING

The Right's politically tinged view of climate change facts is but one symptom of the broader ideological wave that has swept through the United States during the past several decades, driven in part by extremely divisive political events, such as Clinton's sex-and-perjury scandal and Bush's Iraq War. When ideology takes precedent over science, people extend trust to like-minded politicians, media, and friends who are prone to manipulating the facts to maintain power and exert influence.

Following that transfer of trust, facts are only considered for acceptance if they are unobjectionable within our preferred ideological framework. But political ideology is far more than an uncompromising commitment to a set of shared beliefs. It also serves as a catalyst for social division. That is, in an intensely polarized environment, politics is increasingly likely to determine our personal identity, not just our opinions.

With climate change, for example, personal hostility toward environmentalists is more likely than policy disagreements to drive conservatives' polarized views on the issue, according to a study by psychologist and prejudice expert Gordon Hodson and researcher Mark Romeo Hoffarth of Canada's Brock University.[29] In other words, if you hate the other side, you're susceptible to rejecting whatever your opponents have to say, even if there's obvious validity to their arguments.

On this issue and many other political matters, Americans are increasingly disgusted with each other on a personal level. That disgust breeds distrust and clouds our judgment, restricting our ability to assess the truth. As animosity creeps in, ideological segregation grows increasingly rigid. Political scientists call this disquieting trend "affective partisan polarization."

One practical factor driving the division is the gerrymandering process, which allows party leaders to bolster partisan incumbents by drawing politically lopsided legislative and congressional districts throughout the country. The redistricting practice insulates politicians from the possibility that centrist candidates could come along to dethrone them and instead rewards them for pandering to their more vocal, extreme supporters. This process has largely benefited Republicans in recent years since they control the majority of state legislatures.

"It increases the polarity of the candidates who get elected, especially because the really strong partisans and strong ideologues are the ones who vote in primaries," said Josh Pasek, a political communications expert and professor at the University of Michigan Institute for Social Research's Center for Political Studies. "So if you're going to select somebody to go to Congress and you're a Tea Partier, you're going to pick the person who really matches your strong ideological views instead of selecting the person who's more moderate."[30]

Consequently, politicians, shielded from centrist challenges by politically monolithic districts, are likelier to circulate fringe views or outright falsehoods that appeal to their extremist supporters. One obvious example is the aforementioned false rumor that Obama was not born in the United States, known as the "birther" conspiracy, which for several years was circulated by many, including Donald Trump himself before he became president.[31]

Empowered by ideological division, Americans are much more likely today to hold views that line up with their preferred political party.[32] The result is large groups of close-minded, partisan devotees who are often committed to their cause—such as the Obama birther conspiracy—regardless of the facts. They use what researchers call motivated reasoning to reinforce their views.

And it's not just conservatives. It's liberals, too. "We see that across the ideological spectrum," said Dan Kahan, a Yale law and psychology professor whose work for the Cultural Cognition Project has shown how people assess the world around them.[33]

Motivated reasoning drives us to filter the truth through the prism of our group identity. Remaining faithful to our chosen group means remaining faithful to the group's worldview. When presented with the facts on any particular topic, we are unlikely to speak up if our private assessment of the material contradicts our group's consensus. It's tantamount to what others have called a spiral of silence.

Simply presenting people with the facts won't necessarily help if the facts conflict with their group identity. Instead, conspiracy theories flourish when fueled by the accelerant of partisanship, especially now that the internet has made them easy to ignite and spread.

People's "ideologically motivated cognition" is aimed at "forming and maintaining beliefs that signify their loyalty to important affinity groups," Kahan concluded in one of his several studies on this topic.[34] Put another way, the intellectual capacity to examine an issue often leads people down an ideologically motivated path, rather than the road that leads to unvarnished truth.

That's one reason why the Left is not immune from the tendency to ignore the facts or openly skew the truth. While conservatives are more likely to dispute the science on climate change, liberals are prone to rejecting science on certain issues, as well.

Take food, for example. According to the Pew Research Center, 71 percent of liberals believe that genetically modified organisms, or GMOs, are unsafe to eat. But 68 percent of scientists who are members of the American Association for the Advancement of Science say GMOs are indeed safe to eat.[35]

An identical share of liberals, 71 percent, say that food grown with pesticides is unsafe to eat. But the same share of AAAS scientists, 68 percent, say that in fact these foods are also safe to consume. Although conservatives are also wary of pesticides, liberals hold these incorrect views to a greater degree, demonstrating that adherence to scientific principles is often selective.[36]

Rush Holt, president of the AAAS, a former eight-term Democratic congressman, and a physicist by training, said the underlying problem is an increasing willingness to substitute opinion for evidence. "I don't want this to be dismissed as just a Republican or a Democratic matter. I also don't want it to be attributed just to Donald Trump and Kellyanne Conway," he said, referring to the Trump campaign chairperson and White House adviser who famously promoted consideration of "alternative facts" early in Trump's administration.[37] "I do think that candidate Trump especially—and to some extent President Trump—have been pretty creative in their handling of evidence," Holt added. "But I think you miss the depth of the problem if you just assign it to a few politicians or one political party. It's a problem that is very widespread and goes very deep."[38]

Respect for evidence is lacking in many issues spanning the political spectrum, he noted. "The reason people deny the evidence on gun violence is different than the reason they deny the evidence on needle exchange, [which] is different than the reason they deny the evidence for climate change," he said. "When was the last time you heard an argument in economics that cited evidence as opposed to some pre-baked opinion, which might be ideology, might be a political platform or a plank of a political platform, or might just be this phenomenon where opinion is just as good as evidence?"[39]

Still, although people of all political persuasions have the tendency to ignore evidence when it's contradictory to their worldview, empirical research suggests that conservatives are generally more likely to dismiss scientific information as a guiding light. In an experiment designed to gauge how conservatives and liberals assess matters, a team of researchers led by University of Alabama social psychologist Alexa Tullett gave test subjects the ability to access scientific data to help them answer a set of questions. "We tried to be very clear about this—that you can get more information at no additional cost, and the perk of more information is that you get a clearer picture of the phenomenon that you're looking at," Tullett said.[40] But on the whole, Tullett's team found that conservatives were more likely to discount scientific data and answer questions based on their instincts or opinion.[41]

"It's a little bit odd, in a sense, that everybody is not just picking the maximum amount of information," Tullett said. "So we considered a couple of plausible explanations for why this might be. We thought perhaps conservatives are more defensive than liberals and they're saying, 'Okay, I don't want to look at this data because it might disprove what I think. The researchers are biased,' or something like that. And we didn't find evidence for that as an explanation for the relationship between political orientation and disinterest in information."[42]

Rather, a divide along political boundaries revealed itself. "What we did find was that conservatives were more likely than liberals to say that they just weren't 100 percent convinced that science was the best way to learn about the world," Tullett said. "And that's not to say that conservatives think that science is useless or you can't learn anything from science. But liberals just think science is a better way of learning about the world than conservatives do."[43]

It was a stark realization for a trained researcher. "As a scientist, I'm used to prizing empirical data over all else," she said. "And I've spent a lot of time in a system that tells me that that's the only valid way to learn about the world. Not everybody subscribes to that belief."[44]

For these reasons, Trump often escapes political punishment from his fervent base of supporters for his consistent stream of misstatements and outright falsehoods. His backers are not proactively fact-checking his assertions. Instead, they often plainly accept many of these statements as truth because to reject them would require his fans to disavow their group identity.

But the desire for a meaningful sense of belonging is not a function of politics. It's a basic, human impulse that extends into areas that aren't ideological at all—at least not by traditional political definitions.

A SENSE OF BELONGING

Minnesota resident Karen Ernst was on prolonged maternity leave from her job as an English teacher when she went to pick up her five-year-old son from preschool one day in 2008. With her husband deployed to Iraq, she had to do it all, so she brought along her ten-day-old baby. They hung out at the preschool with the other kids for a while before going home.[45]

The next day, the preschool receptionist called Ernst to inform her that one of the students had been diagnosed with chickenpox. Fearing that her newborn baby had been exposed before the baby was old enough to get the vaccine, Ernst confronted the mother of the sick kid at the next available opportunity. "How did that happen? Didn't she get vaccinated?" Ernst inquired.[46]

"No, that's not really important," the mother replied.[47]

Flabbergasted by the mother's flippant attitude, Ernst told the woman about how one of her English students had died a few years earlier from chickenpox. "Well, I see how not getting vaccinated is scary for you," the mother responded.[48]

"No, that should make it scary for everyone," Ernst replied.[49]

But the mother of the kid with chickenpox had made up her mind that vaccines were to be avoided. "The fact that she had exposed my newborn wasn't alarming to her," Ernst said. "The fact that I knew someone who had a child who had died wasn't alarming to her. She was fine with it."[50]

Not long after that, the global outbreak of the H1N1 influenza, or swine flu, called further attention to the need for vaccinations. "I actually did go online, and I was shocked to see what I found there," Ernst said. "I was laboring under the assumption that if you just told people facts, they would see that they were wrong and change their minds, which I now understand is not actually how the world operates at all."[51]

That was when Ernst started to research the anti-vaccination movement, whose committed followers are often referred to as anti-vaxxers. In 2010, Ernst and fellow concerned parent Ashley Shelby launched a blog called *Moms Who Vax* to highlight pro-vaccine resources, stories, and advice. Three years later, they volunteered to serve as parent leaders of a nonprofit called Voices for Vaccines, which fights the anti-vaccination movement.[52]

As she began studying the anti-vaccination mind-set, Ernst recognized that it was furthered primarily by a sense of belonging. Although the movement's followers often cite dubious scientific evidence to dismiss the legitimate research proving that vaccines are safe, bogus science was not necessarily the backbone of the movement. "It really is tied to emotion, to these gut-level feelings, to tribalism—that I belong to a tribe of parents, and this is where I fit in, and not vaccinating is part of that," Ernst said.[53]

Online—and particularly on social media, where Facebook groups provide the structure for conversation and companionship—anti-vaxxers find affirmation among like-minded believers, fueling that rush of tribalism.

"I actually became a mother before social media. I had my first baby in 2003 and my second in 2008. So I can compare raising children both in and out of social media," Ernst said. Before, "unless you knew people around you weren't vaccinating, you didn't have the space to talk to other people" to gain emotional support for your decision, she said.[54] But "with the advent of social media, what happened is people who might be alone by themselves in a previous time not vaccinating suddenly have access to all these people who are just like them, who aren't vaccinating. And they can listen to all those reasons, and they can have all their reasons reinforced."[55]

One of the only major anti-vaccination Facebook groups that doesn't block nonmembers is the Vaccine Resistance Movement, which proudly proclaims that it is "exposing vaccine fraud," rejecting the authority of the World Health Organization, and funding a study to show links between vaccines and autism.[56]

"Never has a groundswell of this magnitude been so prescient, never has the urgency of our times demanded greater action, or threatened the very fabric of our existence to such an extent," the Vaccine Resistance Movement declared on its Facebook page. "And the people are finally waking up and discovering the real meaning of freedom!"[57]

Many of the group members, numbering more than thirty thousand, use the page to promote conspiracy theories, circulate dubious news articles, share personal stories, and comfort each other. "Within one generation autism will be commonplace in most homes," one anti-vaxxer posted in summer 2017. "Not in this home, no way in hell are vaccines allowed here," a supporter responded.[58]

The sense of belonging and community that anti-vaxxers find through social media is self-sustaining, fueling their version of ideological empowerment. "That's a built-in support system that a lot of people crave, especially women when they first become mothers and they find out that motherhood operates differently than it seems to from the outside," Ernst said. "It's really true that they try to insulate themselves from what the rest of the world is saying. They insulate themselves from criticism about how they want to perceive the science."[59]

When Ernst speaks to doctors and nurses, she points to the insular and supportive nature of the conversation in the Vaccine Resistance Movement group. "Some of it is kind of nutty, but the thing I want people to look for is the echo chamber effect of it," she said. "No matter how preposterous something they say is, everyone around them will agree."[60]

The political diversity of anti-vaxxers illustrates how anti-science ideologies are not purely rooted in partisanship. It's "a mishmash of libertarians, people who distrust mainstream medicine, people who've got natural foods instincts, and people who have certain parenting views," including some extreme religious beliefs, said Brendan Nyhan, a Dartmouth professor who has studied the movement. "It's all over the map."[61]

The fundamental driver connecting those disparate groups is a pulsating sense of togetherness. Because of this, simply providing anti-vaxxers with accurate information won't necessarily cause them to change their behavior. Nyhan, in fact, has proven this empirically in his research. "Anytime you have an existing directional preference, it can affect the way you interpret information," Nyhan said. "It's important to be clear—this applies to all of us as human beings."[62]

Providing people with correct scientific data about, for example, the life-saving influenza vaccine is insufficient. Some 43 percent of Americans—most of whom support childhood vaccines and would never consider themselves part of the anti-vaxxer movement—still incorrectly believe that the flu vaccine can give them the flu.[63] After Nyhan gave flu vaccine skeptics accurate information from the Centers for Disease Control and Prevention dispelling the myth, the study subjects were less likely to believe the lies. But, critically, they were even less likely than before to say they planned to get vaccinated. The same counterintuitive interplay has been observed for information about the measles, mumps, and rubella (MMR) vaccine that parents authorize for their children.[64] Nyhan said,

> So if you already have a hesitation about vaccines or fears about vaccines, with some new piece of information you're not going to process that dispassionately. Our interpretation of that finding is that even when people's beliefs are changed, it doesn't mean the way they interpret that information—or the opinions or behaviors that result—will be altered in the way that you might expect. Instead, our interpretation of the results of these vaccine studies is that people buttressed their existing beliefs by thinking of other hesitations or concerns they had about vaccines. "So maybe the MMR vaccine doesn't cause autism, but I've heard these other things."[65]

Kahan, the Yale professor and member of the Cultural Cognition Project, has shown in his research that increased education on scientific issues does not necessarily equate to accurate assessment of the facts. "The more science comprehending somebody is," he said, "the more vulnerable they are to these kinds of dynamics."[66]

In fact, anti-vaxxers include many "people who are pretty well educated and have advanced degrees," said Ernst, the Voices for Vaccines leader. "I think part of that is the way that we, as an entire society, perceive healthcare. We think of healthcare as something that we should research and dig into and make these individual decisions about what's best for us. For example, before you even have your baby you usually interview pediatricians. I remember doing this with my own first child—interviewing pediatricians—and I remember thinking, 'I don't even know what I'm looking for. What am I supposed to know about having a pediatrician for a child?'"[67]

The internet has empowered us to put ourselves on par with medical professionals, even though we lack the training. "You get parents who are interviewing pediatricians and researching the best breast pump, researching the best hospital, and reading up on the best midwives, and making the best health choices that way about their babies. And when it comes to vaccinating, it [seems] reasonable for them to go ahead and research each vaccine," Ernst said.[68]

The problem is that even people who are educated in their respective fields—"maybe they're lawyers, or maybe they have advanced English degrees, or maybe they have science degrees," Ernst said—aren't necessarily equipped to assess the safety profile of vaccinations.[69]

"Immunology is just one of the most difficult things in the world to understand," she said. "I always triple-check with all the immunology experts that I know anytime I'm saying anything to parents that requires any nuance at all. I always say, 'Can I say it this way?' It's just hard. So there's this false sense of, 'I made it through graduate school. I know how to research things. I'm supposed to make all of these decisions for my child, so I can go and figure it out.'"[70]

People with greater scientific comprehension are better able to pick out facts that align with their preconceived notions about the world, and ignore the material that doesn't. Kahan used the term "motivated numeracy" to describe this capability and propensity to selectively use mathematical data to support your established beliefs.[71]

Readers of this book will inevitably "say, 'Well, I'm educated. This doesn't apply to me,'" Nyhan predicted. But "in some cases it's more knowledgeable people who are more likely to hold misperceptions, rather than less," he added, confirming Kahan's conclusion. "The reason is they're more likely to know about the misperception because they're more politically aware, and they're better able to organize their beliefs in a consistent manner, including their factual beliefs. That's not always the case, but knowledge and education aren't necessarily a panacea. They can help us build better ideologues, too, so it's a tricky thing."[72]

In one experiment, Kahan and several fellow researchers tested this concept by presenting randomized data on two sets of questions to their study participants. In the first set, they asked their subjects to assess whether a new skin rash treatment was effective. In the second set, they asked their subjects to assess whether gun control measures had increased crime or decreased crime in cities.[73]

In the skin rash treatment case, which had no political implications, people with high capability for numeracy were much more likely than people with low capability to reach the correct conclusion from the data set.[74] But in the gun control case, a politically divisive issue, people with strong data comprehension skills were not more likely than people with low skills to accurately assess the study results when the correct outcome did not fit comfortably within their preset ideologies.[75]

In essence, the advantages of data comprehension evaporate when the issue to be examined arouses political passions. Simply put, people often can't think scientifically when politics are involved.

That's because, in those cases, people genuinely believe the science is on their side, Kahan said.[76] Which is why no one will admit to being anti-science. They use heuristic strategies to examine the truth. That involves gauging circumstances through easily recalled knowledge and experiences, which are naturally vulnerable to personal biases. And when those personal biases are governed by ideologically zealous politicians who perpetuate strategic rhetoric that's not faithful to the facts, danger abounds.

"If you think your group doesn't agree with your view, you won't speak up. People self-censor," said Lee Rainie, the Pew Research Center's director of internet and technology research, who has studied the flow of information online. "The original work on this was done in Germany. Why did so many Germans back the Nazis even though they later claimed they didn't? The spiral of silence became the term to describe this self-censorship and attachment to the group being paramount."[77]

That concept "still applies in the internet age," Rainie continued. "But the new thing now is if people think that their Facebook friends disagree with them on a subject, they also don't bring it up at work or in neighborhood gatherings. So, all of a sudden there's a compounded spiral of silence as people worry, 'Well, gosh, I'm really out of the mainstream here. Everybody's going to disagree with me. Why do I want to lose friends over this issue?'"[78]

CHAPTER 5

"THE CONTEMPORARY FACE OF ISOLATION"

The day that Noelle Lilley's Instagram account was inadvertently deleted was emotional. After accumulating thousands of followers while capturing personal moments in photos as a high school student in San Bernardino, California, her account suddenly disappeared in an unfortunate mix-up. Instagram, which is owned by Facebook, had apparently mistaken her authentic account for fake accounts that anonymous users had created to harass her. Then eighteen years old, Lilley couldn't hold back the tears.[1]

"I was really upset and super devastated, probably more devastated than I should have been, considering it's just a social media platform," she recalled three years later while attending Arizona State University as a junior. "I had invested a lot of time into getting followers, uploading photos, and there were certain pictures that would be gone because I didn't have them saved elsewhere."[2]

In the immediate aftermath, she felt frantic that she wasn't connected with her peers and her family. "I was like, 'What are people posting? What are people saying? What are they talking about?'" she said. "I couldn't keep up with that."[3]

But as the weeks passed and the emotions faded, she said she gained perspective. She began to realize that on Instagram, many of us are engaged in an endless pursuit of shallow interactivity. "The number of likes you have, it almost seems like it corroborates . . . your popularity," Lilley said. "At my high school, the kids that were really well known, or maybe had a lot of friends, or were really outgoing—they always got a lot of likes on Instagram. And the people that were maybe a little bit quieter, maybe not as well known, or not as popular, didn't get a lot of likes on Instagram. So naturally that causes the individual to feel that the number of likes they get is what's going to determine their value and how they feel about themselves."[4]

Like many of her contemporaries, she would go to digital extremes to chase popularity, even when it meant distorting her social media presence. "There's other external apps, and you can download them, and [they] will give you fake likes, basically," she said. "So if I were to sign in to one of those apps and connect it to my Instagram, then other users through the app would be automatically liking my photos. It's not something they have to do manually. It's something the app does for you, and it makes you like each other's photos. That way, before you know it, you're boosted up to forty, fifty likes. People take it very, very seriously."[5]

For a long time, she maintained a personal threshold. "People will tell their friends, 'Hey, go like my new photo.' I used to be the same way myself," she said. "I needed to get a minimum of, like, eighty likes; otherwise I would delete that picture. And when I think about that now, that's just ridiculous, and it just seems so toxic in a way."[6]

Her experience is extremely common among young millennials and people born later, known as Generation Z. Social media allows them to create a veneer of beauty, hilarity, success, or coolness, often divorced from reality. But let's not act like this is exclusive to kids these days. Social media, in fact, gives us all the tools to do this. And many of us are quite proactive about it.

When I consider my own social media persona, I am acutely aware of how I'm portraying myself to the digital world at any given moment. In fact, it's part of my job. As a professional journalist, I'm generally expected to remain active on Twitter, Facebook, and Instagram. I regularly update my LinkedIn account, upload occasional blog posts to Tumblr, broadcast live video through Periscope, and hold onto a forlorn Google Plus account.

Suffice it to say, I have long recognized that my online persona greatly affects my professional reputation and my image in the eyes of friends, family, and strangers who follow me online. I have significant control over their perception of my marriage, family life, accomplishments, failures, religion, state of mind, ethics, personal views, sensibilities, and basic humanity.

Like others, I think hard about the exact timing of when to post something. When will it get the most action? If I post it now, will it generate engagement? I will confess that I've even asked my wife to "like" my important posts right away to fool Facebook's algorithm into believing that my content is popular or to help my tweets take off.

But what am I not posting? What am I pretending hasn't happened? How does that affect my friends' and followers' perceptions of me? And, perhaps most importantly, how do my posts affect their perceptions of themselves?

Lilley has considered these implications, too. "This applies to almost all social media platforms in general, in my opinion," she said. "You don't post on Instagram when you fail a test or when you don't get a job offer. You post when you get straight A's. You post when your child gets on the dean's list."[7] She recently didn't land a journalism internship that she had wanted:

> Did I post that anywhere? No. But the current program that I'm doing now, when I got into that, you can absolutely believe that I posted that everywhere. So when you're looking at someone else's account, and you're only seeing all these positive things in their life . . . you think about all the negative things that are going on in your life, and you start to feel down about yourself, when the reality is it's not as though they're not experiencing [bad] things. They're just not outwardly sharing that. It's like you're constantly absorbing the good in other people's lives, which makes you reflect on the bad in your life, not realizing that those people have bad in their lives as well. They're just not posting it.[8]

DISGUISING REALITY

Like. Love. Snap. Post. Share. Retweet. Reply. Comment. Tag. Click. Stream. Message. Follow. Friend. Connect. Filter. Pin.

This explosion of interactivity has permanently altered the way we communicate with friends, family, and strangers. In a culture already chopped up along divisive social boundaries—white versus black, citizens versus immigrants, wealthy versus the middle class, urban versus rural, men versus women—conversation over the roots of these chasms often ignores the digital catalysts of our misunderstandings.

If one of the only ways to bridge these societal divides is to promote better understanding and acceptance of each other, then we must grapple with the effects of social media on how we portray ourselves and consume information about others. While pervasive connectivity makes communication easier than ever before on a practical level, the digital age has counterintuitively compromised our ability to recognize reality in each other. Though we may understand intellectually that the way people present themselves on social media is not necessarily reflective of their real lives, that recognition is not top of mind when we're scrolling, sharing, and posting.

In 1956, Erving Goffman wrote,

> Society is organized on the principle that any individual who possesses certain social characteristics has a moral right to expect that others will value and treat him in a correspondingly appropriate way. Connected with this principle is a second, namely that an individual who implicitly or explicitly signifies that he has certain social characteristics ought to have this claim honoured by others and ought in fact to be what he claims he is. In consequence, when an individual projects a definition of the situation and thereby makes an implicit or explicit claim to be a person of a particular kind, he automatically exerts a moral demand upon the others, obliging them to value and treat him in the manner that persons of his kind have a right to expect.[9]

More than six decades after Goffman's assessment, social media has given us the unprecedented ability to perpetuate misperceptions of who we are, incidentally fostering envy and creating an epidemic of disconnectedness against the backdrop of perceived togetherness.

The personal images we carefully cultivate through social media create unhealthy life expectations in others and spawn a gaping divide between our grasp of our own personal reality and others' seemingly untarnished circumstances. This fuels misunderstanding of real-life challenges—such as divorce, miscarriage, financial difficulties, eating disorders, and domestic violence—and triggers personal crises like clinical depression. As a result, the bonds of friendship and family are undermined by jealousy. And lies cross the digital divide into real life.

Why, then, are we surprised that someone who skews the facts about his life could rise to political power? Donald Trump isn't the only one who does it. It's what we do as ordinary citizens every day online—skew the facts, sometimes consciously but often subconsciously.

This paradigm is central to the erosion of truth that has redefined how we relate to one another and how we perceive the world.

EPIDEMIC OF ENVY

To be sure, the desire to be loved and liked is nothing new. It's core to who we are.

"By definition, self-presentation is the act of selecting, out of the entire repertoire of who you are, what you want to come across in view of achieving some sort of impression that you desire," said Catalina Toma, a University of Wisconsin communication science professor and an expert on the effect of technology on image management. "The majority of the time, people want to come across positively. They want to impress in some way; they want to be attractive or likeable, come across as sociable, things of that nature."[10]

But what's new in the social media age is the ease with which we can strategically or incidentally cultivate false images of our lives—whether mildly or completely misleading. "When you go on the internet, your ability to achieve your self-presentational goals is enhanced compared to face-to-face," Toma said. "So we are better able to craft images that are aligned with how we actually want to come across online."[11]

One reason is what Toma calls "editability" before digitally communicating. "Online, you can craft your statements, [and] you can revise and polish in ways which are just impossible face-to-face," she said. In real life, "you've said something, it's out in the open, [and] you cannot take it back. You don't have the luxury of revising and polishing."[12]

Another key factor that distinguishes social media from in-person communication is what she called "asynchronicity." "This is a temporal dimension, which refers to how much time you have to craft your statement. On social media you basically have unlimited time. It's an asynchronous medium, as opposed to face-to-face, which is synchronous and happens in real time," Toma said. "So you don't have a lot of processing ability. You have to react spontaneously or instantaneously—whereas online you can take much more time to think about what you want to say and how you want to say it."[13]

Perhaps the greatest difference, however, is that Facebook, Instagram, and Twitter in particular give users the ability to broadcast their photos, videos, opinions, and mundane material to the masses in an instant. This distinguishing feature makes the publish button equivalent to a digital microphone.

"I give this example to my students: If I talk to any of them one on one, yeah of course I care what they think about me. If I talk to two hundred of them at the same time, it's a whole different beast—I really care about what they think about me, I'm really motivated to come across in a particular way, and I'll definitely put more time and effort into crafting my statements than if I just talked to them individually," Toma said.[14]

With social media, "never in history has an average person had access to such a large audience. Never. We can broadcast our thoughts to hundreds of people really quickly and really easily in a way that was just not possible before. So social media is putting us humans in a completely novel situation."[15]

Amid a flurry of posts depicting happy marriages, joyous children, successful professionals, and glamorous vacations, it's difficult to avoid the trap of social comparison—especially when users are becoming increasingly sophisticated about strategically packaging personal content. In a survey of college students for her book *The Happiness Effect*, Donna Freitas found that 73 percent say they "try always to appear positive/happy with anything attached to my real name,"[16] while only 19 percent say, "I am open about my emotions on social media."[17] All things considered, the message you receive through social media is clear: your friends are living a more fulfilling life than you are.

Utah Valley University behavioral science researchers showed that over time, Facebook users come under the impression that their friends are better off. "Those who have used Facebook longer agreed more that others were happier, and agreed less that life is fair, and those spending more time on Facebook each week agreed more that others were happier and had better lives," researchers Hui-Tzu Grace Chou and Nicholas Edge concluded.[18] It was worse for people who had more Facebook friends they didn't know personally. In other words, it's even harder to distinguish the digital lives of strangers from their real lives, whereas you might be able to recognize when close friends or family members are digitally distorting their personal circumstances.

A concept called the "availability heuristic" makes this particularly problematic. It describes our tendency to judge situations based on experiences and observations that readily come to mind. "When forming impressions of others, it is easy for frequent Facebook users to recall the statements and pictures posted by their Facebook friends," the Utah Valley researchers reported. "Since people are motivated to make positive self-presentations, the information and images posted by Facebook friends tend to be socially desirable."[19] This comparison trap raises the risk of an epidemic of envy in a society that's already brimming with socioeconomic tension, which politicians on both sides of the aisle often use to divide us.

"Comparison emotions can corrupt the comparer. Envy humiliates and angers people," warned Princeton University psychologist Susan Fiske. "Feeling below someone makes people feel ashamed at their own inadequacy. If a peer can succeed, then people feel inadequate for not doing equally well. Envy also makes people angry at the injustice of their low-status positions. Those who succeeded must have had unfair advantages. Envy correlates with depression, unhappiness, and low self-esteem."[20]

Envy "is directed up, toward the rich, professional, and entrepreneurial," Fiske asserted. It "is dangerous, dividing people in a different way than scorn does. Envy can lead to going along with the higher status and with more powerful others, but also to sabotaging and attacking them. Envy is harm waiting to happen."[21]

EMOTIONAL MANIPULATION

Before the internet, when face-to-face conversations, letters, and phone calls were the dominant ways to distribute personal information, people knew exactly what messages they were communicating to their friends and family.

In the social media age, we still control much of what we disclose. But we don't control which of our posts are actually seen.

The algorithmic filtering of our lives has turned software engineers—namely, the anonymous engineers at Facebook and Instagram—into our personal editors. Through complex formulas that reward engagement, their algorithms decide what we see and what we don't see about each other.

Yet many people don't even realize that the Facebook News Feed is promoting or concealing certain content from them based on an algorithmic judgment. In a survey by researchers at the University of Illinois at Urbana-Champaign, California State University at Fresno, and the University of Michigan, more than 63 percent of Facebook users "were not aware of the News Feed curation algorithm's existence at all."[22] Although the survey's sample size was small, perhaps inhibiting its empirical reliability, plenty of other evidence also suggests that general awareness of the News Feed's basic digital mechanics is limited.

The public's reaction to a separate, controversial study—in which a Facebook data scientist and other researchers altered the content of some users' News Feeds to factor out positive or negative expressions in a test of the platform's "emotional contagion" effect—showed how the News Feed has become a foundational element of people's personal lives.[23]

"How dare you manipulate my News Feed!" was a typical reaction, according to Cornell information science professor Jeffrey Hancock, who helped conduct Facebook's study. "This was a really fervent response—and very common."[24]

The wrath that descended upon him following the study's publication was "worldwide," and his "family paid a price for it," Hancock said. He attributed the outrage in part to the fact that "our study violated people's sense of autonomy and the fact that they do not want their emotions manipulated or mood controlled."[25]

The irony is that Facebook's algorithms were already exerting significant influence over people's emotions, often without them realizing it.[26] Hancock's team simply tweaked the algorithmically curated mix of content that people had access to. In a way, that's no different than what Facebook engineers do every single time they tweak the algorithms that govern the site.

"I'm not sure whether this means we need to bring in an education component to help people understand that their News Feeds are altered all the time by Facebook," Hancock said. "But the huge number of e-mails about people's frustration that researchers would change the News Feed indicates that there's just no sense that the News Feed was anything other than an objective window into their social world."[27]

In general, users simply have "a very poor understanding of the algorithm of Facebook," the University of Wisconsin's Toma said. "We don't know exactly how the algorithm works because it's proprietary to Facebook, and they won't release it, obviously. But it does seem like it's a rich-get-richer situation—posts that get a lot of feedback, comments, and likes being more likely to appear in people's News Feeds and accrue even more comments and likes as a result of that. It's also who we click on the most, who we tend to keep an eye on the most."[28]

But users "think that what's presented in their timeline is an accurate reflection of reality," Toma said. "And they don't realize that what they're getting is aggregate news about many people at once. No individual life is all roses and no thorns constantly in the way that the algorithm may make it seem."[29]

Naturally, the most compelling content is the most atypical. It's the engagement announcement, the baby news, the exotic vacation, the work promotion, the strong opinion, the extreme event. The algorithm creators believe these are the items we want to see. And they're right. The problem is that by presenting these outlier incidents to us in a rushing river of content, it's easy to forget that these events are not reflective of everyday life.

THE FACADE OF CONNECTIVITY

Just as Facebook and Instagram deliver an algorithmically filtered view of our friends' lives to us, they also show us a filtered view of the lives of strangers and celebrities. These tools have become professional platforms for the distribution of strategically cultivated content through movements like #VanLife, which has attracted promoters who are paid to craft digital images of life on the road in beautiful locales. It's a form of camping, in which they live out of a van, meandering from place to place to experience the world with limited responsibility and roots.

"God I wish my life was that free and easy and amazing," reads a typical comment on the Instagram account of #VanLife promoters Emily King and Corey Smith, whose sponsors include Kettle Brand potato chips, Clif Bar, Synergy Organic Clothing, and Hydro Flask.[30] On their Instagram account, @WheresMyOfficeNow, the couple describe themselves as "wondering wanderers reclaiming real wealth" under the premise that "wealth by ancient origin is happiness + wellbeing."[31] The *New Yorker*'s Rachel Monroe wrote an article describing the trend:

> The same vanlife pictures get taken over and over: the van's back doors opening onto an ocean vista; a long-exposure nighttime shot of the van, cozy and lit from within, against a backdrop of stars; a woman on the van's roof, in the middle of a sun salutation. . . . One vanlife trope, a middle-distance shot of

a van on an empty, winding road, seems more self-consciously artificial than most: someone clearly had to hop out and run back to get the shot. The ideal vanlife image has something of the hazy impersonality of a photograph in an upscale catalogue, depicting a scene that's both attractive and unspecific enough that viewers can imagine themselves into it.[32]

These types of distorted portrayals of life through social media—including commercial, pseudo-professional, and amateur efforts—have even spawned a cottage industry of satire accounts. A wedding photographer in Oregon racked up more than one million followers on Instagram for her Socality Barbie account, featuring artistic depictions of a Barbie doll prancing on the beach, gazing at an idyllic pumpkin patch, kayaking through a forested river, or sipping a latte. Socality Barbie served as "a critique of a larger slow-living hipster aesthetic" that "includes anyone sufficiently dedicated to their lifestyle to heft fancy coffee-making gear on a hike for the perfect sunrise espresso," the *Atlantic* wrote.[33]

It was "a way to poke fun at all the Instagram trends that I thought were ridiculous," said the creator, Darby Cisneros. "Never in one million years did I think it would receive the amount of attention that it did, but because of that it has open[ed] the door to a lot of great discussions like: how we choose to present ourselves online, the insane lengths many of us go to to create the perfect Instagram life, and calling into question our authenticity and motives."[34]

Unquestionably, social media can provide genuine joy, inspiration, companionship, and wonderment. When a grandparent sees photos of a newborn grandchild, when a friend feels close to a distant colleague, when someone feeling downcast can laugh at an innocent meme—all of these things can be uplifting. In some ways, social media can serve as an antidote to social isolation. Many of us have experienced this in some fashion, myself included.

But for many, it's the reverse. The facade of connectivity and authenticity cultivated through social media can have serious negative consequences. In one study that drew a distinction between "passive" and "active" Facebook use, researchers at the University of Leuven and the University of Michigan found that when people were simply consuming content through the social media platform and not actively posting anything, they were especially susceptible to negative effects, including envy. In their first experiment, the researchers assembled subjects in a computer lab and gave them each a task. Some were instructed to use Facebook actively, which meant "posting status updates or sharing links, reacting and commenting on friends' posts or private messages." The rest were told to use the site by simply browsing—that is, "scrolling through News Feeds, looking at friends' pages and pictures, or a band's page."[35]

"Passive Facebook usage leads to declines in affective well-being: by increasing envy," the researchers concluded.[36]

In their second experiment, the researchers assessed subjects in the real world by remotely monitoring their Facebook activity and asking each participant to answer brief surveys periodically throughout the day about their feelings. Both experiments supported the overall hypothesis. Problematically, the second experiment found that Facebook users engaged with the site passively about 50 percent more often than they used it actively. "This suggests that people spend most of their time on Facebook engaging in a behavior that undermines their affective well-being. It also explains why measures of overall Facebook activity have revealed a negative relationship with subjective well-being," the researchers concluded.[37]

The question then is, why do people continue to engage with social media if it makes them feel worse about themselves? The researchers noted Facebook's addictive qualities as one possibility while also noting that some users simply may not realize the effect it's having on their state of mind. Also, "actively interacting with one's colleagues online may build social ties, but still leave a person feeling badly when they learn about their peers' accomplishments," according to the study, which added that "it is possible that people's motivation to 'stay in touch' outweighs concerns they have over how interacting with this technology influences their feelings." Overall, though, the concern is that "Facebook creates an environment that is difficult to passively navigate without negatively influencing how we feel," the researchers reported.[38]

For some social media users, the effect goes deeper. Many of us seem to be subconsciously convinced that our friends and family are presenting their lives authentically online. The consequences of this are unsettling.

Brian Primack, director of the University of Pittsburgh's Center for Research on Media, Technology, and Health, said the rise of social media has direct implications for our mental health. He has demonstrated in published research that there's "a linear relationship between how much social media you used and whether or not you were depressed."[39]

"We thought it was going to be more of a U-shaped curve. We thought that if you used very little social media, that might make you an outcast and less normative in today's society. Therefore we expected that if you were on either extreme—you were using way too much or you were using very small amounts—either of those would be associated with more depression and that the middle range might be the optimal spot. That's not at all what the data showed."[40] It was a straight line. "Every increase in social media was paired with an associated increase in odds of depression," said Primack. "So we were very surprised by that."

Online, it's simply harder to ascertain the truth about the lives of our friends, family, and coworkers. The more we observe them on social media, the worse we often feel about our own lives. And people who are predisposed to feeling this way are especially susceptible.

"Let's say you're already down on yourself. Let's say you're already starting to feel somewhat depressed. Then those things are probably going to affect you even more," Primack said. "So what it presents is the possibility of a vicious cycle. Somebody who is already in a more sensitive spot is affected by these things and feels a little more like their life isn't ideal."[41]

The paradoxical effect is that "the more you use social media, the more socially isolated you feel," he said. While he acknowledged that for "certain subgroups" this might not be true—say, the grandparents who want to follow the lives of their distant grandkids—the connection is evident in empirical research.[42]

It's even worse when your friends aren't responsive to your activity on social media. When your Facebook friends ignore your status update, photo, or video, you're even more likely to feel down. It's tantamount to "interpersonal neglect," which is "associated with an increased experience of loneliness and a decreased sense of control, self-esteem, and meaningful existence," according to a study by researchers at the University of Innsbruck.[43]

But because the visibility of our personal content is strictly controlled by algorithms, we don't have direct control over our feelings. The algorithms are exerting a significant influence on whether we can meaningfully connect with each other and connect over our feelings of self-worth.

Our ability to develop genuine relationships with others is directly tied to our ability to post snappy status updates, carefully curate photo albums, and broadcast engaging videos. So the worse we are at creating engaging content, the more socially isolated we become—even if it appears to the casual observer that we have hundreds of close friends.

"We have moved from living in a world where social connections required considerable investment of time to a world where connections are widely available and cheap to establish," Stanford University's Paolo Parigi and Warner Henson II wrote in an assessment on social isolation. "Having many friends from disparate corners of the social space is now a common experience. An isolate is no longer [simply] a person without connections but is now somebody who creates connections that carry little meaning. This is the contemporary face of isolation."[44]

Isolation fuels discontentment, which feeds directly into our divisive political environment. Lacking personal validation and genuine connection, many people feel a sense of emptiness.

So they go looking elsewhere for the truth.

CHAPTER 6

BLINDED

The multiplication of ideologically motivated and digitally empowered but socially secluded factions of individuals has severely undermined truth as a pillar of American community and as a linchpin of personal empathy for others. People are increasingly self-segregating and rejecting each other based on politically charged motivations, lies, distorted perceptions, and animosity.

One sign of contagion is a palpable surge of unadulterated rage against outsiders. The inflammation of xenophobia and incivility has fueled a rise of political and social isolationism among increasingly detached communities. That has led to intensely personal and counterproductive conflicts over issues such as immigration, refugees, and racial inequality.

We've already experienced a sharp increase in tension over these issues—much of it inflamed by Donald Trump himself. The policy risks created by this spike in deceitful and uncivil discourse are significant and wide-ranging. Without respectful conversation centered on the facts, common ground is generally elusive, and change is practically impossible. Rarely is progress made when people are yelling at each other.

There are obvious exceptions, of course. Rage is appropriate when social injustice is present—and sometimes it's the only way to bring about transformation in attitudes and laws. But with most political topics, advancement is typically unattainable when people have dropped an anchor in the sea of hostility.

A clear example of where the intolerance of alternative perspectives is occurring is on many American college campuses, where administrators and faculty are allowing or enabling students to wall themselves off from viewpoints and ideas that make them squirm. For instance, many faculty members place so-called "trigger warnings" on syllabi to give ideologically or socially sheltered students advance notice of material that will be discussed during courses that they may find troublesome. That way, the students can excuse themselves if necessary to avoid feeling uncomfortable. Many colleges have also adopted the concept of "safe spaces" where students can commune with others like them and avoid encounters with people with competing perspectives or different life experiences.[1]

It is a puzzling turn of events for anyone who believes in the importance of the college experience to expose students to new ways of thinking and to force them to learn about how the world works. After all, the truth about the world's challenges won't change while students are hiding from it.

But in numerous cases, students have vigorously rejected the suggestion that they should have to listen to views they disagree with. Some have shamed their universities into canceling the speaking engagements of conservatives and have even hurled invective at liberal leaders who believe that discussion, debate, and interaction are critical elements of a healthy democracy. The *Atlantic*'s Conor Friedersdorf dubbed this trend the "new intolerance of student activism" after Yale students erupted at a lecturer and her professor husband in November 2015 for suggesting that they should engage in dialogue with anyone wearing a Halloween costume that they find culturally offensive.[2]

"American universities were once a safe space not only for maturation but also for a certain regressive, or even transgressive, experience; increasingly, it seems, they have become places of censure and prohibition," the lecturer, Erika Christakis, wrote in an email to students protesting the university's guidance on costume wearing. "The censure and prohibition come from above, not from yourselves!" she continued. "Are we all okay with this transfer of power? Have we lost faith in young people's capacity—in your capacity—to exercise self-censure, through social norming, and also in your capacity to ignore or reject things that trouble you?"[3]

She added, referencing her sociologist husband, "Nicholas says, if you don't like a costume someone is wearing, look away, or tell them you are offended. Talk to each other. Free speech and the ability to tolerate offence are hallmarks of a free and open society."[4]

The email sparked a furious response from students, who "circulated petitions" against them, "wrote editorials" airing their grievances, "posted social-media tirades," "scribbled criticisms in chalk" outside the couple's home, and "posted degrading images of them online," according to Yale student Zachary

Young, writing as a fellow for the *Wall Street Journal*.[5] The incensed Yale students wore their intellectual dismissiveness as a badge of honor despite their educational institution's historical reputation for cherishing the exploration of alternative viewpoints.

"Walk away, he doesn't deserve to be listened to," one student spewed in a meeting where Nicholas tried to explain their perspectives. Another student protestor profanely demanded that the professor leave the school.[6]

Soon after the explosion over their suggestion that students should be forced to encounter and grapple with alternative viewpoints, Nicholas and Erika Christakis resigned from their respective posts as master and associate master of Silliman College, Yale's largest residential college.[7] Because they had refused to bend to student demands that they commit to exclusionary discourse, they were no longer welcome at Silliman.

It is, without a doubt, sometimes perfectly acceptable to strenuously condemn alternative perspectives. Indeed it's occasionally imperative, such as when Americans spoke out against racists marching in Charlottesville, Virginia, to promote white supremacy, neo-Nazism, and the Ku Klux Klan in August 2017.[8] Those hateful and intolerant views should be overwhelmed with messages of love, acceptance, and equality.

But there's a serious risk to democracy when we consider anything that makes us uncomfortable as an extreme position and refuse to listen to it at all. This goes for both sides of the aisle.

On most key political issues—such as taxes, healthcare, regulatory reform, education, foreign policy, and the military—reasonable minds can differ. And most people are not extremists. So when we banish others based on their personal viewpoints, we are effectively snuffing out any hope of understanding each other and bridging the wide gaps that divide us. This refusal to even listen to each other worsens the grouping effect that exacerbates isolation. And it stifles the free flow of ideas that leads to progress.

When we shield ourselves from opposing views, we constrain our ability to assess the truth. Naturally, without a thorough investigation of the entire landscape of facts, we become more susceptible to manipulation by our group leaders, who often profit by steering us onto their preferred course.

The natural evolution of this trend is already unfolding geographically and socially, as Americans grow increasingly distant from people of other political views. "Purple America," a term used to describe communities containing a politically diverse mix of constituents, "has all but disappeared," according to *Cook Political Report* analyst David Wasserman.[9]

Our regional divides are becoming more extreme. During the 1992 presidential election, only 4 percent of voters lived in counties that cast at least 60 percent of their major-party votes for one candidate. Although independent Ross Perot's candidacy slightly skewed the 1992 numbers, the share of people living in those landslide counties has increased in every presidential election since then. In 2012, it was five in ten. By 2016, it was six in ten—and about one in five lived in a county in which the most favored candidate won by at least fifty points. It's "an accelerating trend that confirms that America's political fabric, geographically, is tearing apart," Wasserman concluded.[10]

Although the entire trend cannot be explained by politics, primarily because of the economic and educational factors involved, the country's widening urban-rural divide has infected our perceptions of each other as Americans.

"Individuals are increasingly living in communities surrounded by other people who believe basically what they do," said Josh Pasek, the political communication expert and professor at the University of Michigan Institute for Social Research's Center for Political Studies. "So as the distance you need to go from yourself to others who actually disagree with you increases, your exposure to their views decreases. That has a number of pernicious effects because hearing the justification for somebody who supports the other side moderates you at least a little bit. If you don't know anybody like that, that's harder."[11]

Journalist Bill Bishop and sociologist Robert Cushing also brilliantly illuminated the roots of this issue in their 2008 book *The Big Sort*. But the ripple effects of political bitterness go beyond the urban-rural divide and swing-state politics.

Ideological hardening is also disrupting individual relationships. The "gradual encroachment of party preference into nonpolitical and hitherto personal domains" is leading to "increasingly politically homogeneous" neighborhoods and families, according to researchers Shanto Iyengar of Stanford University and Sean J. Westwood of Princeton University. "A standard measure of social distance—parents' displeasure over the prospects of their offspring marrying into a family with a different party affiliation—shows startling increases," the researchers concluded.[12] Amazingly, Americans are more likely to filter out prospective marriage partners based on politics than on physical desire or personality, according to Iyengar and Westwood. In other words, people would rather marry someone they dislike than marry someone they disagree with.

The evidence is clear that personal discrimination based on politics is perfectly acceptable in the minds of most Americans, unlike discrimination based on other factors. "Americans increasingly dislike people and groups on the other side of the political divide and face no social repercussions for the open expression of these attitudes," the researchers concluded.[13]

PUTTING OTHERS AT RISK

Just as ideological hardening undermines personal relationships, it also paves a path to destruction when it consumes scientific discourse. Scientific falsehoods, myths, and misleading material are profitable to only a small group of elites who can leverage the phony information for their political or personal gain. Ultimately, their lies often hurt those who are most vulnerable.

Without action, scientists say that within decades the environmental catastrophe of global warming will likely displace countless people, cause sea levels to rise, trigger economic disasters, and spawn serious health crises. It's well documented that poor communities, indigenous people groups, seniors, people with disabilities, people with preexisting medical conditions, and people of color face the worst consequences, according to the US Global Climate Change Research Program.[14]

Though many affluent Americans likely will be affected by climate change in some way, those vulnerable people groups are most at risk. They are less likely to be able to escape affected coastal regions, access air-conditioning, receive adequate medical care, and avoid exposure to air pollution and waterborne pathogens, among many other challenges. Even the Department of Defense has launched a climate change adaptation plan to adjust to the increased medical risks of vulnerable US soldiers, who may face more heat illnesses, infectious diseases, and other health hazards.[15] But the reality of these scientifically projected ramifications is of course not accepted by politically charged groups that have banded together to fight policies on this front.

For Bob Inglis, the former Republican congressman from South Carolina who was voted out of office after endorsing budget-neutral federal action on climate change, it's a harsh reality to stomach. "Some people would say, 'Inglis and his kind of people brought in this problem,'" he said, reflecting on his period as a rigid ideologue in the 1990s. "And I think there would be some truth to that."[16]

To be sure, he continues to identify himself as a steady conservative, often proudly citing his record of supporting pro-life policies and backing gun rights. Still, Inglis now speaks openly about the dangerous grouping effect of ideology on people's perceptions of climate change and other critical scientific issues. "We live in a time where there's so much information, and so much available to know and to be known that you need some filter for it, and ideology becomes a pretty effective filter," said Inglis, who is now pursuing a consensus for climate action through his nonprofit group the Energy and Enterprise Initiative at George Mason University and its online community at RepublicEn.org.[17]

Ideological filtering also serves as a propellant of staunch opposition to genetically modified organisms (GMOs) among certain left-wing activists. GMOs—which liberals are more likely to believe are unsafe to eat, as previously established—offer significant global health and economic benefits.

But much as climate change is poised to hurt the most vulnerable, campaigns against GMOs are especially hurtful to poor communities throughout the globe. Nations in sub-Saharan Africa that are in dire need of improved agricultural production are at grave risk as GMO opponents seek to block the technology despite its widespread acceptance among scientists as being safe. The technology has reduced the use of pesticides, increased crop production capability, and bolstered farmer profits, scientists have concluded.[18]

Yet concerted efforts to oppose the technology, by organizations such as Friends of the Earth International and various left-wing groups, have effectively blocked global progress, according to the nonpartisan Information Technology and Innovation Foundation (ITIF). As of 2016, only three of fifty-four countries in Africa were growing any crops improved by biotechnology, in part because of European governments exerting "manipulation via foreign aid and trade pressures," ITIF reported. The foundation asserted that these efforts have formed "significant barriers to the development of the poorest nations on earth," costing low and lower-middle-income countries up to $1.5 trillion in economic gains through 2050.[19]

The aggressive campaign to fight GMOs has roots in the United States, too. In a letter to Greenpeace, more than 120 Nobel laureates exhorted the environmental group to end its campaign to block genetically engineered golden rice. The crop "has the potential to reduce or eliminate much of the death and disease caused by a vitamin A deficiency, which has the greatest impact on the poorest people in Africa and Southeast Asia," the Nobel laureates wrote.[20]

Some 250 million people worldwide suffer from vitamin A deficiency. Altogether, vitamin A deficiency leads to one million to two million preventable deaths every year, the Nobel laureates wrote, "because it compromises the immune system, putting babies and children at great risk." It's also the leading cause of childhood blindness throughout the world.[21]

"I find it surprising that groups that are very supportive of science when it comes to global climate change, or even [appreciate] the value of vaccination in preventing human disease . . . can be so dismissive of the general views of scientists when it comes to something as important as the world's agricultural future," one of the signatories, Nobel laureate Randy Schekman, a cell biologist at the University of California at Berkeley, told the *Washington Post*.[22]

Greenpeace retorted that the benefits of golden rice are unclear, said efforts to commercialize it have "failed," and called instead for the adoption of sustainable agricultural practices that protect the environment while increasing crop yields. The organization had previously blasted genetically engineered products for "manipulating genes in a way that does not occur naturally," possibly "contaminating . . . environments and future generations in an unforeseeable and uncontrollable way."[23]

The catastrophic ramifications of rejecting scientific principles are not exclusive to environmental or political circles, however. People who group together to deny the science on vaccinations find consolation in each other, as demonstrated in chapter 4, but they are doing considerable harm to the most vulnerable among us: young children, who in this case aren't getting the vaccinations they desperately need.

In Minnesota, an outbreak of measles among American children of Somali descent occurred in 2017 after vaccination rates plummeted amid concern over autism diagnoses. Children of Somali descent in Minnesota weren't always at risk, though. In 2004, they had higher rates of measles, mumps, and rubella (MMR) vaccination than non-Somalis. But by 2014, their MMR vaccination rate had dropped to 42 percent, compared with 89 percent for other Minnesota children.[24]

Many of the children's parents had become concerned about vaccines after encountering widely circulated but debunked research by Andrew Wakefield, a champion of the anti-vaxxer movement.[25] Wakefield's material has become gospel to the cloistered anti-vaxxer community, providing the dubious confirmation that many parents seek when they're pursuing information linking autism and vaccines.

"In the midst of this measles outbreak you really can tie a one-to-one connection between the anti-vaccine movement targeting the Somali community, the vaccine rates dropping in the Somali community, and measles spreading," said Karen Ernst, the parent leader of Voices for Vaccines and a Minnesota resident.[26] She added,

> And in the midst of that measles outbreak, the anti-vaccine movement is doubling down. They're going in with school exemption forms and notaries to help people opt out of vaccines. They're encouraging people not to go to their doctors and to not listen to the health department. Even when they're starting outbreaks, they're feeling very bold right now. We're at a juncture where it could get really bad, where we could really see a lot more power moving toward the anti-vaccine movement.[27]

Even in the highly educated and technologically advanced city of Austin, Texas, bustling with progressive politics and culture, vaccine rates have declined sharply. Rates elsewhere in the state have plunged, too. By 2015, Texas had nearly forty-five thousand children whose parents had exempted them from school immunization laws. That was twice as many as 2010 and nineteen times as many as 2003. Some Texas counties were dangerously close to dropping below the immunization rate at which communities lose what experts call "herd immunity."[28]

"WEAPONIZED NARRATIVE"

Perpetuating lies that undermine our communal values and our collective commitment to scientific principles typically requires someone at the helm leading the charge. Although organic, grassroots opposition to basic facts is not impossible, it's much more likely for a community of like-minded believers to form around a charismatic or influential leader who circulates falsehoods and determines what beliefs are acceptable to maintain membership in the group.

To be sure, the strategic construction of narratives to achieve policy goals, gain votes, build movements, or stir up dissension is nothing new. But amid a cacophony of information in our digitally saturated world, our desperate search for truth makes us acutely susceptible to lies perpetuated by our group leaders. Examples include the aforementioned discredited beliefs that climate change is a hoax, GMOs are dangerous, and vaccines cause autism.

Brad Allenby and Joel Garreau of the Center on the Future of War, a partnership of Arizona State University and nonpartisan think tank New America, have labeled this threat using a term historically associated with military strategy but increasingly applicable to modern politics: "weaponized narrative."[29]

"By offering cheap passage through a complex world, weaponized narrative furnishes emotional certainty at the cost of rational understanding" and "inoculates cultures, institutions, and individuals against counterarguments and inconvenient facts," ultimately dividing people along politically strategic boundaries, wrote Allenby and Garreau, who serve as codirectors of the Weaponized Narrative Initiative.[30]

Within cloistered communities, we feel "strengthened through media tools and messages that reinforce the narrative—crucially, by demonizing outsiders," they said. And "trust is extended only to those who believe, leaving other institutional and social structures to erode. In the hands of professionals, the powerful emotions of anger and fear can be used to control adversaries, limit their options, and disrupt their functional capabilities. This is a unique form of soft power. In such campaigns, facts are not necessary because—contrary to the old memes of the Enlightenment—truth does not necessarily prevail. It can be overwhelmed with constantly repeated and replenished falsehood."[31]

The overarching risk is that as weaponized narratives allow political leaders, partisan media, and ordinary folks on social media to reinforce group boundaries, those of us who consume these tainted messages will become increasingly distrusting of others outside of our own social circles. Indeed, in politically polarized societies, people are less likely to trust one another on a personal level. In a study examining the comprehensive World Values Survey, Switzerland political scientist Carolin Rapp culled data from more than forty-eight thousand individuals in thirty-nine countries. Using a novel technique to assess the connection between polarization and trust, she focused on people's opinions about the morality of three social issues: abortion, homosexuality, and euthanasia.[32]

On each issue, people were asked "whether you think it can always be justified, never be justified, or something in between." They were also asked, "Generally speaking, would you say that most people can be trusted?"[33] For each question, the respondents were asked to plot their answers on a range. Rapp found that higher divisiveness on these moral issues was connected to greater distrust across society.

THE DECLINE OF EMPATHY

When trust breaks down, empathy also deteriorates, which plays to the advantage of anti-outsider political impulses. For example, during his campaign and the first months of his presidency, Trump inflamed political opposition to allowing international refugees from war-torn areas to enter the United States,[34] citing national security concerns despite a lack of evidence of any substantive threat from immigrants.[35] But signs point to a decline in empathy extending beyond politics and affecting our basic humanity.

One concerning trend is a decline in volunteerism, which serves as a practical gauge of American togetherness. The percentage of Americans who serve as a volunteer in any capacity has steadily declined since the US Bureau of Labor Statistics began tracking the figures in 2002. In 2015, only 25 percent of Americans volunteered at any given point, marking an all-time low and the fourth consecutive year of decline.[36]

There's other concrete evidence that we care less about the plight of others. In a 2010 meta-analysis of seventy-two different studies, experts at the University of Michigan Institute for Social Research found that college students were about 40 percent less empathetic than college students twenty and thirty years earlier.[37]

The exercise, led by social psychologist Sara Konrath, involved parsing data from the Interpersonal Reactivity Index, which asked respondents to answer questions designed to gauge "empathic concern," "perspective taking," and the ability to identify with others.[38] For example, respondents were asked to what extent they agreed with statements such as, "I sometimes try to understand my friends better by imagining how things look from their perspective," and, "I often have tender, concerned feelings for people less fortunate than me."[39]

The largest drop in empathy in college students came after the year 2000.[40]

As it happens, this period of declining empathy encompasses my own college career. So while writing this chapter, I wondered the following: Am I also less empathetic than students of days gone by? Have influences in my life prompted me to care less about others than generations that went before me? Do I ignore the problems of others because I'm so focused on my own narrow corner of the world?

Online, the University of Michigan researchers offered a condensed version of the Interpersonal Reactivity Index survey given to students to gauge their level of empathy. I clicked and started answering. Each statement asked me to say whether it "does not describe me well," "describes me very well," or somewhere in between.[41]

"I often have tender, concerned feelings for people less fortunate than me."

Yes, certainly.

"Sometimes I don't feel very sorry for other people when they are having problems."

Well, it depends.

"When I see someone being taken advantage of, I feel kind of protective towards them."

You bet. Usually.

"I would describe myself as a pretty soft-hearted person."

I guess so. But does it show in my daily actions? I'm not sure. I know it should.

After completing the survey's sixteen non-demographic questions, I wasn't sure what to expect. I clicked for my results. It turns out my score was approximately equal to the average of college students over the last thirty years. I guess I'll take it, though clearly I'm not brimming with empathy.[42] But what are the exact reasons for this general decline in concern for others?

Political scientist Robert Putnam famously explored the roots of our increasing individualism and declining community engagement in his groundbreaking work *Bowling Alone*.[43] Surely the trends Putnam identified in his 2000 book—namely a general decline in social capital because of changes in family, work life, popular culture, and other factors—formed the early stages of this erosion of empathy. But I suspect that if Putnam were to conduct his analysis again today, he would find an even more dramatic shift.

Common theories on the drop in empathy often focus on a pandemic of narcissism and entitlement attitudes among me-first millennials—that is, my generation. Our parents, the theory goes, have coddled us and made us believe that we are the center of the universe. So, naturally we don't care that much about others. There could be some truth to that.

But the Michigan researchers pointed to the revolution in personal interaction brought about by technology as a potentially foundational culprit. "With so much time spent interacting with others online rather than in reality, interpersonal dynamics such as empathy might certainly be altered," they concluded. "For example, perhaps it is easier to establish friends and relationships online, but these skills might not translate into smooth social relations in real life."[44]

When others aren't part of our geographical, social, or political groups, we are now even less likely to trust them or consider their views because our digital connections to them are surface-deep. Thus, it's easier to ignore the truth that contributes to the plight of others.

PART 3

DISRUPTED

CHAPTER 7

FABRICATION NATION

A few days before Donald Trump was elected, digital designers, film-makers, software developers, photographers, and editors gathered together for a symposium on technological creativity at the San Diego Convention Center. With plenty of distance from the maelstrom of fabricated or distorted news stories rocking the foundations of American democracy, the crowd of hundreds was geeked for the annual Adobe Systems MAX conference, where the company often reveals new technologies. Much like events in Silicon Valley where Apple, Google, and Facebook show off new consumer tech products, the MAX conference allows Adobe to demonstrate its prominence in the field of creativity software.[1]

On this particular day, the tech giant that famously enabled people throughout the world to edit pictures seamlessly with its Photoshop software had a surprise to share. "We have already revolutionized photo editing," developer Zeyu Jin told the crowd, smiling widely. "Now it's time for us to do the audio stuff."[2]

With his laptop hooked up to a video feed, Jin opened a secret software application, internally dubbed Project VoCo, to perform a demonstration.[3] He proceeded to show the crowd how he could use Project VoCo to rearrange people's words from audio clips, making it sound as if they had said things in a different order than they had actually spoken them. That specific function wasn't particularly novel because there was already similar technology on the market. But what Jin said next sent a murmur through the crowd.

"We can actually type something that's not here" into Project VoCo, and the system will make it sound as if people have said words they've never actually spoken at all, Jin explained. With twenty minutes of sample audio from anyone's voice, Project VoCo could synthesize new words in the speaker's precise pitch and intonation.[4]

"We're not just going to do it with words. We can actually type small phrases," Jin said. "It mirrors how you speak."[5] After a flawless demonstration, the gobsmacked crowd rose up in thunderous applause. Jin, a Princeton University developer working with Adobe, flashed a big grin and raised his arms triumphantly, soaking in the moment.

Seemingly anticipating concerns over the potential for abuse, conference moderator Jordan Peele, an actor-comedian and director familiar with sound editing, spoke up. "If this technology gets into the wrong hands," he interjected, his voice trailing off.[6]

"Don't worry, don't worry," Jin responded, clearly prepared for the question. "We have actually researched how to prevent forgery. . . . We're working harder trying to make it detectable."[7]

The technology, he assured, was not designed for anything nefarious. "It's just for you to edit, like, audiobooks, podcasts," he said. "Really not for bad stuff."[8]

Yet the possibility for the technology to be misused was immediately obvious. Abuses could include, for example, making it sound as if a public figure said something provocative with the goal of stirring confusion, generating controversy, inciting violence, or slandering someone. If the technology is made available to average consumers, it is not difficult to envision the spread of fabricated audio turning into an excuse for politicians to deny anything they are caught saying on a recording or enabling them to smear an enemy. Imagine, for example, a world in which Trump could have believably denied the recorded comments he made to *Access Hollywood* in 2005 about groping women,[9] under the premise that the clip was faked.

After the initial Project VoCo demonstration was uploaded to YouTube, it was clear the public did not share Adobe's optimism about humanity. "This is going to get horribly abused," one commenter said on YouTube after watching the video.[10]

"Suddenly courts are gonna be filled with recorded proof of [stuff] you didn't say at all," another viewer declared.

Sarcasm was thick. "Yeah, this will not be abused. Not at all," one watcher quipped.

"I can't wait to make Trump supporters hate him," another person confessed.

"Let's make this world full of LIES!" one commenter wrote.

"Great!!!! Now we can't ever believe anything!!!!!" another said.

"This is NOT a good thing to enter the world," one concerned viewer concluded.

"I can't wait to horribly abuse this," another disclosed.

One observer, with history in mind, tepidly praised Adobe. "Wow, amazing technology. Kudos to the developers. However I think we all know what all good technology ends up being used for."

Adobe, which did not respond to requests for comment for this book, pressed ahead. In a video demonstrating Project VoCo's progress six months after the MAX conference, the developers from Adobe and Princeton revealed that they had already reduced the amount of audio they needed to imitate a speaker's voice. Instead of twenty minutes, it was now down to "more than ten."[11] With more than ten minutes of audio of anyone speaking, Project VoCo could seamlessly synthesize speech in its target's voice.

"Our fully automatic results are mistaken for real recordings more than 60 percent of the time on average," the developers reported in a video showing off their progress.[12]

In another test, the developers found that it took professional editors using commercially available software about twenty minutes per word to make it sound as if someone had said something they hadn't. For Project VoCo, it took less than one second per word.[13] "And their results are less satisfactory than those of VoCo," the developers said of the commercial editors.[14]

What's more, the new system allows users to manually tweak the pronunciation of falsely spoken words by tinkering with the sound quality to better mimic the real person's voice. "Our studies suggest that when synthesized words are inserted in the context of a spoken sentence, the modified sentence is often perceived as indistinguishable from other sentences spoken in the same voice," the Adobe developers reported in a published research paper. "With alternative syntheses and manual editing, the 'authenticity' of the synthesized word is further strengthened."[15]

Not long after the first demo of Project VoCo—which several observers nicknamed "Photoshop for voice"[16]—the outcry of concern about possible abuse reached Adobe's top executives. Seeking to quell the consternation,

Adobe vice president for creativity Mark Randall acknowledged that seamless voice-editing technology could be "scary."[17]

"But new technology can be like that—full of positive potential to educate, entertain, or inform on one hand, or yet another tool unscrupulous people might twist for nefarious purposes on the other," Randall said in a blog post. "That's because, at its core, technology is an extension of human ability and intent. Technology is no more idealistic than our vision for the possible nor more destructive than our misplaced actions. It's always been that way."[18]

He noted that the printing press "democratized thought and drove the spread of literacy throughout the world, but it also enabled societal upheaval and religious division." Similarly, the automobile "allows us to travel great distances quickly and conveniently, but it is also a leading cause of fatal accidents."[19]

Social media, he noted, gave rise to meaningful connections but also to the spread of fake news. Most notably, he acknowledged the company's own role in reorienting how society views the validity of photographs, which should today be questioned in virtually any format, even though they're often subconsciously accepted at face value. "In the era of silver plates, and later film, we thought of photographs as objective truth—as reality captured and frozen in time. Never mind that negatives could be altered in the darkroom, or that the photographer's use of framing or cropping could alter the perception of reality through omission or chosen perspective," the Adobe executive said.[20]

Technology has been developed to track photo manipulation, though it's not "perfect," Randall admitted. Audio editing, he noted, was already possible, though Project VoCo could bring it to the masses. But will it become a product that anyone can purchase? The Adobe MAX conference often serves as a place for the company to demonstrate real-life products and others it's still testing or considering. It "may never become a product feature," Randall said. "But now we have better insight into the benefits our customers find most useful. We also have new feedback to consider as we participate in discussions with professional organizations and standards bodies about the use of digital media."[21]

Whether Adobe brings seamless syntax editing and fabrication to life, however, is perhaps irrelevant. If not Adobe, someone else will do it.

In 2017, Montreal start-up Lyrebird demonstrated a voice-imitation algorithm that "can mimic a person's voice and have it read any text with a given emotion, based on the analysis of just a few dozen seconds of audio recording," the company said. "Users will be able to generate entire dialogs with the voice of their choice or design from scratch completely new and unique voices tailored for their needs."[22] Formed using deep-learning systems first developed at the University of Montreal, Lyrebird counts artificial intelligence pioneer Yoshua Bengio as one of its advisers. The company said its technology could be used for voice assistants, audio books in famous voices, animation, video games, or speech for people with disabilities.

In a transparent demonstration of its still-nascent AI system, Lyrebird released fabricated audio of Trump, Barack Obama, and Hillary Clinton. While for now the clips remain obviously fabricated to the casual listener, Lyrebird is quickly improving the system. "This is huge—it can make us say anything now, really anything," the bogus Trump says on the recording. "I wish them good luck. I'm sure they will do a good job."[23]

Although the promise is clear, the democratization of such technology is poised to compromise the believability of what we see and hear on an everyday basis. It's only a matter of time before convincingly fabricated audio is commonplace.

But that's just the start of the explosion of misinformation that's coming.

"INDISTINGUISHABLE FROM REALITY"

Within a few years, the emergence of accessible artificial intelligence enabling the fabrication of video footage and other media will dramatically blur the lines between visible fact and fiction. This technology will worsen the spread of false and misleading material online. And it could even undermine our collective faith in certain core elements of a healthy democracy, including the validity of criminal evidence and the trustworthiness of news segments.

"I think that it will not be too long before we are generating all sorts of media that is indistinguishable from reality—and that goes for pictures; it goes for audio, such as fake speeches given by politicians that are put in their voice and in their style. It goes for fake news broadcasts, fake radio broadcasts, potentially entire fake magazines, fake novels, fake news stories, the whole nine yards," said Jeff Clune, a computer scientist and director of the Evolving Artificial Intelligence Laboratory at the University of Wyoming.[24]

The implications aren't all bad, Clune promised. Artificial intelligence will enable the creation of virtual reality environments that are "tremendously realistic," he said.[25] It will foster a new wave of creativity in artistry, architecture, film, music, dance, photography, writing, video games, interior design, and many other areas. Technology will allow users to conjure up entirely new media based on their imagination. Clune said,

> You could say, "I would like to stand on a beach with a blood-red ocean and a green sky and a yellow moon with dragons flying in front of it shooting large flames." And you say, "Make the flames pink—no, make the sky blue," and you could iteratively ask for and customize the world that you want. And as the AI gets better and better, you could say, "I would also like a friend, and I would like her to be wearing clothes of this style and have this sort of personality." And poof, there you are—a character to interact with that's realistic and customized. So you can imagine a potential for video games and for interactive movies and virtual reality experiences.[26]

"But," he added, "you can also imagine the trickery that can ensue when it doesn't require ten to fifteen years of [photo-editing] skills and machine-learning skills and computer science skills to generate this well-crafted . . . version of, say, Trump with his arm around Putin accepting a cash bribe. If anybody can just say, 'Computer, make me a picture of Donald Trump receiving a cash bribe from Vladimir Putin with a smirk on his face,' boom, now I have the image, now I can Facebook it, [and] now I can put it on social media. And it can spread." The prospects are "scary," he said, because with "the power of the technology in the hands of the masses," there's "much more chance for mischief."[27]

One obvious example of the advancements in photo manipulation is the popularity of a relatively harmless smartphone application called FaceApp. The app allows users to alter the appearance of a photo by, for instance, making an old person look young, making a young person look old, turning a frown into a smile, improving someone's appearance, or making a subject look distorted. The app uses the concept of neural networking, a form of artificial intelligence modeled after the human brain that enables a computational system to improve its performance by observing and gleaning insight from the transmission of digital signals.[28] Transforming photos through FaceApp accomplishes in an instant what was a laborious process not long ago.

Historically, "pixel by pixel those are extremely challenging transformations to make in Photoshop—and you had to go to school for a long time and be an artist and an engineer, or at least technically savvy and experienced with software, to make those transformations," Clune said. "Now my grandmother can make them with the tap of a button."[29]

For now, the outcome is clearly fake and just for fun. But an accelerated pace of change is sweeping through artificial intelligence, and it will bring more dangerous applications with increasingly advanced fabrication capability.

"Give it a couple years and these transformations won't look pretty good, and they won't look like they have potential—they will just work. But they will work to such an extent that you won't be able to tell the difference between the products of these tools and the real thing," Clune said.

Clune has personally used artificial intelligence to demonstrate the early stages of completely fabricated pictures. In a 2017 project designed to illustrate the power of machine learning and to advance the technology, Clune, fellow researchers at the University of Wyoming, and computer scientists at the Montreal Institute for Learning Algorithms and Uber AI Labs designed an AI system that can create novel images on its own. The "plug-and-play generative networks" concocted by the researchers delivered high-resolution, artificial photos depicting, for example, birds, ants, monasteries, and volcanoes that don't exist in real life. All of them look remarkably authentic. And none of them look the same.[30]

"It basically allows you to generate synthetic images that look very real for any type of image that you want. So if you want a fake motorcycle or a fake tulip or a fake cheetah, you just ask the AI and it will draw it for you," Clune said.[31]

That's impressive. But what's even more astounding is that the system is not fetching an image from a database and altering it. "It is legitimately creating a new picture of a cheetah that looks like a real photo of a cheetah, on the fly, that the world has never seen before," Clune said. "One way you know that that's true is you can ask it for things that don't even exist in the world. So I can say, 'Make me a bell pepper on fire,' and it will totally render a green bell pepper on fire or something that looks like a bell pepper candle that has flames sitting in the middle of a chopped-open green pepper. So that's very cool. It allows you to see what the computer thinks about the world."[32]

The system could have helpful commercial applications in many areas, such as furniture design. "So you could train it on a whole bunch of tables and then say, 'Show me a bunch of tables,'" Clune said. "Many of them will look like the tables you're used to, but a couple of them will look like wild and crazy, new types of tables that you've never thought of or seen before. So as an artist or designer, that might spark you to go build that table. Or maybe the table itself looks ugly, but it's got a new wrinkle or a new kind of motif that you never considered before, and you can expand on that."[33]

It could even generate new rock songs or novels, he said. "It might invent the next dance craze because it does something wild and crazy that humans never would have conceived of, but once we see it, we can recognize that it's very interesting and cool," he added. "So it unlocks entirely new creative landscapes, which I think is fascinating."[34]

The promising applications of such technology are likely what will propel it forward. In a capitalist economy, someone will find a way to make money off of it. And if someone can make money off of it, technological innovation will follow.

In a demonstration of a new, real-time, motion-capture system in 2016, researchers at the University of Erlangen-Nuremberg, the Max Planck Institute for Informatics, and Stanford University showed how they could falsify facial expressions on real people seen in videos already uploaded to YouTube. Grabbing clips of political leaders, including Obama, Trump, Putin, and George W. Bush, the researchers showed how they could seamlessly transpose unique expressions onto the speaker while maintaining the person's facial structure. Their software absorbs an actor's facial expressions, frame by frame, via a video camera. Then the system believably transfers those expressions onto the face of the targeted speaker. The resulting altered footage shows the person speaking with the actor's facial expressions instead of his or her own.

"We aim to modify the target video in a photo-realistic fashion, such that it is virtually impossible to notice the manipulations," the researchers said in a study reporting their results.[35] Justus Thies, the lead researcher on the project, said he hopes it serves to educate the public about the billowing risk of phony footage.

"Otherwise they might get fooled by fake video," he said. "Most people do not know that such video-manipulation tools exist. They consume movies that are full of special effects, but they do not realize that such techniques can also be used to produce fake videos. Showing the simplicity of facial reenactment in our published videos leads to an increased awareness of such manipulations."[36]

Taken together, these technological developments show how the era of trustworthy video and audio clips is coming to an abrupt end. "It shows that we have to re-think the value of video material and that we have to develop algorithms to detect such manipulations," Thies said.[37]

DISTORTING MEMORY

The impending onslaught of altered and fabricated media will challenge our basic instincts about how to assess the validity of what we see and hear. But even when we instantly recognize the content's questionable nature, encounters with misinformation linger in our minds.

People "often feel like, 'I only trust what I see with my own eyes.' But your own eyes can be so deceiving," said Linda Henkel, a cognitive psychologist and memory researcher at Fairfield University. "Everything that you perceive is filtered through your cognitive expectations, your cultural conditioning."[38]

To examine how watching video and listening to audio affects people's memories, Henkel and researcher Isabel Lindner of the University of Kassel designed a study to gauge what people recall about actions they've previously performed. In the first phase, subjects were told to perform mundane tasks, such as breaking a toothpick or pouring water into a glass. In the second step, they were shown video or audio of other people doing tasks they had performed and some tasks they had not performed. Some were shown video with audio, while others were shown footage without sound. And in some cases, people heard audio of the tasks but did not see video. In the third phase, participants were asked two weeks later to recall whether they had completed certain tasks, including some they had done and others they had not.[39]

In each scenario, the subjects regularly professed to remember doing things that they had not done, simply because the participants had seen video or heard audio of another person completing the tasks.[40] These results confirmed what Henkel and Lindner referred to as the imagination-inflation effect, the observation-inflation effect, and the sound-inflation effect. In other words, seeing or hearing something that didn't happen can later make you believe that it did take place, even when you initially realized it had not occurred at all.

When considering these results in the context of a future world overrun by fabricated and misleading video, audio, and photos, it's not a stretch to conclude that our collective subconscious is susceptible to manipulation by partisan actors seeking to profit from deception.

"We remember that something happened but how it happened" is harder to recall, Henkel said, adding,

> Was it something we imagined or actually saw? Was it something I read in the newspaper or heard on the radio? Was it something this person said or that person said? I've done a lot of research looking at how our imagination—the things we just think about or infer—can create memories that we swear happened in the actual world. So I can get people saying, "Oh yeah, I remember breaking that toothpick," when all they did was see a couple of photos of a broken toothpick. But in their memory they can reconstruct what it must have been like to break that toothpick because they can see the aftermath of it.[41]

Because of this reality, doctored videos, photos, audio clips, and text are "fertile ground" for delivering false messages, Henkel said. "We don't have the ability to figure out very well where our memories came from," she said. "So you can definitely create memory distortion."[42]

SPINNING THE STORY

For professional news media that have so far survived the industry's contraction, fabricated or highly misleading content—ranging from videos, audio clips, and photos to simple text—represents both an opportunity and a serious threat. As doubts about the reliability of online material grow exponentially, some consumers will seek refuge in corners of the internet containing genuinely trustworthy content. Indeed, this opportunity is already presenting itself. After the early stages of fake news became well known to the general public following the 2016 election, paid subscriptions surged for several serious, traditional watchdog journalism outlets, including the *New York Times*, the *Washington Post*, the *New Yorker*, the *Atlantic*, and the *Financial Times*.[43] This significant increase in online subscriptions, in particular, was especially encouraging because it's increasingly clear that digital advertising alone won't sustain many journalism jobs.

But while additional digital subscriptions to venerable national news organizations are good news, the forthcoming boom in fabricated and seriously slanted online content threatens to suck those organizations into a believability crisis. Today's fake videos, audio clips, and photos are often distinguishable from authentic news if the observer is looking closely or applying a skeptical lens. Clune said,

> Every single time you turn on the radio right now [and] you hear Obama saying something, you believe it's Obama because you have a good [internal] voice-recognition system. When that stuff is perfectly faked, the ultimate solution, which is a solution that's been known for a long time in human history, is trust. Brand trust. You'll have to know that if it came from the *New York Times*, then it's trustworthy. But then you have the problem of people faking stuff that looks like it came from the *New York Times*. That's a whole extra level of problems. You just get into this situation where so much stuff is fake [that] you can't trust anything. And so then you just start believing whatever you want to believe because you don't have checks on your epistemological beliefs.[44]

This situation plays directly into the hands of political and corporate leaders who want to evade scrutiny. Trump has already made it his mission to discredit the traditional news media, unfairly and inaccurately labeling CNN, NBC, ABC, CBS, the *Washington Post*, the *New York Times*, and other outlets as "fake news" whenever he disagrees with their legitimate journalism.[45]

Those attacks encourage his followers to question responsible reporting as well. It is common for Trump supporters to barrage journalists on social media with accusations of "fake news."[46] Trump, recognizing an opportunity to get more than just the vocal support of his base, has even trumpeted the erroneous accusations in fundraising. "It's up to us to get things done and drain the swamp in Washington. I have been listening to the REAL America, and I know you're with me. Join me in FIGHTING THE FAKE NEWS and get your sticker with any contribution today," Trump declared in an early reelection campaign fundraising push on his website in summer 2017.[47]

With Trump's accusations and the coming outbreak of fabricated material posing a serious threat to journalism's reputation, it's vital for news outlets to double down on credible content. Unfortunately, although much content in mainstream outlets is vetted through journalistic processes that adhere to ethical standards based on the pursuit of the truth, journalism's financial crisis has prompted many outlets to lower their standards, which threatens to compromise the entire industry's believability.

For example, with fewer reporters and fewer editors, many organizations have resorted to inviting extensive contributions from outsiders to beef up their websites and generate advertising dollars. These types of contributions can certainly offer value when they're clearly demarcated and forced to meet stiff editorial standards. After all, op-eds and letters to the editor, which are usually fact-checked before being published, have been part of the news business for decades. But the proliferation of contributed content raises the serious possibility that news companies are lending the credibility of their brands to people with an agenda to mislead, misconstrue, or misinform.

In 2017, the Securities and Exchange Commission (SEC) filed charges against three publicly traded companies, seven stock promotion firms, two chief executive officers, six corporate employees, and nine business writers for allegedly publishing seemingly legitimate stories through established business news sites with the goal of promoting favored stocks in exchange for compensation from the companies that benefited from the publicity.[48] The stories, published from 2011 through 2014, "left investors with the impression they were reading independent, unbiased analyses on investing websites, while writers were being secretly compensated for touting company stocks," according to the SEC. In more than 250 articles, the writers allegedly falsely claimed that they had not received payment from the companies they were promoting.[49]

In one of the most egregious cases, owner Kamilla Bjorlin and associate Andrew Hodge of the stock promotion firm Lidingo Holdings hired business writers Brian Nichols and Vincent Cassano to "deceive investors into believing that the articles were impartial," SEC investigators alleged. According to the government, in some cases, the company published articles under made-up bylines to avoid getting caught. Altogether, Lidingo pocketed at least $1 million in cash and stock for publishing articles promoting penny stocks, the government said.[50] Writers profited, too, with one pulling in about six hundred dollars per published article, according to a settlement document.[51]

Lidingo published articles on many trusted business news sites, including *Forbes*, Yahoo! Finance, Seeking Alpha, Benzinga, TheStreet, Fool.com, and Investing.com.[52] Companies that allegedly benefited from the bogus publicity included Arch Therapeutics, Assured Pharmacy, Galena Biopharma, NeoStem (later Caladrius Biosciences), OncoSec Medical, and Stevia First (later Vitality Biopharma).[53] The allegations suggest that the perpetrators capitalized on the aching news industry's weakness for free content.

Some outlets are already pivoting to limit their reliance on free content. The *HuffPost* announced in January 2018 that it would end its section that featured regular outside contributors, which totaled more than one hundred thousand since the feature launched in 2005. Editor in Chief Lydia Polgreen praised the section for providing a public voice to "a huge number of people who weren't previously afforded one." But she also acknowledged that "open platforms" are risky. "One of the biggest challenges we all face, in an era where everyone has a platform, is figuring out whom to listen to," Polgreen wrote. "Open platforms that once seemed radically democratizing now threaten, with the tsunami of false information we all face daily, to undermine democracy."[54]

What's more, the substantial decline in news coverage of numerous issues has created a vacuum for public relations officials to openly spin the facts with little consequence, for corporate executives to sway consumers through social media, and for elected leaders to escape notice altogether or control the message more effectively. In many cases, the onus is almost entirely on them to adhere to the truth because there's no watchdog to sound the alarm when they're engaging in campaigns of deceit.

I don't want to act like anything that doesn't come from a journalist is deceitful. That would be disingenuous and just plain wrong. For many companies, teams, politicians, nonprofits, community groups, and governments, reaching their intended audience has become much more difficult in recent years without journalists to tell their stories. They previously relied upon the news industry to communicate with the public, and now that is often no longer possible. Therefore, many of their efforts to publicize their news by circumventing the media are entirely defensible, ethical, and even necessary.

In the past, "we basically made a deal with the news industry," said Matt Friedman, a public relations executive at Tanner Friedman in metro Detroit, with whom I've often worked as a reporter. "In exchange for their audience, which was significant and influential in a marketplace, we would cede control of the message. . . . Now, it's often the case that we don't get that audience anymore. So we have to take back editorial control of the message."[55]

The traditional relationship between brands and news media has largely collapsed, save for the most newsworthy of companies, towns, and sports teams that still garner traditional coverage. All of Tanner Friedman's clients today get less professional news coverage than they did five or ten years ago, Friedman said, citing an internal grid through which the firm tracks that information. Now, he said,

> Companies have to start filling the gaps and communicating directly to their audience about what they want their audience to know. It can be done in a very credible, attention-getting way, similar to the way in which news is constructed and communicated. And I think there's a great opportunity for business. At the same time, of course, you have to look at the societal impact of that. There is no independent arbiter of fact. However, there is an imperative, still, to communicate. And if the news business doesn't give you that opportunity to get your stories covered, then you go for the next best thing.[56]

Consequently, communications professionals have gained more authority to strategically weave their own stories, sometimes even enabled by the vestiges of professional news media. Following the decimation of Michigan's local news industry through newspaper closures, job cuts, circulation decreases, and broadcast ratings declines, many of the state's shrunken news organizations are publishing Friedman's client's press releases almost word for word.[57]

"If not verbatim, pretty close," he said. "They just have to crank out news as efficiently as possible. So we have to be able to write the press releases so that they are ready to go, ready to become news. And that's new. It used to be we would put press releases together to help journalists get facts straight. And maybe we'd try to sneak a few messages in there. But it's like now we have to write the story.

So the quotes better be quotable. And they better communicate a message and have some kind of benefit for the audience."[58]

Friedman, a former local TV producer, is known for his candor and credibility among Michigan news media. And he is often critical of companies that aren't transparent and truthful. But we should not expect ethical practices to take precedent everywhere else, with the balance of messaging power having shifted to organizations and people who often have incentives to slant the story.

Amid the decline of the news media, US employers have aggressively beefed up their spending to control the message, adding more than 40,000 public relations specialists from 2004 through 2013 for a total of 202,530 nationwide. Public relations specialists outnumbered reporters by a ratio of 4.6 to 1 in 2013, up from a ratio of 3.2 to 1 in 2004.[59] And the gap is expected to widen. The US Bureau of Labor Statistics projected that the number of reporters would decline at an annual pace of 9 percent from 2014 through 2024,[60] while the number of public relations specialists increases at an annual pace of 6 percent.[61]

Empowered by reduced scrutiny from the news industry, companies can deliver their own version of distorted news that's more palatable than the outright concoctions that are easily identifiable on social media. This tendency is apparent in the increased frequency of questionable earnings figures reported by publicly traded corporations.

While public companies are still required to report their revenue, profit, and expenses using generally accepted accounting principles (GAAP), the SEC has tracked "a significant and, in some respects, troubling increase over the past few years in the use of" alternative data known as non-GAAP figures. That strategy gives companies significant discretion on how to track sales and profitability, allowing them to brag about transactions that should not necessarily be considered revenue and downplay the impact of costs that potentially should be factored into their overall performance. Instead of scrutinizing those figures, the weakened business news media have given the figures "prominence" in their reporting, SEC chief accountant James V. Schnurr said.[62]

"I am particularly troubled by the extent and nature of the adjustments to arrive at alternative financial measures of profitability, as compared to net income, and alternative measures of cash generation, as compared to the [GAAP] measures of liquidity or cash generation," Schnurr said.[63]

Through social media, companies are also able to exert more control over their messages and images, build digital relationships with consumers, and deliver personalized marketing. While official corporate social media accounts reflect a fairly transparent form of communication, a more underhanded form of messaging involves surreptitious sponsoring of influential users who agree to post positive things about brands in exchange for compensation.[64]

Although the Federal Trade Commission (FTC) requires promoters to post the hashtags #ad or #advertisement alongside sponsored material, many often leave it off—sometimes unintentionally but often purposely. This is particularly common in the fashion, beauty product, fitness and weight loss, and food and beverage sectors.[65] In fact, about one in four online "influencers" acknowledged in a nonscientific survey by marketing firm SheSpeaks that they had been asked to post positive messages without disclosing their commercial ties to their respective brands.[66]

"Lesser-known celebrities and influencers with smaller followings are dominating the influencer market on Instagram," said Robert Weissman, president of watchdog group Public Citizen, in a letter to the FTC signed by other similarly concerned groups. Digital word-of-mouth marketing sites, such as Influenster and BzzAgent, often promise to "send users free products in exchange for reviews and social media posts," Weissman said. "Once a user receives a free sample, they are encouraged to post a photo on Instagram to advertise the product to their friends. The more posts promoting a product that a user makes, the more free products they receive."[67]

Those types of posts are especially deceptive because "people generally place more trust in recommendations made by their peers and have no reason to believe that their friends, colleagues, and family are engaging in paid-product promotion," Weissman said. "Thus, companies are preying off of the trust and relatability of smaller level influencers."[68]

Parasocial relationships—in which an ordinary person feels invested through social media in the life of the influencer, but not the other way around—have a significant impact. Research has demonstrated that parasocial bonds bolster trust, meaning that a semblance of authenticity in the promotion of products and services can often lead consumers to spend money or take action to support brands.[69]

Parasocial trust also extends to individual corporate leaders on social media. Elon Musk, the charismatic innovator and CEO of Silicon Valley automaker Tesla and rocket-maker SpaceX, is a prime example of a corporate executive who has mastered Twitter to exert influence over public perception. His tweets ricochet throughout social media, garnering a fiercely loyal following among consumers and sometimes even boosting Tesla's stock price.

WHERE TO GET NEWS

Much like corporations, politicians also use social media as a propaganda machine to establish trust and subvert the truth. Trump, of course, has famously used Twitter aggressively to connect with voters, influence the news media, and circulate inaccurate statements about his opponents, including journalists. His tweets fire up his political base without any help from reporters, who often end up publicizing the posts anyway.

Not surprisingly, the most ideologically rigid politicians are typically the most influential on social media. On Facebook, the most conservative and most liberal US senators had a median of 140 percent more followers than moderate members, while the most liberal and most conservative House members had a median of 59 percent more followers than their moderate counterparts. For example, archconservative representative Trey Gowdy, the South Carolina Republican who defeated enlightened climate change believer Bob Inglis in a 2010 primary, has racked up more than 1.3 million followers, many of whom liked his page as he was leading a controversial congressional investigation targeting Secretary of State Hillary Clinton over the Benghazi, Libya, disaster.[70] Inglis, by contrast, had about fifteen thousand followers as of fall 2017.

Using the internet to communicate directly with constituents is not exclusive to Trump or Republicans. Although Trump has taken political communication through social media to a new extreme, at least in terms of volume and content, his predecessor also made a habit of communicating directly to the public. Obama's White House communications strategy relied heavily on delivering messages through social media, blogs, video, and other digital channels. Though the material was generally less provocative than Trump's tweets, the

Obama White House often still circumvented the traditional arbiters of truth that once filtered most political material for public consumption.

Though these types of messages are often reliable, occasionally engaging, and perhaps even politically imperative in the digital age, the increased frequency at which politicians communicate directly with their constituents is tantamount to a twenty-first century version of state-sponsored media. While Americans have long derided authoritarian governments for their state-controlled media—such as China's Xinhua news agency, which happens to operate an active Twitter feed in English[71]—we cannot ignore the effects on our democratic values of political propaganda delivered through social media. It is content designed to achieve a specific agenda, plain and simple.

Although many Americans may snub Obama's videos or Trump's tweets, social media communication by people in power is a proven way for them to tinker with the facts. In a scientific study tracking the sway of executives who actively post to social-networking platforms such as Facebook, Twitter, and LinkedIn, researchers found that "perceived CEO authenticity and approach-ability" bolster trust among consumers. This was especially true of CEOs who elicited engagement through social media. In other words, leaders don't neces-sarily need to engage with the press to appear trustworthy. They can cultivate an aura of truth through social media, avoiding the uncomfortable scrutiny of professional journalists.[72] After accumulating trust, it's easier to mislead.

In a speech on the floor of the House of Representatives not long after Trump took office, Representative Lamar Smith, a Texas Republican and chairman of the House Science, Space, and Technology Committee, ripped into the news media for supposedly ignoring the president's accomplishments. "The national liberal media won't print that, or air it, or post it," Smith said. "Better to get your news directly from the president. In fact, it might be the only way to get the unvarnished truth."[73]

CHAPTER 8

CRAP DETECTION 101

S tanford University is one of the most selective higher-education institutions in the world. It rejects 95 percent of its applicants, choosing only the best of the best for undergraduate admission.[1] These students are academic stars in high school, elite performers in Advanced Placement courses, and top-notch scorers on standardized tests. They have extensive extracurricular involvement, volunteer experience, and leadership skills.

"These are not merely good students," said Sam Wineburg, a Stanford history and education professor. "These are the cream of the crop, and they define critical thinking by all of the metrics that our society prizes."[2]

But that does not mean they are proficient at assessing facts in a digital context. When Wineburg set out to test the online civic-reasoning capability of students throughout the country—including Stanford's best—the outcome was disheartening. Amid a profound shift in how we encounter information, our first instinct should be to prepare students to enter a world in which authenticating facts is a basic skill they need to be productive citizens. But Wineburg's research shows that young people, whom we often assume to be digitally savvy, are not faring well in our suddenly chaotic information universe.

Wineburg's Stanford History Education Group, backed by the Robert R. McCormick Foundation, conducted a study spanning eighteen months from 2015 to 2016 that involved more than 7,800 responses from students in middle school, high school, and college. Students at each level were asked to validate information on various digital platforms, including social media, organization websites, and news articles, by completing a series of tasks. The students' performance, across the board, was "bleak," Wineburg's team of researchers concluded.[3]

In one task, fifty-eight undergraduate students at three large universities were asked to decide whether the website of the American College of Pediatricians—ACPeds.org—was a trustworthy source of information about children's health and to explain how they arrived at their answers. On a polished page with modern design and graphics, the American College of Pediatricians described itself as "a national organization of pediatricians and other healthcare professionals dedicated to the health and well-being of children." It claimed it produced policy "based on the best available research, to assist parents and to influence society in the endeavor of childrearing." It linked to a standard "About Us" page, a blog with regular updates, a "member login" page, and a mailing list.[4]

At first glance, it appeared to be a reputable source of information from a large, scientifically grounded, national association of industry professionals. But a few minutes of independent research into the group's agenda revealed that the Southern Poverty Law Center estimated that the organization had no more than two hundred members and often supported the promotion of "utter falsehoods about LGBT people," according to the Stanford researchers. The widely respected group in this field is actually the American Academy of Pediatrics, which has some sixty thousand members.[5]

But this distinction escaped nearly half of the undergraduate students asked to assess the validity of ACPeds.org, including many of the Stanford students.[6] They decided the fringe group was trustworthy, despite the fact that, at the time of the exercise, the organization was openly linking to news releases with dubious titles such as "Know Your ABCs: The Abortion-Breast Cancer Link."[7]

The students' reasons for deeming the group legitimate revealed pervasive naivety at how to authenticate digital material. "The first thing that I noticed was that the website ended in .org," one college student wrote afterward. "This was a sign that it was a trustworthy source."[8] Information on any website, including pages with domain names ending in ".org," can be falsified or skewed, of course.

Another student took a similarly straightforward approach. "I searched through the 'About Us' section of the website," the student wrote. "It looks formal and provides a legit means of contact. Searched Google to make sure the website even came up. Objectives and goals of website are clear, as well."[9]

In a separate task, the college students were asked to assess the trustworthiness of material in a tweet. "New polling shows the @NRA is out of touch with gun owners and their own members," read the tweet by the liberal group MoveOn.org about the conservative National Rifle Association. The tweet listed a link to the results and a photo with text describing the survey: "Two out of three gun owners say they would be more likely to vote for a candidate who supported background checks."[10]

Accompanying the tweet was "#NRAfail," underscoring MoveOn.org's political motives for publicizing the results. The photo accompanying the tweet listed, in small, difficult-to-read lettering, Public Policy Polling as the source of the survey and provided the dates it was conducted. The tweet's link revealed that the liberal Center for American Progress sponsored the survey, which suggests it might have been designed with a political agenda in mind. The undergraduates, including the Stanford students, were asked to determine whether the tweet was a "useful source about NRA members' opinions on background checks" and to explain their reasoning, including listing any other sources they used to reach their conclusions.[11]

Of forty-four students at three universities who completed the exercise, less than one-third successfully noted that a liberal political agenda might have skewed the presentation of the results. Moreover, more than half of the students who completed the task didn't even click on the link to assess the source of the poll. Many "simply scrolled up and down within the tweet," according to the researchers. Some tried a Google search on their own, but many came up short with an inadequate search for "CAP," the acronym listed in the bottom left corner of the tweet with no clear indication of what it represented.[12]

The Stanford History Education Group study also showed how middle school and high school students struggle with simpler digital tasks. In one exercise, middle school students were shown a comment posted to a news article by a random member of the public who was relaying supposed study data on health issues without any documentation. More than 40 percent of the students said they would cite the commenter's data in a research paper, even though no source was presented to back it up.[13] "The person included many statistics that make me think this source is reliable," one student wrote after assessing the commenter's contribution.[14]

Wineburg's provocative findings reflect a kindergarten-through-twelfth-grade education system that teaches "out of textbooks with a single unambiguous answer," he said. "We ask kids to analyze the text, but they're not analyzing the same kind of text the minute they go into recess and open up their Twitter feed.

We protect them from what they find on the web. We protect them from pseudo texts, we protect them from biased texts, [and] we protect them essentially from all of the experience and practice they need to be thoughtful observers and participants in democracy."[15]

Which is why Wineburg does not criticize the students who participated in his study for their inability to authenticate online material. "I do not blame my Stanford students for doing poorly on a set of tasks that no one in their high school experience prepared them to do," he said.[16]

But his results show that our education system must be overhauled to force students to grapple with the mistruths, deception, and misdirection that make up our disorderly digital landscape. "Should school be a prophylaxis that protects us from the world? Or should it prepare us to deal with it?" Wineburg asked.[17]

Cursing the digital revolution is fruitless, he said, adding, "It's like complaining about the genie after you've already rubbed the bottle, and he's escaped."[18] Doing so "diverts us from the central question we have to face as a society, which is, what are the ways of thinking that are necessary to operate effectively in a world where information comes to us in zeroes and ones?" he said, referring to binary code that's familiar to computer programmers. "That is not a question that Facebook, a moneymaking operation, particularly cares about. That is an educational question. That's a social question."[19]

The questions we should be asking, Wineburg said, are, "What type of system will serve us into the future? Should we do what we've always done in the past? Will that serve us? No. We are in a very difficult moment at this point. What's going to make the difference? What's going to make the difference is how we as a society respond educationally."[20]

STUDENTS AS CUSTOMERS, NOT THINKERS

If we stipulate for a moment that many adults are a lost cause in the post-fact era—that those of us with preconceived notions of the world are entrenched in our own digital, ideological, and social bubbles that collectively color our views of the truth, and that there's little chance we'll change—then hopefully students can still be influenced in a positive direction. Indeed, any concerted effort to combat misinformation almost certainly must begin at a young age, when the ways we learn how to process information are still taking shape.

As anyone can attest, though, millennials and Generation Z are more reliant on technology than any previous generation. The smartphone rules our world. And that will not change.

So we must adjust our educational strategies accordingly to give young people the intellectual tools to enter a world in which facts are constantly in dispute, mistruths spread rapidly through powerful digital engines, and ideological segregation undermines our collective commitment to true community. But instead of equipping students with the skills they will need to survive amid unfamiliar terrain—in which historical arbiters of facts, such as the mainstream news media, have declined precipitously in prominence—K–12 schools and higher-education institutions have transformed into educational factories designed to manufacture kids who can beat the test, nail the college entrance essay, score good grades, and assemble résumé bullet points that appeal to employers.

Rather than emphasizing the intangible skills that will help young people tread water in the misinformation age, schools and colleges are catering to parents and tuition payers who demand good grades and practical job skills. The irony is that while it's commendable to help students prepare to enter the labor market, technology is changing so rapidly that the skills students learn in high school and college are often obsolete shortly after they reach the workforce—if they were ever relevant at all.

Consequently, students emerge from high school and college without the lifelong-learning capability and analytical-reasoning skills they need to navigate both the scourge of mistruths and the rapidly evolving knowledge economy.

In a survey of more than 1,600 recent college graduates, Project Information Literacy executive director Alison Head found that about three-quarters "believed that their college experience had taught them information competencies, such as searching, evaluating, and presenting" material. Yet at the same time, "far fewer" claimed to know how to ask "questions of their own."[21]

In other words, the students graduated with the technical knowhow to navigate the digital world but without the fundamental critical-thinking skills necessary to discern truth in the material they encounter and experiences in which they find themselves. Nearly two-thirds of the recent grads said they found it challenging to stay "motivated to keep up with learning in their personal and professional lives."[22]

An interview Head conducted with a recent grad who landed a job as an engineer at a major aerospace company starkly illustrated the issue. In college, when presented with a problem, his philosophy was that "either the professor knows the answer, or the answer's in the back of the book," Head recalled him saying. "Then I got a job as an engineer, and I was working on a launchpad, and it malfunctioned, and we were really under the gun, and it was a federal project," the recent grad relayed. "So we had to hire consultants to help us figure out how to ask questions because we couldn't get beyond, 'Well, we did X, Y, and Z, but this didn't happen.'"[23]

The engineer, although brilliant from a technical perspective, was not equipped with the intellectual skills needed to challenge the rigid path that had been presented to him. "Being able to develop questions of your own is lacking—in institutions we've lost that as students feel pressure to get out in four years and the tuition costs have increased," Head said.[24]

Many students are what she called strategic learners. They are masters at completing coursework, answering exam questions, delivering spotless projects, and landing impressive grades, but they do not necessarily develop the ability to trek beyond the narrow framework of a syllabus. "A strategic learner is the student who shows up, they take your exam, and you really can't give them a C, but they don't have an original thought in their head. They haven't processed the information. And I think . . . the challenge of learning is how to create learners that take chances and do embrace their curiosity," Head said.[25]

In an analysis of data from the Collegiate Learning Assessment exam, often called CLA+, which is administered to college students throughout the country to gauge their critical-thinking, analytical-reasoning, problem-solving, and writing abilities, the *Wall Street Journal* found that the average graduate at some of the "most prestigious flagship universities" displayed "little or no improvement in critical thinking over four years." The ninety-minute test requires students to assess information by combing through spreadsheets, research papers, news articles, and various documents to "make a cohesive argument" or evaluate an assertion. But at least one-third of seniors at more than half of the schools, numbering more than one hundred, failed at the task.[26]

This should not come as a surprise. Amid skyrocketing tuition costs and increased demands on colleges to prepare students for the workforce, an emphasis on what researchers call fluid intelligence, which describes the ability to use analytical reasoning to assess and solve problems, is a casualty. The increased emphasis on career-ready skills—from nursing to robotics to software coding—simply leaves little room for abstract exercises, such as the thoughtful exploration of the liberal arts and casual encounters with new ideas.

When students are paying thousands or tens of thousands of dollars per semester, they naturally expect to emerge from college with the earning capability that makes their investment worthwhile. To avoid alienating their customers, higher-education institutions are essentially selling grades and degrees in exchange for nominal performance. This formula devalues academic accomplishment. Instead of assessing college students based on their abilities and genuine achievement, educators are rewarding students based on whether they put in the minimal effort.

Former Duke University professor and geophysicist Stuart Rojstaczer has been tracking college student performance for years, having assembled a database of several decades of grades from more than four hundred institutions. His research shows that the average grade-point average at four-year, American colleges increased by 0.1 points on a four-point scale every decade since the early 1980s. In the early 1960s, fewer than two in ten grades were A's. Today, it's well over four in ten. An A, in fact, is the most common grade today, despite scant evidence that students have improved academically.[27] Rojstaczer said,

> What appears to be driving rising grades over the last thirty-five years is rising tuition. As students pay more and more for a degree, and their parents pay more and more for a degree, they expect more for that degree. And that includes a high grade upon graduation. They also expect to graduate. So when you raise tuition like the United States has raised tuition, on average nationwide, for a college degree, you're going to see an ethos develop on college campuses where students are no longer acolytes in search of knowledge, but they're customers in search of a product. And that product is a college diploma.[28]

He called it the student-as-a-consumer era. "So what we've done on college campuses, with the blessing of college leadership—and actually the leadership of college leadership—is instill an ethos where the students are the customers, and the customer is always right," he said. "And if the customer wants a high grade for a class, the professor needs to deliver."[29]

Simply making the minimal effort—doing the required work—is typically enough for students to get by, regardless of the quality of that work. Rojstaczer said,

> What an A or a B increasingly means is that you showed up, you were diligent, and you didn't insult the teacher. And C is substandard performance. So if you're putting in the effort, you're going to get a B or better. If you don't put in the effort, you might get—horrors of horrors—a C, which is what used to represent more or less average behavior. Average seriousness and just showing up means a B or better at most any school or any college. That's a change in how we evaluate students. In some classes, just showing up means you get an A, an A minus. And that's a change.[30]

By some measures, even the effort required of students has waned during the same period in which grades have risen. "The amount of time that students spend on homework is down considerably from previous decades. And the amount of writing and reading required for classes is down," Rojstaczer said.[31]

But one reason for that is rising tuition itself. "Some of that diminishment in expected student workload is caused, or probably caused, by the fact that students are increasingly taking part-time jobs, trying to make ends meet, and universities and colleges have to take that into account in ways they didn't before," he said. "Students have to pay their way."[32] As a result, many college educators feel pressure to not maintain high standards for their students.

DRIVEN TO TECHNOLOGICAL HEIGHTS

At the high school level, the relentless emphasis on preparing kids for standardized tests, college, and careers leaves little room for helping them gain the critical-thinking skills they need to grapple with misinformation.

Although most students don't pay tuition to attend high school, their parents pay taxes that fund public schools and elect the officials who run local districts. And voting parents are demanding high school experiences that prepare their children for college admission. They're not demanding that school board trustees and state policy makers design curriculum and performance assessments to ensure their kids can authenticate facts. Rather, they are demanding an à la carte approach to education, expecting specialization at a young age under the premise that our dynamic, technological age requires specific skills and abilities that must be cultivated over many years.

To be sure, skills such as software programming are excellent to gain at a young age. I wish I could code. But the rapid evolution of technology shows how specific skills are increasingly irrelevant in the digital age. Instead, the ability to gain skills—that is, learning how to learn—is what matters most.

From a practical perspective, politicians and elected school board leaders won't overhaul education to reorient curriculum and performance goals toward critical-thinking skills until they view it as contributing to their mission of promoting students' wage-earning prospects. Until education policy makers can show their constituents that change will benefit students economically, any hope for a substantive shift is futile. This applies to both K–12 schools and higher education.

"One could say that you need to have an external threat that forces us to pursue knowledge for societal good," said Andrew Rotherham, cofounder of the nonprofit consulting firm Bellwether Education Partners. "When was college particularly rigorous in the United States? Well, when the Russians launched Sputnik in the 1950s, there was a sudden inward look by the nation as to what colleges were doing and that what we needed was to catch up to the Russians. Otherwise, they were going to dominate the world. So we started to make college tougher. We started to be concerned about engineering programs and science programs because of this fear of the Soviet Union. We used to think, 'The Russians are getting smarter than us. We can't allow that to happen.'"[33]

Indeed, after the Soviet Union's Sputnik satellite reached space in October 1957, Americans panicked, believing that their Cold War opponent had usurped the United States in technological prowess. In the several years leading up to that seminal moment, the Senate had passed bills to federally fund higher-education initiatives, but the House had failed to follow suit, leaving the nation without a cohesive strategy to bolster collegiate enrollment. But after Sputnik launched,

Senate Education and Labor Committee chief clerk Stewart McClure suggested to committee chairman Lister Hill, an Alabama Democrat, that he revive the push by rebranding the education bill as a matter of national security.[34]

Amid a groundswell of demand from the public for action on education following Sputnik, lawmakers adopted the National Defense Education Act, which authorized federal funding for higher education, along with low-cost student loans. From 1960 to 1970, the number of US college students more than doubled from 3.6 million to 7.5 million.[35] At the same time, policy makers put extensive thought into "re-conceptualizing how to create the kind of scientists and mathematicians that we would need for our national defense," Stanford's Wineburg said.[36] "If there was leadership [today] the way there was leadership after Sputnik, there would be a recognition that we are facing a threat that we've never faced before."[37]

That threat, of course, is misinformation in the digital realm. But without a crisis that transcends political boundaries in a polarized world, our K–12 schools and higher-education system will continue to drift away from an emphasis on analytical reasoning and critical thinking toward skill-specific outcomes.

As it happens, however, such a crisis exists. But it has nothing to do with foreign powers.

AUTOMATION REVOLUTION

The rise of automated factory equipment, self-driving vehicles, service robots, and artificial intelligence threatens to undermine the US economy in profound ways. Indeed, the onset of the automation revolution is already upon us, though many Americans don't realize it yet. Although skeptics often dismiss concern about automation's economic destruction as something that is commonly predicted but never happens, many robotics and AI experts say that automation is approaching an inflection point, whereafter it will consume our daily lives and disrupt our jobs.[38]

Separate studies by consultancy McKinsey and accounting firm PricewaterhouseCoopers each estimated that about 45 percent of worker activities can be automated based on currently demonstrated technology.[39] Automating those processes would lead to an estimated $2 trillion reduction in global spending on labor.[40]

Major advances in computer vision, sensors, gripping, processing power, and AI algorithms will enable entire job categories to be wiped out. At least 90 percent of activities in more than seventy entire professions can be completely automated, including mail clerks, food preparers, ophthalmic lab technicians, and tire repairers, according to McKinsey. And a high percentage of activities in many other professions can also be turned over to technology.[41]

This is not exclusive to labor-intensive, repetitive, blue-collar factory jobs. Numerous white-collar professions are at grave risk, as well. Many manual functions in accounting and law, for example, can be handed over to software. Walmart in 2016 slashed seven thousand bookkeeping and in-store accounting positions as it automated cash management.[42] Nearly six in ten CEOs said in 2016 that they planned to cut jobs over the next five years because of robotics.[43]

In fact, any job that involves a significant amount of predictable work, ranging from burger flipping to data processing, is susceptible. Yet according to the Pew Research Center, an astounding 80 percent of Americans believe their current job will definitely or probably exist in its current form in fifty years.[44]

"When we ask people about the future, they say, 'Oh yeah, disruption is inevitable. Lots of jobs are going to be taken away by robotics.' Things like that. 'But my job isn't,'" said Lee Rainie, director of Pew's internet and technology research. "There's this built-in optimism bias that people have about their own worth and the uniqueness of their skills."[45]

It's misplaced optimism. Even my own profession is at risk, as if the news industry didn't already have enough economic strife. A company called Automated Insights has developed software called WordSmith that is already writing thousands of automated news stories per month, including corporate-earnings articles for the Associated Press (AP), basketball game recaps for Yahoo! Sports, and financial content for many other clients.[46]

For a while I could easily tell when I saw a newswire story written by a robot. The wording was clunky, and the story structure was highly formulaic, clearly suggesting that a human professional had not written it. But when I recently encountered an AP earnings story about fast-food chain Dunkin' Donuts that one of my editors had posted to *USA Today*'s website, I was briefly fooled into thinking the piece had been written by a real person until I read the disclaimer at the end of the story, noting its automated author.[47]

The robots are approaching the city gates. The only way to prevent them from invading and conquering—that is, to survive the automation revolution—is to adapt quickly. But the only way to adapt quickly in a rapidly evolving economy is to continuously reinvent yourself, to learn how to learn.

Which is why the threats posed by the post-fact era go far beyond politics. In a dynamic economy in which static skills will quickly become outdated, training workers for specific jobs is admirable but won't lead to enduring prosperity. Instead, we must equip students with an entrepreneurial mind-set, along with flexibility and a willingness to teach themselves long after they've finished college. Under this new paradigm, curiosity is even more important than knowledge. A desire to learn more about the world—which means learning more about each other—comes with a spirit of openness to new ideas and new ways of thinking.

When Cultural Cognition Project researcher Dan Kahan of Yale set out to ascertain why certain people are better than others at removing their personal biases when assessing scientific information, he found that people who registered higher on a key measurement of curiosity were "less polarized" and "much more likely to examine evidence that was contrary to their views."[48] He added, "People will tend toward the media sources they think support their position and shun the rest. But not the science-curious people."[49]

Even if they have opinions, people who exhibit high rates of curiosity are able to set aside their biases when filtering new information. "They're the ones who are going to be listening in an open-minded way," Kahan said. "Science curiosity is the opposite of the defensive reasoning people engage in. Typically when their group's position is attacked, they want to push [contradicting information] away, whereas the science-curious person is looking for a surprise. So if you could induce that in a greater part of the population, that would be good."[50]

Stimulating curiosity is indeed critical if the United States is to remain competitive in a global economy. But that requires a major emphasis on self-directed learning and fact authentication. In a nonscientific survey in 2016, the Pew Research Center and Elon University's Imagining the Internet Center asked more than 1,400 technologists, scholars, educators, strategic thinkers, and practitioners to predict how US workforce retraining programs would evolve over the next decade. Respondents said new courses would be available, but many "will be self-directed" and "workers will be expected to learn continuously," especially through online classes.[51]

"Tough-to-teach intangibles such as emotional intelligence, curiosity, creativity, adaptability, resilience, and critical thinking will be most highly valued," the respondents said. But many doubted whether the political will or funding exists to promote these objectives, while others worried that "some people are incapable of or uninterested in self-directed learning."[52]

The "ability to adapt to changes" is paramount because "any given set of skills will become obsolete quickly as innovations change the various economic sectors: precision agriculture, [advanced manufacturing], precision medicine, just to name a few," one respondent, Calton Pu, a software professor at the Georgia Institute of Technology, told the researchers. "Therefore, the challenge is not only to teach skills but also how to adapt and learn new skills."[53]

Disconcertingly, this reality threatens to deepen socioeconomic inequality—a major source of polarization in America today—as people with access to a better education and stable home life are likelier to gain the crucial skill of life-long learning. "Students who are self-directed often have had a very good foundational education and supportive parents," Muhlenberg College professor Beth Corzo-Duchardt told the researchers. "They have been taught to think critically and they know that the most important thing you can learn is how to learn. And they are also . . . more likely to come from economic privilege."[54]

TEACHING SKEPTICISM

When Philadelphia technology teacher Mary Beth Hertz was instructing kindergarten-through-eighth-grade students several years ago on how to navigate the internet, she quickly realized that giving them the technical tools to track down information online is insufficient. Equipping them with the right mind-set with which to conduct basic research is far more important. That requires teaching students how to evaluate the legitimacy of information instead of just regurgitating facts. But teachers often find it difficult to carve out time to focus on these types of intellectual exercises because of the litany of material they must cover to prepare students for standardized tests.

"There wasn't a lot of time for research projects. It killed me," Hertz said. "You're still stuck teaching discrete skills rather than teaching kids how to learn on their own."[55]

After she transitioned to teaching ninth graders at a magnet school in Philadelphia where one of the "core values is research" and "inquiry-based learning" is a priority, she had more flexibility to design curriculum to give students the capacity to ascertain truth.[56] So she created a lesson plan modeled after the ideas of technologist and internet critic Howard Rheingold.

Evaluating source credibility is among the fundamental skills in what Rheingold called "Crap Detection 101,"[57] a phrase he co-opted from something the *Atlantic* once quoted Ernest Hemingway as saying: "To invent out of knowledge means to produce inventions that are true. Every man should have a built-in automatic crap detector operating inside him. It also should have a manual drill and a crank handle in case the machine breaks down."[58] To provide practical ways to develop an automatic crap detector, Rheingold posted an online lesson and a collection of links to digital tools to help people "test the veracity of information."[59]

Using Rheingold's resources, Hertz deployed a new strategy that involves presenting students with opinionated articles that may contradict their beliefs. This forces them to "understand that what they're reading is biased," so they'll be more likely to view other information they encounter through a critical lens, she said.[60]

Indeed, one of Rheingold's core beliefs is that students need to be exposed to lies, not shielded from them.[61] When kids are forced to reckon with misinformation, they learn how to investigate source credibility, embrace skepticism, and challenge their own ways of thinking. Rheingold said,

> So many schools are afraid to allow [unfiltered] internet access at all because they're afraid bad things are going to happen. I think bad things are already happening, and the bad thing of believing everything you see on the web greatly outweighs the possibility that some kid is going to access a porn site or something like that. Schools need to face the reality that they need to teach online skills. It's weird that almost a hundred percent of what is taught in K

through eight and high school has nothing to do with the world that everybody, including kids, lives in online. And I think that you can teach—you can call it critical consumption if you don't want to call it crap detection—pretty early just by making kids aware that there's bad information out there and just a little bit of inquiry can eliminate a lot of the bad stuff.[62]

That will be especially critical as fabricated and highly distorted videos, audio clips, and photos explode onto the digital scene amid technological advances that make such content easy to create and spread. Students will need to be taught that just because they see it doesn't mean they can believe it.

"We need to arm the next generation with the intellectual tools to be skeptical about what they see, to try to get to the bottom of what's real versus [what's] fake," said Jeff Clune, the Wyoming computer scientist mentioned earlier. "It's simple when said that way. The devil is in actually pulling that off. But at the end of the day there is already a segment of society that doesn't get duped by fake images and news now—or at least they get duped far less frequently because they've been trained to be skeptical, and they've had a great education. And we need to do that better and do that for everybody."[63]

Exposing students to inauthentic material is crucial, he agreed. "I think you've got to be fooled repeatedly," he said. "You have to simulate this—where somebody looks at something they think is real, and then you show them that it's fake—so this isn't an intellectual thing that they think they one day might encounter. They emotionally realize how easy it is to be duped."[64]

Rheingold acknowledged that it's much easier said than done to overhaul the largely decentralized US education system and orient it toward a common goal. "We've got these issues we've identified—none of them are insoluble. But where is the political will and the willingness of teachers and administrators and parents to teach their kids to look at the world in a new way? It's just happened so rapidly," he said. "When the printing press vastly increased the number of literate people, it took, really, decades for the habits of reading to establish themselves, and we haven't had that long."[65]

K–12 schools and higher-education institutions won't completely change overnight, but some rapid changes are feasible. One productive shift would be to set aside longstanding qualms about *Wikipedia*. The crowd-sourced online encyclopedia has been reviled in many classrooms, libraries, and college courses since it was founded. But the reality is that *Wikipedia* has developed a set of core principles, editing standards, and authentication processes that make it a strong starting point for basic research on millions of topics.[66] Besides, teaching students how to interact with *Wikipedia* is more realistic than banning it altogether. It's not going away.

Professional fact-checkers already rely heavily on *Wikipedia*. Many often use the "Talk" tab at the top of *Wikipedia* to track debates among the site's editors about the content of a particular subject. "The 'Talk' entry, once you get past the obligatory prose, is essentially watching the argument over knowledge develop in real time," Stanford's Wineburg said. "It does precisely what no textbook could ever try to do, which is to show and reveal how arguments of knowledge sometimes reach consensus and sometimes reach divergence."[67]

One of the common criticisms of *Wikipedia* is that anyone can make a change to an entry. But the site has established processes to neutralize agenda-driven contributions. To prove it, Wineburg said, "Go to 'Israel-Palestine.' Make a change." Then wait a moment. "Here, I'm going to start my stopwatch, and let's see how long before your change is eliminated," he said. The change likely will disappear within minutes, if not seconds. "What a lot of educators do is they just say, 'Well, we don't allow *Wikipedia* in here because *Wikipedia* has errors.' Yes. Guess what? *Wikipedia* has errors and so does *Encyclopædia Britannica*," he said.[68]

Artificial intelligence entrepreneur Paul English, who is often seeking to hire recent college grads with the ability to adapt their skills and assess dynamic material, feels the same way. He made the case that guidelines for the proper use of *Wikipedia* and Google should be integrated directly into school curricula. English, who founded travel site Kayak.com, said students must be taught how to navigate the world of information as it exists—not as we wish it existed. Without those skills, students won't survive in the era of automation and artificial intelligence. And if they don't have those skills, companies like his will suffer.[69]

"Kids should be taught that some sources are more accurate than others," English said. "If I were an educator, I would just show some really egregious examples of how wrong some news outlets can be to make sure the kids get critical-thinking skills."[70]

These skills have universal applicability. English's nonprofit Summits Education has invested in teacher compensation, training, and curriculum through a network of forty schools in Haiti, where about ten thousand rural students are getting access to an education that may one day help them escape poverty. In one of the world's poorest regions, Summits is teaching primary school students how to assess the truth because it's a skill they need to survive.[71]

"These schools are in very remote areas in the Central Plateau," English said. "Some of them are hours away from roads. You literally have to hike up a mountain for three hours to get to the school because there's no way to get a vehicle to it. There's definitely no electricity and definitely no internet. For the primary kids, we're just teaching them the basics of literacy and critical-thinking skills. We have the kids interview each other. So it's not just the teacher lecturing to the kids."[72]

Summits is teaching skepticism, showing the Haitian students how to "get information from multiple people," and how to assess the reliability of the material, he said, adding,

> The kids in rural Haiti don't get the advantage of getting information from remote people because there's no internet. All they can do is take information from their family and students and teachers and elders. But even though their information comes just from local people, we can still teach them that some local people are more reputable than others on certain topics. So part of critical-thinking skills is being aware that you should trust different sources differently. The thing that would be dangerous in Haiti would be if people just trusted what comes from "authority" and what comes from a politician. What we're trying to do in Haiti is to have a lot of learning be discussion-based rather than authority-based.[73]

In that respect, the skills that students in Haiti need are no different from the skills that students immersed in the digital age must also acquire.

DEEPER LEARNING

For schools in the developed world, the emergence of a new field predicated on what proponents call deeper learning offers a path that enables students to grapple with misinformation and dynamic economic changes.

Marc Chun, a program officer in education at the Hewlett Foundation, which has funded deeper-learning initiatives, described deeper learning as a set of cognitive competencies. "The world is changing, and our schools have not," Chun said. "The types of skills you need are the ability to solve novel problems, to deal with unstructured situations, [and] to be able to apply new knowledge. A lot of that is how you make sense of that knowledge."[74]

Strategies to develop deeper learning in the classroom include promoting collaboration among students, encouraging students to direct their own learning, empowering students to provide feedback to each other, emphasizing projects and problem-solving, and favoring long-term assessments over short-term quizzes and tests. "You have to know content, you have to critically think, you have to be able to work with others, communicate well, both written and oral," and then to "learn how to learn and to maintain a learning or academic mind-set," Chun said.[75]

Preparing schools to help students adopt this mind-set involves revolutionary change. "In many ways, we're asking the education system to do something that they've never had to do before," Chun said. "Folks aren't adequately equipped to do this because the world of how you get information has changed so radically. How do you vet a source—how do you tell what's truth from nontruth—is a key challenge. That is the place we're entering. So I don't blame anyone. I just think our system was not set up for doing what we need folks to do today."[76]

Deeper learning gives students the skills to solve problems by completing projects or exercises that force them to assess unfamiliar material. But from a practical perspective, students won't be motivated to gain these skills unless they can see how it applies to their lives. That's why real-world experience such as internships, job shadowing, and volunteering can be crucial to empowering young people to exercise their capacity to learn while also appeasing parents who want their kids to graduate with specific skills.

"Students are more motivated to learn if they see the reason why they're learning something and if you can tap into their interests," Chun said. "If they really care about something or it's something they're passionate about, they're going to totally engage. I think that's more than half the battle."[77]

A Hewlett-funded study by the nonpartisan American Institutes for

Research examined data from more than twenty thousand students in twenty-seven public high schools. Students at high schools that deployed deeper-learning techniques were eight percentage points more likely to graduate on time than students at other schools. The benefits extend beyond high school, however. Another American Institutes for Research study funded by Hewlett examined more than twenty thousand students in twenty-five schools. It concluded that students at deeper-learning high schools were more likely to attend college and more likely to attend selective institutions.[78]

And there's reason to believe that the benefits of deeper learning extend into the workforce, as well, where adaptability is central to success. "Young people today are going to have ten, fifteen, thirty different jobs," Chun said, noting the "jobs you see posted today, like social media analyst, that didn't exist when I was in college. So the ability to be able to learn something new and apply that—I think that's the most crucial skill that someone needs today."[79]

THE ROLE OF JOURNALISM EDUCATION

One profession dedicated primarily to learning new material on a daily basis, authenticating facts, and analyzing issues as objectively as possible is journalism. Despite the news industry's many challenges, the fundamental principles of sound journalism are highly applicable for anyone in the digital age. Yet in many schools, journalism education is virtually nonexistent.

While some schools still offer a newspaper class or broadcast course, few kids receive comprehensive instruction on the basic principles of news reporting. With little understanding of what journalists actually do for a living, students are more susceptible to lies and distortions about the news media, such as Trump's persistent labeling of reports he dislikes as "fake news."

But a little journalism education can go a long way. At its core, basic training on news reporting requires students to sideline their own biases, embrace skepticism, give all sides a fair shake, and prioritize the truth over spin.

In a 2015 study of more than nine hundred high school journalists in Kansas and Missouri, University of Kansas journalism professor and former high school newspaper adviser Peter Bobkowski found that student reporters were more likely to be civically engaged than their classroom contemporaries.[80] "One of the clear findings was that students in journalism classes had a better understanding of the First Amendment than students who had never taken journalism," Bobkowski said. "Whether or not they had to deal with First Amendment issues, at least they were exposed to it more than students who weren't in journalism, and had a greater appreciation for freedom of speech, freedom of the press, [and] freedom of expression."[81]

To be sure, we cannot and should not expect many students to become professional journalists. The number of jobs in the industry is dwindling, after all. But for students to become citizens who can successfully navigate the misinformation age, they must have a basic understanding of how to separate fact from fiction on their own. "By teaching young people journalistic skills, we teach them how to more effectively function in a society that relies on digital information for civic engagement," Bobkowski said. "An extension of that also is the ability to look at information, verify information, find information, [and] find the accurate sources of information—just the idea to question your sources. All of that is definitely something that journalism has always strived for. These are professional standards that we certainly teach students and [that] journalists practice."[82]

Here again, though, socioeconomic inequality threatens to exclude entire populations of students from access to the type of education they need to thrive. In a separate analysis of student media programs throughout the country, Bobkowski found that, unsurprisingly, "schools that were most likely to have a more robust student media program were the better funded," large schools in suburbs. "Where there's a dearth of media programs are both [in] urban schools and small, rural schools, just because the resources are not there. It's almost like journalism and media programs, to a certain extent, are a luxury item. And it's only when schools reach a certain threshold of resources that they're able to dedicate the teachers and space and technology toward media programs."[83]

Luckily, schools don't need to muster resources to form student media programs to combat the post-fact era. They can simply find ways to integrate the core principles of journalism education into classroom lessons on other subjects.

The processes of "finding information, evaluating information, [and] communicating information" aren't exclusive to journalism, Bobkowski said, adding,

They're language arts skills, they're social studies skills, [and] they're math skills. I think we should have a more concerted effort to make sure that our students are doing those three things well and being critical about the information they find—not blindly critical but being able to evaluate it using some standards. The principles are pretty basic and pretty universal—being able to find and locate information, locate sources of information, know where to look beyond Google or maybe even using Google, and being able to say, "If I'm looking at this type of source of information, I should be looking here."[84]

Clune agreed that the skills of an old-fashioned news reporter are what students need to spot falsehoods. "Learning the tools and the tricks of the journalist's trade, such as figuring out if your source is trustworthy, getting multiple, independent sources to verify facts, doing basic fact-checking—those are great things to have," he said.[85]

School librarians are often "at the forefront of this," said Neal Goff, founder of education publishing consulting firm Egremont Associates and former board president of the Association of Educational Publishers, who has studied the role of libraries in promoting student growth. "They're all over this issue. Librarians' charter traditionally has been to teach kids research skills. And in the pre-digital age that meant how to use print sources and do bibliographies and find your way around a physical library. Now, doing research is very much about teaching them digital skills and teaching kids that there are more ways to get information than" searching it on Google.[86]

Librarians recognize that the belief that students, as digital natives, have strong digital-research skills is misguided. Kids typically "don't know how to do [research] beyond using Google, and sometimes they don't know how to structure Google searches so it yields the kind of information they want," Goff said. "Teaching kids that there are all sorts of digital sources beyond Google that are very useful and worth checking is exactly what libraries do these days." Yet "in this age of very constrained school funding, there are fewer school librarians than there used to be," he said. "It used to be it was a given that every school building would have a librarian. That's no longer the case."[87]

While investments in journalism education and school librarians could yield lasting benefits, simply requiring students to write more often could also eventually help reverse the post-fact tide, said education consultant Rotherham.

"The ability to write is the ability to think," he said. "Clear writing is a result of clear thinking. One thing we can do is we can leave more time in school for kids to write."[88]

But that's also easier said than done. To enable more writing in school, English classes "should be substantially smaller," he said. Right now, he added, high school English teachers can have 120 students at any given time, spread out among several classes, making it practically impossible for them to grade effectively, let alone help students become better writers. "You can't assign any real amount of writing to that many kids. The classes should be smaller, or if they're going to be large like that, there should be support on the grading," Rotherham said.[89]

One development that was potentially promising—but has since been politically demonized—is the creation of the Common Core State Standards for English Language Arts & Literacy in History/Social Studies, Science, and Technical Subjects. Known as Common Core, the standards were developed by states—and incentivized by the federal government—as a suggested set of education benchmarks that promoted critical-thinking, problem-solving, and analytical skills. While states retain the authority to implement their own K–12 learning goals and curricula, the Common Core standards are aimed at developing "cogent reasoning and evidence-collection skills that are essential for success in college, career, and life" and offer a "vision of what it means to be a literate person who is prepared for success in the twenty-first century."[90] But the standards have been caught up in a whirlwind of rhetoric after critics raised fears of political indoctrination and federal interference with state affairs. Goff said,

> The politicization of the Common Core was truly unfortunate because in addition to the fact that it is not a curriculum and is not mandated by the federal government, I think what happened was—with all of the backlash of teaching to the test and what was happening in schools because of mandated testing—the Common Core became a lightning rod for that backlash. Most of the people who are very much against the Common Core probably don't know what the standards say and continue to conflate the concept of standards with curriculum. Common Core, well applied, comes down on the side of better equipping kids to tackle the kind of challenges we're talking about here.[91]

That caveat, however—"well applied"—is significant.

The Common Core standards are admirable and worthy of implementation, Rotherham said, adding that they "are exactly what you would hope people can do," forcing students to consume content critically and "really think about things."[92] But successfully implementing the Common Core standards is a tall order for the K–12 education system, particularly under a framework in which "we don't get serious about teacher quality," Rotherham said.[93]

To do so would require not just teaching students how to deploy critical thinking and analytical reasoning but teaching the teachers how to do so, as well. "You need a good background yourself to be able to teach like that," Rotherham said. "We're asking teachers to teach stuff that a lot of them don't know. That's not fair. But it is the kind of teaching you want."[94]

It's a good sign that various efforts to promote media-literacy coursework gained momentum throughout the country after Trump ascended to the presidency.[95] Better late than never.

But whack-a-mole education won't accomplish much. What's necessary, instead, is to reexamine whether schools should seek to equip students with specific skills or whether they should instead prepare students to acquire skills on their own.

CHAPTER 9

FINDING COMMON GROUND

As an evangelical Christian and climate change scientist, Katharine Hayhoe straddles a bitter fault line dividing disparate worlds. Trying to bridge the gap inevitably involves enduring a steady stream of hostility.

"I do get disheartened," she admitted. "I get very disheartened by the constant, excessive, aggressive, negative feedback I get. How can I say it?"[1]

She paused to gather her thoughts. "Certain days, I'm convinced, are just spiritual attacks," she said, using a biblical term for a confluence of unseen forces that come together simultaneously to undermine your peace of mind and wellbeing. "There are just certain days when you cannot explain what's happening other than it really is a spiritual attack because it's the intensity and coordination and how I feel in response."[2]

The assault from conservatives on her commitment to the cause of promoting climate change awareness and action can be relentless—especially after she was catapulted into the public spotlight when she spoke on the subject during a panel discussion with President Obama and actor Leonardo DiCaprio in October 2016.[3] "It's really challenging to be, every single day, attacked by somebody who calls you names, who disparages you, who accuses you of all kinds of things you've never done, and who basically tells you you're a liar—the shared arrogance of people who know nothing about what you do always telling you that they know more about it than you do," she said.[4]

But Hayhoe does not let those attacks compromise her devotion to her cause. She believes, in fact, that bringing Republicans and Democrats together may be vital if the United States—and indeed the world—wants any chance of curtailing carbon emissions and thus preventing environmental catastrophe.[5]

And she's right. Without a successful effort to bridge ideological divides, the country faces profound economic, political, and social crises that will fester amid rigid polarization. Regardless of your political persuasion, it can feel like our society is hopelessly infected with disunity. But it would be dangerous to stipulate that all of our differences are irreconcilable. Instead, we must never stop seeking common ground because it's the only route to progress in the American political system, which was specifically structured to promote compromise and pragmatism.

People like Hayhoe show how this is possible, even in the most divisive arenas. Her strategy for reaching evangelicals on climate change involves several stages of action. First, she seeks to understand the stance of her fellow evangelicals by reading and listening to their arguments. "I try to figure out what frame they're using," Hayhoe said. "And then I try to figure out, would that frame work for me?" Usually not. "So what I do is I go in and I completely disrupt that narrative so that they can't use it anymore, and they have to look for a new narrative," she added. "And while they're searching for a new narrative, that's when they're actually going to listen to me. I have this finite amount of time where I can actually get information out or communicate and share and have them actually listen before they pigeonhole me again."[6]

The narrative her fellow evangelical Christians typically use, she said, often overtly or implicitly labels environmental activists as spiritual enemies. "I do think that we can only communicate effectively and persuade people effectively if we understand what is the narrative in their heads and what role we are playing in that narrative. A lot of conservative Christian audiences I talk to—the narrative they're using is that of a false prophet and a true believer. I'm the false prophet, and they're the true believer," she said.[7]

In the biblical narrative on the end-times, false prophets play a crucial role in deceiving Christians into turning their backs on their religious principles. "That's a test of your faith. You're actually going to prove your faithfulness to God by rejecting the false prophet," Hayhoe said.[8]

So when she enters a room in which she is viewed as the enemy, she starts immediately by finding common ground. It requires her to commit what would appear to be heresy among climate activists. "I sometimes even start off by bluntly saying, 'I don't believe in global warming,'" she said. "And everybody just looks at me like, 'What planet are you from?'"[9]

She laughed. Her point was that her beliefs—that is, her spiritual beliefs— rest in a higher power. "I go through a statement of faith of what I do believe in that I know the people I'm talking with share: 'I believe in God. I believe that God created this amazing world we live in. I believe what it says in Genesis—that God gave it to us to care for. I believe that God delights in his creation.' Creeds or statements of faith are very familiar and comfortable ways to talk to people" in the church, she said. "So I go through this statement of faith, as well as a personal witness" or what Christians would call her "testimony."[10]

Once she's explained that she's on their side from a spiritual perspective, she has an opening to dive into climate change. Though she does not believe in climate change in the same way she believes in God, she still believes that climate change is real, is caused by humans, and is a massive threat that must be addressed.[11]

"I transition from that and say, 'Here's why I care. Here's what's happening to this planet God gave us. Here's what's happening to all these people put on this planet that we're told to care for,'" she said. "Then I say, 'Well, why is this happening?' That's where I come in as a scientist. . . . I don't say, 'This is what science is telling us.' I say, 'This is what God's creation is telling us.' And so we're already two-thirds of the way down the road together before I even get to anything that they might potentially have a problem with."[12]

People, to put it in spiritual terms, don't like to be preached at—even Christians. They want to know that you value them and appreciate their perspective, even if you don't agree with them. "You have to have mutual respect," Hayhoe said, "otherwise it just doesn't work."[13]

USING SHARED LANGUAGE

Finding common ground also means using shared language from a political perspective. Former South Carolina Republican representative Bob Inglis knows this innately because he used to explicitly reject environmental activism on ideological terms. Now, as a conservative proponent of action to combat climate change, his clear-eyed view on the dysfunctional conversation focuses on the need for a shift in how both sides speak to each other.

"There's a lack of respect for the other position or the other point of view, or a sense of superiority that creates the equal and opposite reaction," he said.

"'You just told me that you don't like me and somehow you're morally superior.' It's very predictable. If you tell me you don't like me, well I don't want to hear any more from you."[14]

To persuade political conservatives of the need to embrace the science on climate change and pursue action, Inglis believes it's critical for climate activists to learn how to speak the language of the other side, as painful as that might sound. "We learn things from people we know and trust," he said. "We don't learn things from people we don't know and trust. We don't trust them, and therefore we don't want to learn from them, and we can't learn from them because we don't have anyone to vouch for them. If somebody walks up to you and says, 'Here's what you need to do about your loved one that's in the hospital,' you would say, 'Now, how do I know you're telling me straight?'"[15]

Unfortunately, many environmental activists "are not aware of the language they're using," he said. "They don't realize that the language they're using is just [for] their tribe."[16]

After an environmental activist delivered a speech at a recent conference, Inglis confronted the person over his word choice and tone. "One of them was saying essentially, 'This is what you can do to be a good boy: you will get solar cells on your office roof; you will turn down the thermostat,'" Inglis recalled. "That's not what conservatives want to hear. They want to hear . . . 'You can have energy freedom on the top of your roof. It's your roof, and you tell that power company that you're going to put it up there, and you'll finance it with whomever you wish. This is America.' That's a completely different language."[17]

Many Republicans resist climate change science and activism due to what Inglis called "solution aversion" because the potential fix hasn't been adequately explained to them as something that aligns with their political values.[18] "Therefore they doubt the existence of the problem. Which sounds strange, but it's what all of us do every day. I mean, if you tell me, 'Let's go from here to there,' well, I'll go look over there to see how good it looks. If I think, 'No, I don't want to go there,' I come up with reasons why the journey isn't worth it," Inglis said.[19]

Realizing the importance of pursuing common ground, Inglis staffed his climate action group, RepublicEn.org, with five Republicans and one Libertarian. His group favors eliminating all energy subsidies, including those benefiting fossil-fuel extraction, and assigning a price to carbon emissions as a market-based solution leveraging the forces of capitalism to trigger a private-sector assault on global warming.[20]

"So we start by saying, 'Now listen, does this make sense to you that we should eliminate subsidies for all fuels? No more Solyndras,'" he said, referring to the solar energy company funded by the Obama administration that went bankrupt. "'No more production tax credit for wind, no more investment tax credit for solar, no more electric car credits, no more—and this gets a little dicey—no more under-market leases on public land for the extraction of minerals.' Then the diciest move we have to make is, 'no more of the biggest subsidy of them all, which is being able to dump into the trash dump of the sky without paying the damages you're causing there.'"[21] In other words, charging companies for their greenhouse gas emissions, which cause climate change, would be necessary.

"That gets a little bit hard. But once you get agreement that, at a principle level, we want to eliminate all the subsidies, no more of the government picking winners and losers—this is where our Libertarian friends say a hearty 'amen, all right'—then once we establish this commonality of purpose, that we're with you, that we believe the same things, these are our fundamental values of accountability. Isn't that a key concept for conservatives?" he said.[22]

The next question he poses to conservative audiences is whether, in the spirit of accountability, Americans must assume responsibility for the harm that our carbon pollution is causing to others. "Is it right that coal-fired electricity gets to do that to my neighbors?" Inglis asks them. "Then you have a moral discussion—that, no, that's not right. [We are] not being held biblically accountable."[23]

Despite the bitter political divide over climate change, Inglis believes that people can—and will—change. He believes that ideologically isolated groups can find common ground. And he does not believe change will be gradual. Instead, he believes it will happen suddenly, albeit after a long struggle. An apt comparison is the political debate in Washington over marriage equality, he said. For ages, "you could get some real applause at Republican conventions" for opposing gay marriage, Inglis recalled. "Then it changes. Now we have Peter Thiel speaking at the Republican National Convention," he said, referring to the gay venture capitalist and Trump supporter. Many Republicans have dropped the issue from their platforms, often saying that the Supreme Court's ruling authorizing gay marriage decided the matter.[24] "So you don't talk about that anymore," Inglis said. "My point is the tipping point is reached, and then those talking points are dropped like hot rocks."[25]

But change must come about through a groundswell of public sentiment. It must be from the bottom up. If it's forced from the top down, it won't stick. "Our whole thesis is that politicians follow; they don't typically lead," Inglis said. "In order to get them to take a bold stand like pricing carbon dioxide, you've got to show them support. And we've known all along that we might have to step out on the street by ourselves, singing solo, gather a couple people out on the street, have a little choir, and then finally get the brass band there. And once the brass band is striking up on Main Street, then you'll find the politicians stepping off the curb and leading the parade where it's already going. But we've known all along that we need to be first out in the street, risking the oncoming traffic."[26]

THE POWER OF STORYTELLING

Establishing common ground and a shared language is helpful in breaking through ideological barriers. But on social media, that's not enough because many people aren't listening at all. They're cloistered in their own groups, walled off from information about scientific findings. Even if they realize that their views aren't representative of expert consensus, they find comfort and affirmation among people within their social circles. Swaying those isolated groups is extremely difficult because simply presenting the facts is insufficient.

That's why Karen Ernst, pro-vaccine activist and mother from Minnesota, believes in the power of storytelling as a persuasive tool to help reach people who are skeptical about the efficacy and safety of vaccines. One reason she believes that storytelling works is because it's working for the other side—the anti-vaxxers. "What we noticed is that parents a lot of times are being drawn into vaccine refusal because they heard a scary story. The quintessential one is Jenny McCarthy. 'I vaccinated my child, and the light left his eyes'—that's what she said on *Oprah*," Ernst recalls. "It's a heart-tugging story. It stays with you. And it certainly stays with you much longer than remembering some statistic about how many lives vaccines have saved or understanding how memory cells

help create immunity. There's a stickiness to the story that plays on your emotions and remains with you. So parents might not know consciously that they're
basing their decision on that, but that certainly plays a role in it."[27] Now Ernst's
group, Voices for Vaccines, is using storytelling to promote vaccinations.

"Everyone's got a story about vaccines and vaccine-preventable diseases.
Everyone does—whether they realize they do or not—and we need to start
getting these ideas out into the public," she said. "Also, when doctors are talking
to parents, they need to share some stories with them, too."[28]

For example, doctors and nurses often tell her frightening stories about their
days treating epiglottitis before the Hib vaccine eradicated most instances of the
life-threatening condition, which blocks the flow of air through the windpipe
into the lungs. "It was terrifying. They'll never forget the time a child came in
with their throat closing, and they just couldn't intubate," she recalled. "Parents
deserve to hear those stories when they're saying, 'I'm not sure about this
vaccine.' I think that a doctor can say, 'Well, you know, let me tell you about this
time I dealt with this disease or this story I know about this disease, because ultimately that's what we're doing when we're vaccinating. We're trying to prevent
that from happening.'"[29]

One particularly poignant account of a woman from the countryside in Lake
District, England, helped underscore the power of storytelling for Ernst. Amy
Parker, a then thirty-seven-year-old music teacher and mother of two teenagers
with another child on the way, told her story in 2013 in a compelling post on the
Voices for Vaccines website. Parker was a self-proclaimed "child of a health nut"
from the 1970s, groomed to repel any unnatural substances. "I wasn't vaccinated,"
she wrote. "I was brought up on an incredibly healthy diet: no sugar til I was one,
breastfed for over a year, organic homegrown vegetables, raw milk, no MSG, no
additives, no aspartame. My mother used homeopathy, aromatherapy, osteopathy,
we took daily supplements of vitamin C, Echinacea, cod liver oil."[30]

Despite the seemingly healthy lifestyle, much of which she continued
into early adulthood, Parker fell prey to numerous serious illnesses, many of
which would have been prevented by vaccines. She contracted measles, mumps,
rubella, whooping cough, and chickenpox, as well as other serious conditions.
In her twenties, she was diagnosed with precancerous human papillomavirus.[31]

Eventually, faced with overwhelming personal evidence of the scientific necessity of vaccines and modern healthcare, she began to question her preconceived notions. "It was only when I took control of those paranoid thoughts and fears about the world around me and became an objective critical-thinker that I got well," Parker wrote. "It was when I stopped taking sugar pills for everything and started seeing medical professionals that I began to thrive physically and mentally."[32]

She exhorted other anti-vaxxers to see how she was personally affected. "Anecdotal evidence is nothing to base decisions on. But when facts and evidence-based science aren't good enough to sway someone's opinion, then this is where I come from. After all, anecdotes are the anti-vaccine supporter's way," she wrote. "Well, this is my personal experience. And my personal experience prompts me to vaccinate my children and myself."[33]

Not long after Voices for Vaccines published Parker's story, Ernst went to log in to her email. "And I couldn't get there. So I called the guy who does IT for us. 'Why can't I get into my email?'" she inquired. "He looked into it and said, 'The website's crashing because so many people are trying to read this story.' So we had to quadruple our web capacity."[34]

The story continues to reverberate several years later. "It's really shared among vaccine-hesitant and anti-vaccine people," especially people who are seeking confirmation that they should use vaccines after reading something "scary" elsewhere, Ernst said. "I really think a compelling story is a good [way to spread truth], especially among people who aren't making decisions based purely on fact. They're making decisions that are emotionally charged. We have to lead them to the facts through emotion."[35]

For the same reason, Voices for Vaccines launched a page on its website, "Why I Choose," to highlight images of healthy pro-vaccine families. "People can just submit a photo of their vaccinated family and a couple sentences about why vaccines are important to them. That's a visual demonstration of vaccine-positive messaging," Ernst said. "It's in a shareable format."[36]

Voices for Vaccines also records a podcast to help create a community of supporters for pro-vaccine parents, much like anti-vaxxers find community through isolated social media groups. And the organization maintains an active social media presence to counterbalance the vortex of misleading material online.[37]

"People are there, and they feel part of the community," Ernst said. "People feel not like it's a place they're visiting but a place they belong to."[38]

LACK OF ACADEMIC DIVERSITY

From a practical perspective, dismantling the rigid barriers that prevent conversation and understanding among politically divided groups is extremely difficult. Shared language and telling stories are helpful for breaking down those barriers. But because of social media, people can find a community of like-minded colleagues without ever meeting others in real life.

College campuses, however, present one tangible opportunity for breaking down barriers. Despite an increase in online courses, most college students are usually forced to interact with others in person for extended periods of time. This happens in classrooms, dormitories, and general campus life.

By its very nature, college is a place where people are supposed to encounter others who aren't like them and who have views that conflict with their own. But US colleges and universities, in the aggregate, are increasingly devoid of conservative faculty members. The ratio of liberal to conservative faculty members at US colleges and universities was two to one in 1995, reflecting a natural proclivity toward left-leaning politics among academics. But that ratio had grown to nearly three to one by 2004 and ballooned to about five to one by 2010, according to Heterodox Academy, a group of college professors devoted to promoting political diversity on campuses.[39] Moderates are also increasingly difficult to find in academia.

Reasons for the shift are up for debate. Some liberal critics say the gap is not surprising because conservatives have drifted further away from academic principles and demonized professional researchers.[40] Though that line of criticism may carry some weight, it's hard to believe it completely justifies the gaping political divide at institutions that are supposed to educate students on how the world works.

Evidence suggests that professors, on average, have become increasingly liberal while the political makeup of the general populace has remained fairly stable. Sam Abrams, a research fellow at Stanford University's Hoover Institution on War, Revolution, and Peace, and a faculty fellow at New York University's Center for Advanced Social Science Research, analyzed data on the political beliefs of tens of thousands of professors throughout the country. His findings, drawn from information collected by the University of California, Los Angeles Higher Education Research Institute, showed that while professors were 11 percentage points more liberal than the US population in 1990, that gap had tripled to more than 30 percentage points by 2013. During that same period, there was "little change" in the percentage of Americans identifying as conservatives, liberals, and moderates.[41]

"While the data confirms that university and college faculty have long leaned left, a notable shift began in the middle of the 1990s as the Greatest Generation was leaving the stage and the last Baby Boomers were taking up teaching positions," Abrams wrote. Since then, "members of the academy went from leaning left to being almost entirely on the left. Moderates declined by nearly a quarter and conservatives decreased by nearly a third."[42]

If scientists want conservatives to respect science—which, of course, would benefit society and help bring about consensus on critical issues such as climate change—then they could start by nurturing more conservative academics. It's only natural for conservatives to bristle at politically monolithic university departments. But if they can see that their worldview is at least respected and represented among elite academics, they will be more likely to accept the fundamental basis of academic accomplishment and scientific assertions.

Even if this proposal seems unreasonable to the nation's elite academics, however, there's a pragmatic reason to consider it. If colleges and universities continue down a narrow political path toward the exclusion of conservative viewpoints and faculty members, they risk alienating a massive population of Americans and devaluing the inherent worth of the higher-education experience in the eyes of conservative tuition payers.

A disconcerting 58 percent of Republicans told the Pew Research Center in 2017 that they believe colleges and universities "have a negative effect on the way things are going in the country," compared with 36 percent who said those institutions have a positive effect. That represents a sharp reversal from 2010, when 58 percent said colleges and universities had a positive effect, while 32 percent said they had a negative effect.[43]

Higher education already faces a crisis—proving its worth to Americans who are concerned about student loans and job opportunities, irrespective of politics. In a 2016 survey by the nonpartisan nonprofit group Public Agenda, 57 percent of Americans agreed that "there are many ways to succeed in today's world without a college degree," up from 43 percent in 2009.[44]

Colleges and universities should not underestimate the crisis of credibility they will face if political division worsens and the automation revolution renders their traditional coursework increasingly irrelevant. For some institutions, the threat could be existential if they can't demonstrate their relevance.

Also, amid the proliferation of online courses—such as free classes offered by experts at Khan Academy—Americans are accumulating alternatives. In fact, the 2016 survey (see chapter 8) of technologists, scholars, educators, and other experts conducted by the Pew Research Center and Elon University's Imagining the Internet Center concluded that within the next ten years, "new credentialing systems will arise as self-directed learning expands."[45] And companies frustrated at the continuous influx of recent graduates who aren't capable of smoothly transitioning into the workforce and don't have basic critical-thinking skills may begin to discount the value of traditional higher education.

"While the traditional college degree will still hold sway in 2026, more employers may accept alternate credentialing systems as self-directed learning options and their measures evolve," the researchers wrote in a summary of their findings. Having "real-world work portfolios" will serve as "proof of competency" because "education systems will not be up to the task of adapting to train or retrain people for the skills most prized in the future."[46]

If the essence of the post-fact era is the diminishment of intellectual relevancy, then this outcome should not surprise us.

FOSTERING RELATIONSHIPS

One of the first steps toward overcoming the massive divide between any ideologically disparate groups is to find ways to foster new relationships. I know it's a simple plea. Call me an idealistic millennial, but I believe that building personal relationships helps people understand and respect each other, even if they continue to disagree on the issues.

Even historically divided groups can find common ground. In May 2016, Catholic and Muslim leaders came together in Rome to discuss their commonalities during a two-day meeting organized by the Pontifical Council for Interreligious Dialogue, Vatican City, and the Royal Institute for Inter-Faith Studies.

Delegates from more than a dozen different countries discussed their shared commitment to "inclusivity" and pursuing cooperation aimed at benefiting the good of humanity, said Anne Leahy, former Canadian ambassador to the Holy See. "We hear too much about what our differences are," she told Vatican Radio, so the meeting was designed "to witness that there are basic values we share that can counter the negativity."[47]

The gathering concluded with an agreement on a list of values shared by everyone at the table despite the history of war and division between Christians and Muslims. The two sides emphasized shared beliefs, including "principles of worshipping God and loving and caring for the other." Those values include a belief that "God bestowed upon every person dignity and inalienable rights," that people in need must be helped, that "sharing the resources of the universe" must be done in a mindful manner, and that armed conflict is not necessary to "achieve peace and harmony."[48]

Pope Francis said that basic conversation could accomplish much. "Dialogue is going out of ourselves . . . to hear the word of the other," he told the leaders at the summit. "It is the first step of a journey. Following this meeting of the word, hearts meet and begin a dialogue of friendship, which ends with holding hands. Word, hearts, hands. It's simple! A little child knows how to do it."[49]

CHAPTER 10

RECONNECTING WITH REALITY

Having cultivated a headline-obsessed culture, my industry now has a choice of two routes. As journalists, we can embrace and perpetuate the status quo—in which content grazing has usurped in-depth reading; trending topics carry more weight than serious news; and social media clout is prized above credibility—or we can choose to pursue brand integrity and to steadily rebuild trust with our readers and viewers.

As President Trump's false accusations of fake news undermine the industry's reputation, the only hope for the media to rekindle trust with the public is to esteem unmitigated truth and to present it responsibly to consumers. In the newly minted age of web metrics, this will require a recognition that the relentless pursuit of clicks, views, likes, and shares will not necessarily deliver sustainable value. With the industry crumbling, there's no time to waste. Using the resources that we have left, we must take a principled stand for credible journalism that makes a difference in the lives of our readers and viewers.

Debunking one of the biggest myths in journalism—the misconception that all clicks are created equal—can help the industry steer back on course. This fallacy, which is deeply ensconced in newsroom culture despite plenty of talk by industry leaders of de-emphasizing traffic volume, springs from the early days of web metrics.

Metrics are "impossible to ignore, but they're often poorly interpreted," said Nikki Usher, a George Washington University journalism professor. "The biggest issue is not that things are being quantified in terms of analytics—because that's helpful," she added. But "you've been in all these meetings where they're like, 'We got seven thousand video views, and that's good.' That doesn't . . . mean anything."[1]

Chartbeat, the real-time traffic tool that allows newsrooms to monitor their trending stories and gauge reader loyalty and depth, can be used for good. And so can Dataminr, the real-time tool that analyzes tweets and identifies viral, newsworthy, and sensational posts for potential coverage.

However, many newsrooms misuse these tools as de facto editors that dictate coverage decisions. More thoughtful usage of web metrics is possible and needed to ensure data is used to make decisions that ground our relationship with readers in the bedrock of credibility rather than in the sand of sensationalism and clickbait.

There's certainly room for whimsical stories, creative headlines, and viral content. But maintaining and growing readership in the long run is largely predicated on cultivating trust and loyalty through serious, dependable journalism. Without that deep connection, the reader won't hesitate to go elsewhere.

"In print, to switch from a subscription with one publisher to another—or even at the newsstand to change your habit from reading one publisher to another—costs you some money," Chartbeat CEO John Saroff said. "Now, the ability to switch from one publisher to another is essentially infinite, and the cost is essentially zero."[2]

In other words, people can click over to a competitor's site in a split second. Loyalty is thin when the relationship between the source and readers is built on misleading or overhyped headlines and paper-thin stories. But readers will actually devote considerable time to news sources that invest in credible, creatively presented journalism that leverages the best principles of engagement learned from tools such as Chartbeat. In fact, it's the only way to distinguish one news source from another following the proliferation of histrionic headlines geared toward social media and search engines' transformation of news into a cheap commodity.

"There's so much content out there and so much choice for readers that everyone is content grazing and tasting a ton of content at a time," Saroff said. "But when they find something that they really want to sink their teeth into, they do."[3]

For example, a jaw-dropping investigation published in 2016 by *Mother Jones*, featuring reporter Shane Bauer's account of four months spent undercover as a prison guard, earned multiple visits per reader. Astonished by Bauer's doggedness and captivating prose, people kept coming back to the site to read more of the approximately thirty-thousand-word story.[4]

In 2015, the most popular story tracked by Chartbeat, based on a metric designed to measure engagement, was Graeme Wood's sophisticated, in-depth *Atlantic* analysis, "What ISIS Really Wants."[5] In 2016, it was the dynamic and interactive map projecting the November election outcome by data journalist Nate Silver's FiveThirtyEight.[6]

Encounters with substantive journalism leave a lasting impact on readers in a culture inundated by surface-deep information. The lesson for the news industry is to place greater emphasis on the average time readers spend on content—which promotes depth and engagement—and less time on pure traffic volume and moment-to-moment shifts in trending topics. "The best stuff really does get a tremendous amount of attention," Saroff said.[7]

What's more, Chartbeat data demonstrates that simply catering to the vagaries of social media and making decisions based on Google's constantly evolving list of trending topics is problematic. Journalists often brag about the number of "shares" a story has accumulated on Facebook or other social media platforms. But Chartbeat data shows there's "very, very little, if any, correlation between news consumed and news shared," Saroff said. In fact, chances are high that readers scrolled past it in their social media feeds without clicking.[8]

"A like, or a reaction, or a comment, or a share on Facebook—or anything having to do with social engagement—has very little to do with whether or not somebody actually read the article," Saroff said. "They tell you whether or not people liked the headline or the image on Facebook, maybe whether they liked the little bit that's excerpted. They don't tell you whether or not people actually delved in and dove deep."[9]

To be sure, Facebook remains a major traffic driver to news websites. And newsrooms can't escape that. But subordinating professional news judgment to trending metrics will only go so far. Traffic from social media isn't driving reader loyalty. About 40 percent of readers who arrive at a news page from a social media platform stick around for fifteen seconds or less, according to Chartbeat.[10]

Two hours after reading a news article accessed through social media, only 52 percent of consumers can recall the source at all, according to the Pew Research Center. But when they go to a site directly through the news organization, 78 percent of readers remember the source.[11] "So you have to be able to understand both what works on social [media] and what works editorially," Saroff said.[12]

This is not meant to be a sanctimonious screed about proper journalism. There's actually a pragmatic element here. Amid the news industry's sharp contraction, we have fewer resources than ever to devote to credible, watchdog, enterprise journalism. As fate would have it, though, emphasizing depth and substance actually boosts the bottom line. When readers spend a full minute on a story instead of just fifteen seconds, the percentage of advertising on a page that is seen by the reader increases from 37 percent to 57 percent, according to Chartbeat.[13]

Some news organizations are already adjusting their business models accordingly. In 2015, the *Financial Times* embraced a new digital advertising metric, "cost per hour," which is designed to charge marketers based on how much their ad is actually seen. If the ad isn't seen for at least five seconds, the marketer doesn't pay anything. The more the ad is seen, the more revenue the publication gets. The new metric, developed in partnership with Chartbeat, effectively forces the publication to pursue meaningful content. In 2014, the news organization had tested the metric with ten clients, including BP and IBM, and earned $1 million in revenue that it said it would not have received otherwise.[14]

"For the nearly three decades of commercial internet history, advertising has derived its value from one measure: how many people click on an ad," *Financial Times* ad sales director Dominic Good said in a statement announcing the change. But "low viewability scores and questions about advertising placement . . . have increased the need for better measurement and transparency to demonstrate the actual outcome an advertiser is seeking."[15]

The development of new forms of web metrics to help news organizations quantify the impact of clickbait on their brands, compared with the impact of serious journalism, would also be helpful. "Metrics are essentially quantitative tools. They're taking two different things, like articles, and they're using the same numerical standard to rank them," said Caitlin Petre, a media scholar at Rutgers who previously studied web traffic at Columbia's Tow Center for Digital Journalism. "But there's this fundamental underlying issue. To us, intuitively, a story about the Syrian refugee crisis is a qualitatively different thing than a story about Kim Kardashian but also a Trump tweet. These are all apples and oranges. What we would all want would be a tool that could compare a story about the Syrian refugee crisis not to a story about a Trump tweet but to a story that was similar to that story. But that becomes a very devilish problem of measurement. It's just a huge challenge."[16]

It's a huge challenge that the industry needs to confront. Following its obsessive focus during the presidential campaign on Trump's antics—a focus that drove considerable traffic and ratings for news organizations but also helped him win—the industry desperately needs to undergo a period of soul-searching.

"I'm sure we're still going to do cute cats, and we're going to do sensational stuff and tabloid stuff from time to time," said John Wihbey, former National Public Radio syndicated show producer and *Newark Star-Ledger* reporter turned journalism scholar at Northeastern University. "We're not going to get rid of the soft news because that's attractive, and you want to be able to build an audience and entertain people. That's part of news, too."[17]

But "can we refocus the news budget a little more on topics that are truly important from a public interest perspective?" he said. "That's doable for a lot of organizations, like CNN, that really tipped over into giving way too much airtime to candidate Trump. A lot of local papers and TV stations should take a hard look, too, at the way they're dividing up the public's attention."[18]

EMBRACING A NONPROFIT BUSINESS MODEL

While more responsible use of metrics to guide news coverage can help restore trust for the news industry, a desire for more substantive journalism may fall flat without a new twist in the sector's broken business model. Although a select few national outlets have capitalized on paid online subscriptions, including the *New York Times*, the *Wall Street Journal*, and the *Washington Post*, meaningful local journalism is reaching the end of its financial rope. Facing never-ending declines in print advertising and circulation revenue, local newsrooms are at risk of extinction.

In fact, there's a good chance that history will record the emergence of the internet as the deathblow to profitable, independent, local news reporting. Which is why the only way to survive may require collaboration and nonprofit models.

Thankfully, the philanthropic community is slowly waking up to the role it can play in preserving journalism as a core element of a healthy democracy. Encouraging the development of nonprofit news outlets that exist to inform the public and have little incentive to chase after frivolous traffic offers a promising route to preserving watchdog reporting.

The Institute for Nonprofit News counted more than 120 members as of summer 2017. National nonprofit news organizations include ProPublica, the Center for Public Integrity, the Center for Investigative Reporting, Chalkbeat, and the Marshall Project. Locally focused nonprofit news outlets include the Arizona Center for Investigative Reporting, Michigan's *Bridge Magazine*, Carolina Public Press, Georgia Health News, Hidden City Philadelphia, Honolulu Civil Beat, MinnPost, NJ Spotlight, Oklahoma Watch, western Pennsylvania's PublicSource, San Francisco Public Press, Tucson Sentinel, Voice of San Diego, and WyoFile.[19]

In 2016 alone, nonprofit news outlets uncovered numerous stories that could have gone completely unnoticed without their efforts. A report by New Hampshire's InDepthNH.org "helped free a man who was locked up for seven years even though he wasn't convicted of a crime," according to the Institute for Nonprofit News. Reporting by the Connecticut Health Investigative Team revealed that more than 860 children had been given up to state custody since 2011 "because their families could not access specialized care," prompting a push for reform. And the Midwest Center for Investigative Reporting exposed "deplorable living conditions and few housing protections for migrant farmworkers in six states."[20]

Perhaps the highest-profile example was the International Consortium of Investigative Journalists' coordination of newsrooms throughout the world on a massive project published simultaneously in April 2016 after months of reporting. The "Panama Papers" project revealed how numerous officials used offshore bank accounts to conceal lavish lifestyles and potentially illicit activities, such as evasion of sanctions, tax avoidance, and money laundering. The newsrooms that collaborated on the project included the United Kingdom's *Guardian* newspaper and McClatchy newspapers in the United States, such as the *Miami Herald*.[21]

The Panama Papers reports illustrated the power of collaboration in preserving vital investigative journalism. Gone are the days when newsrooms could operate in isolated competition, spurning cooperation to pursue the glory of a big scoop or project. Instead, they must now collaborate often with each other—and with nonprofits—to fulfill their journalistic calling. This is already happening on a local level, such as *Bridge Magazine*'s collaboration with *Crain's Detroit Business* in Michigan,[22] and on a national level, such as ProPublica's collaborations with the *New York Times*, *USA Today*, *60 Minutes*, *Time* magazine, and dozens of others.[23]

Encouraging newsrooms to collaborate and trust each other is admittedly harder than it sounds. In the case of the Panama Papers, the *Guardian*'s editors wanted to publish first, said Stephen King, a partner at the nonprofit Omidyar Network, which helps to fund the International Consortium of Investigative Journalists. "They just found it very difficult to accept that they may have to collaborate with journalists from other papers and then all publish on the same day," he said.[24] In the end, the collaborating organizations published concurrently, shocking readers with their findings and eventually winning the Pulitzer Prize for Explanatory Reporting.[25]

"It's an intensely competitive thing," said King, who leads the global governance and citizenship initiative at the Omidyar Network, which was founded by eBay creator Pierre Omidyar. In the news business, "you don't share your stories that you're working on generally with other journalists. What I think was the breakthrough—and is something we'll start to see more of, partly because people's budgets are going to shrink—is more collaboration. Journalists will see the benefits of collaborating and keeping the information—and the data they're all working on—secure right up until an agreed-upon point."[26]

Although nonprofit funding can play a key role in sustaining the free flow of information, philanthropic resources are finite, and competition for funding is fierce. That's why the Omidyar Network is also funding for-profit journalism outfits throughout the world to spur innovation. Its investments include, for example, social impact news start-up Rappler in the Philippines, which CEO, cofounder, and former CNN journalist Maria Ressa has built into one of the country's most popular news sites.[27]

"We think there's a blended or mixed model out there," King said. "We're great proponents of nonprofit investigative journalism in that context. But we also realize that the for-profit models are more sustainable and potentially can still deliver the same kind of impact."[28]

Philanthropic funding can also play a productive role in educating the public about journalism at a time when the industry's trust is eroding and the president is spewing invective about the integrity of reporters. About six months after the 2016 election, a coalition of nineteen organizations and individuals—including Craig Newmark, founder of online classifieds site Craigslist, and Facebook—pooled $14 million to pursue research, events, and projects to "help people make informed decisions about what they read and share online."[29] The project, overseen by the Tow-Knight Center for Entrepreneurial Journalism at the City University of New York, is geared toward reversing the public's erosion of trust in the news media.

"In high-school US history, I learned that a trustworthy press is the immune system of democracy. As a news consumer, like most folks, I want news we can trust. That means standing up for trustworthy news media and learning how to spot clickbait and deceptive news," said Newmark,[30] who also donated several million dollars to other similarly minded initiatives, such as the establishment of an ethics chairperson at the nonprofit journalism group Poynter Institute.[31]

THE PRESENT AND FUTURE OF FACT-CHECKING

Another promising journalism trend is the rise of fact-checking as a core element of news coverage. The tiresome, longstanding approach of he-said-she-said journalism—minted in the past era dominated by print and traditional broadcast journalism—has failed to serve readers in the digital age. CNN, for example, has taken to proactively fact-checking bogus statements by displaying the truth in an on-screen caption,[32] while print and online reporters are increasingly feeling emboldened to immediately and authoritatively fact-check quotes and statements in everyday stories.

Plus, news organizations are assuming the responsibility of fact-checking stories that are circulating online, rather than pretending they don't exist. "We're looking at the collapse of the idea that a story that isn't being reported in the mainstream media shouldn't be fact-checked because you're giving it oxygen," said Alexios Mantzarlis, director of the International Fact-Checking Network at Poynter. "The old recognition of the media's role as a gatekeeper is gone, so at least it should try to offer a role of filtering this enormous amount of information we're bombarded with daily. To the extent where there are verifiably false claims, they are and should be called out within news stories. And we saw that a lot in 2016."[33]

Official fact-checking services such as PolitiFact and Snopes add value, too. It's vital to counteract misinformation wherever possible. Unfortunately, however, in-depth, manual fact-checking efforts take considerable time.

In 2016, researchers at Indiana University created a new tool called Hoaxy to collect, detect, and analyze online misinformation. Their new platform showed that the distribution of fact-checking material on social-networking platforms typically occurs within ten to twenty hours after the bogus information first breaks out. This is partly because misinformation is "dominated by very active users, while fact checking is a more grassroots activity," the researchers, including fake-news foreseer Filippo Menczer, concluded in a paper on their creation of Hoaxy.[34]

In one example of how misinformation outruns dedicated fact-checkers, several sites known for perpetuating fabricated or highly distorted content stirred outrage when they published bogus stories on November 22, 2015, asserting that President Obama had ordered the aerial dropping of leaflets, giving militants for the group that calls itself the Islamic State forty-five minutes to flee the area of upcoming airstrikes. The initial reports by fringe right-wing sites such as *FrontPage Magazine* and Gateway Pundit were quickly followed by similarly false claims on other skewed sites such as InfoWars. But it took about a day after the initial stories surfaced for Snopes to publish a detailed, polished breakdown of the distortions underlying the reports.[35]

"WHO, ME?"

Any effort to bolster trust in journalism and steer people toward the truth will fall flat if fabricated or highly distorted material increasingly compromises the believability of content from real news organizations.

Days after the 2016 presidential election, Mark Zuckerberg, facing heat over Facebook's role in allowing fake news to spread, contended that "of all the content on Facebook, more than 99 percent of what people see is authentic" and that "only a very small amount is fake news and hoaxes." He said the company was already exploring ways to allow users "to flag hoaxes and fake news" but pledged to "proceed very carefully" because "identifying the 'truth' is complicated."[36] It was a stance that fit comfortably within the company's strategy of prioritizing political neutrality, aiming not to offend one side or the other.

"There's been a real reluctance on the part of these tech companies to take seriously that they are playing a really strong editorial role in shaping our public sphere and our democracy," Petre said before revelations about Russia's interference forced the industry to pledge a few changes. "They have this, 'Who, me?' attitude, where, when it's convenient, you're just a platform and you don't have to take any responsibility for what happens on your platform."[37]

Zuckerberg's initial "who, me?" response eventually gave way to an increasing realization on his and Facebook's part that the company must take at least some responsibility to help prevent the spread of falsities and distortions. In early 2017, the company announced algorithm changes—without offering technical specifics—that would give greater weight in the News Feed to what it called "authentic content." Facebook said the changes would downplay accounts that post spam or attempt to "game" the site by requesting likes, comments, or shares. Facebook also tweaked its algorithms to spot certain "signals" from users to help better prevent the spread of nefarious material. Those signals could include, for example, the frequency with which users dismiss a certain piece of content by hiding it from their feeds.[38]

Zuckerberg pledged to combat fake news, nurture online community, and promote trust. "For the past decade, Facebook has focused on connecting friends and families," Zuckerberg wrote in a manifesto detailing his new way of thinking. "With that foundation, our next focus will be developing the social infrastructure for community—for supporting us, for keeping us safe, for informing us, for civic engagement, and for inclusion of all." Facebook, he said, must help cultivate "an informed community that exposes us to new ideas and builds common understanding in a world where every person has a voice" while discouraging "divisiveness and isolation."[39]

Acknowledging "sensationalism and polarization leading to a loss of common understanding," Zuckerberg said the company should "help people see a more complete picture" but "must be careful how we do this" by showing "a range of perspectives" and letting people come to their own conclusions. He said the company would find ways to alter its structure accordingly.[40]

However, he made it clear that Facebook would not stamp out misleading material altogether.[41] "In a free society, it's important that people have the power to share their opinion, even if others think they're wrong," he said. "Our approach will focus less on banning misinformation, and more on surfacing additional perspectives and information, including that fact-checkers dispute an item's accuracy."[42]

This new commitment to fact-checking took the form of a list of "related articles" adjacent to some stories posted by Facebook users, which "helps give people more perspectives and additional information, and helps them determine whether the news they are reading is misleading or false," Facebook News Feed product manager Sara Su wrote in an August 2017 blog post. She said the company would roll out the new feature "more broadly" after having tested it for several months.[43] The new feature was set to use artificial intelligence "to detect more potential hoaxes to send to third-party fact-checkers," and "if an article has been reviewed by fact-checkers, we may show the fact-checking stories below the original post," she said.[44]

Changes like these "are good things and steps in the right direction," Indiana University fake-news technology expert Menczer said. "They are absolutely necessary. But they're probably not sufficient."[45]

For starters, people don't necessarily change their opinion when confronted with the facts. As demonstrated earlier, for example, many conservatives who relentlessly circulated the Obama birther conspiracy were generally aware of the evidence disproving their claim. They simply discarded it or used their knowledge to skew the evidence. Their commitment to ideological purity transcended their willingness to let the facts sway their actions.

From a technical perspective, however, Facebook's strategy also falls short. Artificial intelligence will help identify offending content that goes viral. But the sheer size of Facebook means that the human fact-checkers cannot sift through everything the AI doesn't catch, Menczer said. "There are a lot of things that are not necessarily going viral. . . . If each one is only seen by a hundred people, it's not going to rise to the point where some fact-checkers will give it attention. But if there are a million of those, that's still a hundred million exposures," he said. Facebook's approach simply "has a scalability limitation."[46]

He also cautioned against any plans to rely on crowdsourcing by asking users to flag offending items. "Anything that's based on people reporting can be gamed," Menczer said. "So right now if I'm a fake-news person, I would hire people from developing countries" and "give them a couple of pennies to report things from the *New York Times* and CNN" as false "so that fact-checkers are flooded with this junk. And then of course this makes it harder for them to do their work. Fact-checking is very time consuming."[47]

What Facebook and other social media companies need to effectively combat fabricated and highly misleading content is a sophisticated, futuristic system of AI that can aid in providing real-time assessment of content with minimal human involvement, Menczer said.[48] With an onslaught of falsified videos, audio clips, and photos on the horizon, technology companies will need to develop "generative adversarial networks," said Wyoming computer scientist Jeff Clune, part of the team that created an AI system that could manufacture novel photos of real-life objects.[49]

A generative adversarial network uses two competing neural networks—one to generate counterfeit content and one to learn to detect counterfeits. By connecting the two in a loop, the detector can learn from its results to avoid getting fooled by increasingly convincing counterfeits, without needing the costly human labor of selecting fake content to feed to the detector. Social media companies can use this technology to help spot fakes at scale, and Facebook is indeed said to be already pursuing this.[50]

But it's not easy to use technology to distinguish between fact and fiction without causing a firestorm because of innately human disagreements over what's truly misleading. "Everything gets complicated the more you look at it," Clune said. "There are many shades of gray in terms of what counts as fake versus real."[51]

Does "a slightly [edited] image where I went through and removed, like, an offensive sign in the background" qualify as fake? What about a "slightly [edited] model?" he asked. "How do you differentiate between things that are massively fake and minorly fake? Or fake in important ways? Like, 'Hey, Trump didn't take a bribe from Vladimir Putin in broad daylight with a photographer standing there. That's seriously fake.' Whereas, 'Oh, this person just removed a pimple. Ah, we can let that go.' It gets really, really complicated."[52]

As of October 2017, Facebook has a stock market value of more than $500 billion,[53] and the company's financial performance remains predicated on stimulating engagement by provoking an emotional response in its two billion users. Making them angry, sad, exuberant, amazed, surprised, heartened, fearful, or hopeful is good for business. That includes politically sensational stories, memes, videos, and photos. Nuanced content promoting thoughtfulness and contemplation is not nearly as lucrative. And although totally fabricated material might be unwelcome, slightly distorted content may be harder for Facebook to justify extinguishing. After all, it generates profits—and squelching it would compromise the company's commitment to political neutrality.

If Facebook banned hyper-partisan content, it "would appear like they're blocking opinions," said Benjamin Fearnow, one of the former Facebook trending-news curators.[54] But egregiously slanted material presents a dilemma for Facebook's algorithm developers: "Do you want to appear that you're not censoring it while at the same time just stepping back and allowing people to post absolute garbage?" Fearnow posed. "But at the end of the day, I think people are comforted by the garbage."[55]

Even as Facebook signaled a willingness to change in the months following the election, a close examination of the company's public pronouncements during its apparent period of awakening revealed a renewed commitment to the same, old mind-set.

"Our goal with News Feed," the company said in January 2017 while announcing its new emphasis on authentic content, "is to show people the stories that are most relevant to them."[56] And therein lies the enduring problem. Relevancy is a disconcerting standard when it's measured based on engagement. As long as the News Feed algorithms reward any form of engagement rooted in user activity, we should not expect to see a sudden shift to meaningful content.

Unlike professional news editors of the past several decades, Facebook has long resisted taking responsibility for showing people news they need to know. Rather, Facebook shows them news they want to know—under the assumption that they want to see what their friends and family think is interesting. And with investors constantly demanding growth and engaged users, there's little reason to believe the company will flood the News Feed with information that users don't want to see. That would compromise Facebook's earnings power, and the company has a fiduciary responsibility to its investors to build its business.

To be sure, Facebook announced a change to its News Feed in January 2018 to "prioritize posts that spark conversations and meaningful interactions between people," claiming it expected a reduction in time that users spend on the site as a result. That outcome could theoretically translate into less revenue and profit. But that's doubtful. For one thing, the change was specifically designed to make it more difficult for news companies, businesses, and other organizations to get their posts into the News Feed without advertising or without stimulating comments among friends. Consequently, many organizations that bet heavily on Facebook will be forced to seriously consider paying for "sponsored" posts to reach their respective audiences. Paid posts add to Facebook's bottom line. In addition, Facebook said it would give greater visibility to content that generates back-and-forth conversations between people who already know each other. That would naturally lead to repeated user visits, which typically boost the financial prospects of any organization that relies heavily on advertising.[57]

The latest shift gives friends and family even more control over the news that people see on Facebook—a remarkable move that deepens the algorithmic bet on engagement and threatens to intensify the grouping effect that fosters ideological divisiveness. As shown throughout this book, the information that users are likeliest to find engaging is not necessarily the information that people need to consume to be civically studious citizens with a strong grasp of the truth.[58]

To effectively combat misinformation, Facebook could theoretically restrict the sources of content that users can post, share, and see. That would probably be helpful. As it happens, the company also announced in January 2018 that it would begin giving greater algorithmic weight to some news sources that people deem "trustworthy" and "informative," based on a survey of its users.[59] That might prove to be a good thing. But allowing readers to decide what's trustworthy recycles the company's past strategy of refusing to make its own decisions on what content is reliable. It's also problematic since surveys have consistently shown that readers tend to trust outlets that align with their political values.[60]

Even so, the reality is it's probably too late for Facebook to proactively and aggressively limit the sources of content that people see on the platform without facing a huge backlash. Much like newspapers—which gave away their content online in the early days of the internet—taught readers to believe online news should be free, Facebook has already trained the public to believe its platform is an information-agnostic social utility.

One way to bring about change would be for advertisers to rise up in protest, said one former Facebook executive. "It all comes down to money," the former Facebook executive said. "If there's enough pressure on the advertisers to make it not lucrative anymore to peddle misleading claims . . . those efforts will [make a difference]. And it might take actually making a call on whether something is misleading or not and having standards and policies and guidelines around the type of media they allow on the platform."[61]

But an uprising among advertisers is unlikely for several reasons. First, businesses rarely take a coordinated stand for political purposes. Second, Facebook's advertising base is highly diversified, making a widespread boycott unlikely. Third, advertisers won't revolt unless consumers lead the charge. Fourth, consumers won't lead the charge. Facebook is getting more popular, not less popular. And fifth, advertisers need Facebook to reach consumers these days. It's too big to ignore. In a sense, they can't live without it.

"YOU'RE AT THEIR WHIM"

As previously noted, Facebook and Google took steps almost immediately following Trump's election to crack down on users who were profiting off of fake news or using the platforms to sow chaos for political purposes.[62] For example, Facebook said it had implemented measures, including AI, to improve its ability to identify fake accounts and spot real-life users who use the platform to coordinate campaigns to spread disinformation.[63] Facebook also announced in August 2017 that it would block organizations that "repeatedly" share "false news" from advertising on the platform—a technique, the company acknowledged, that some pages had used to build their following.[64]

But those measures likely won't be effective for long. Like hackers who continuously try to expose holes in software and operating systems, which inevitably prompts developers to patch those vulnerabilities, fake-news purveyors and social media platforms are poised to engage in a digital arms race with no end in sight. The balance of power may have shifted temporarily in favor of the tech giants after the election, but there's reason to believe it will shift back to the illicit content creators after they adjust.

"As long as there is a market, there will be somebody that supplies the product," Menczer said. "Plus, it's hard to set up a place where you will for sure prevent these websites from having a financial gain because it doesn't cost much ... to create a new website or change the name or the domain. It's a moving target."[65]

Moreover, for the tech giants, limiting fake-news creators' ability to make money off of their platforms is a far cry from willingly capping their own earnings power. With a market value of nearly $700 billion as of October 2017,[66] Google parent Alphabet has profited tremendously by perfecting a system that capitalizes on confirmation bias, allowing users to efficiently explore their preferred corner of the digital world. The next evolution in confirmation bias through technology is already underway with the proliferation of voice assistants that provide one answer to an audible request, increasing the odds that the searcher will trust the output of algorithms instead of applying a healthy dose of skepticism to authenticate the results.

These devices, including Amazon's Echo and Google's Home, are already improving the daily lives of ordinary people. Much like Google's search engine, these devices will lead to ever easier discovery of the most convenient hair salon, tax adviser, and sports trivia—all of which is helpful. But voice-assisted search will also exacerbate the post-fact era.

As for how to improve its standard search engine, Google could adjust its algorithms to highlight disconfirming evidence in search results. That would benefit society. Although people might scroll past it, at least they would have a chance to absorb it. But Google has little financial incentive to promote cognitive dissonance. Any sign that it isn't customizing results for its users would open the door for competitors to capitalize.

Even so, inserting disconfirming evidence into the results page sounds good in principle but could prove problematic in practice. It would raise the distinct possibility that Google could someday alter its algorithms to present an intentionally skewed picture of the world for political purposes, business reasons, or other objectives.

Robert Epstein, a Google critic and psychologist who actively monitors the results of the search giant's secretive algorithms, noted that the company is already manipulating people. For example, Google presents search suggestions after users type a few letters, displays boxed information snippets at the top of some pages with answers to search queries, and tailors results based on previous activity. In addition, Google's continuous tweaking of the algorithms controlling its search rankings reflects a degree of human bias that exerts significant influence on the daily lives of most Americans. "These new means of manipulation are completely invisible to people," Epstein said. "They have no idea they're being manipulated. They have no idea that they're being influenced. And that's extremely dangerous because if you don't know you're being influenced, you end up having the feeling that you made up your own mind."[67]

The search engine's subtle influence takes many shapes. European regulators fined Google $2.7 billion in 2017 over allegations that the company illegally favored its own shopping service over retail competitors in search results, which would reflect a measure of digital manipulation.[68] Google has denied it.

Even if the company has done nothing wrong and presents a purely unbiased picture of the world to its users, the fact that the company possesses the ability to skew search results presents a serious risk to the public's perception of reality. Even if today's Google executives are ethical, future executives could view it as their prerogative to alter the search engine's algorithms to their political, economic, or social liking. There could come a day where motivated executives or engineers believe it is, in fact, their duty to skew the results.

"I don't believe they have any intention to do that," said Varol Kayhan, an information systems professor at the University of South Florida St. Petersburg who has studied Google's search results. "But they can definitely do it."[69]

We might not notice if they do. Transparency has limits at Google, whose algorithm tweaks are occasionally disclosed in broad strokes to the public but rarely discussed in detail.[70]

Transparency is better at Twitter, which provides raw feeds to researchers for analysis. That's not the case at Facebook, though the company hired former *New York Times* public editor Liz Spayd in August 2017 to help make the company more open.[71]

"What they still have not done is to open up their data so that other people can actually examine and advise and analyze—people like me, who would like to study" it, said Panagiotis Takis Metaxas, Wellesley College computer scientist. "Unless you're an employee on Facebook—and I'm sure that you probably sign a lot of paperwork that would not allow you to open up your mouth—you're not going to get access."[72]

Not long after leaving his job on Facebook's team of news curators, Fearnow observed the company's seeming lack of transparency from the flip side. In his new role as social media editor for *Mediaite*, a blog on the news industry, Fearnow was assigned the responsibility of posting trending items to the site's Facebook page, which had more than two hundred thousand likes.[73]

But despite whatever tips he might have picked up about Facebook's choices, Fearnow became increasingly frustrated at his inability to control the fate of his new employer's content on the platform. Though he could strategically tinker with the wording, timing, and types of posts to *Mediaite*'s page, Facebook's shrouded algorithms nonetheless retained control over the visibility of his company's content. Despite having direct access to such a powerful content-publishing tool, "you're still answering to the few gods that exist out there in the Valley," Fearnow said. "Anytime they make a change, you're at their whim. I feel like I have no power over any of this information because you're always just [trying to adjust] to whatever stupid algorithm change they made."[74]

News companies are constantly trying to ascertain how the latest Facebook or Google algorithm changes affect their content. When Facebook or Google tweak something, it carries inordinately large implications for news companies seeking to build readership and revenue. Journalists are constantly mystified by Facebook's maneuvering, in particular. They "talk about it like this Old Testament, vengeful God—that Facebook giveth and Facebook taketh away," Petre said. "You could have this boon to your traffic, but you could also lose it. And if Facebook decided that they didn't like certain practices on your site, you were going to be in real trouble."[75]

The vengeful God analogy rang true to Matt Hardigree, a former editor in chief of Gawker Media's *Jalopnik*. He recalled a meeting between *Jalopnik* editors and two Facebook employees after the automobile blog's web traffic suffered due to a mysterious dose of biblical punishment. "One of the editors said, 'I feel like Job. I feel like I was doing everything I needed to do. I was doing everything right. I was following your guidelines for what made a good post, what made a bad post. I was posting what I thought I was supposed to post. I was doing everything right, and I was getting great traffic. And then one day it just all disappeared, and I have no idea what happened to me—other than that God is smiting me,'" Hardigree recalled.[76]

The Facebook employees at the *Jalopnik* meeting looked puzzled, he said. "I think those people earnestly thought they were trying to work with the media and doing the right thing, having no idea the terrible effect they'd have," he added.[77]

REGULATING A "DUOPOLY"

The algorithms that govern Facebook and Google are often treated as if they're living organisms that humans can't control. But that's misguided, of course. Algorithms are the creation of people, and people must take full responsibility for the implications of those algorithms.

"Someone has to make those decisions," Hardigree said. "Everything involves value judgments, and Facebook is making value judgments. And we can say, 'Make Facebook a public utility,'" and try to regulate it accordingly. "But I don't think that's happening anytime soon. So Facebook just has to own up to who they are."[78]

Because Google and Facebook have little to no US government oversight over their algorithm decision-making, no regulatory agency would have the authority to immediately put a stop to it if either company was suspected of intentionally presenting a skewed version of the digital world to their users. That's one reason why some activists, including both conservatives and liberals, have advocated for a regulatory framework that would exert a measure of control over how online giants handle political content, in particular. "The most likely approach would be a supercharged transparency rule requiring clear disclosure of how traffic is treated, and clear specification of the standards used for limiting speech, including any possible viewpoint discrimination," conservative activist Phil Kerpen wrote in a memo advocating a push for oversight that was circulated in certain political circles during summer 2017 and was published by news start-up Axios. "Platforms that represent themselves to the public as neutral would be subject to enforcement actions if they violate those representations through a consumer-protection framework."[79]

Under Kerpen's proposed structure, Facebook, Google, and other platforms could "elect not to be neutral." In that scenario, they "would be free to exercise editorial control but would have to prominently disclose they are doing so" and would then relinquish federal rights to protection from the legal liability associated with any defamatory content published by their users.[80] Those rights are currently codified in Section 230 of the Communications Decency Act of 1996.[81]

The Kerpen proposal may sound appealing to politicos on both sides of the aisle who are frustrated at the stupendous power of Google and Facebook. But from a legal perspective, it could run afoul of the Bill of Rights, which may afford social media companies the same rights that news companies enjoy to decide what information to show the world.

Even if the tech giants could be legally regulated to ensure their algorithms are not used to slant things, it's unlikely that government regulators could match the pace of technological development without throttling innovation. Google and Facebook tweak their algorithms continuously and pivot quickly, which has helped them build their businesses and deliver extraordinary wealth to their investors.

"I'd love to see regulation of these companies," tech critic and researcher Epstein said. But "it would be very hard to keep passing regulation to keep up with changing technology. It's happening too fast, and the legislative process and the regulatory process both are pretty slow."[82]

Antitrust action is theoretically possible if the Federal Trade Commission and Department of Justice decide that the tech giants are too powerful in digital advertising or other areas. Research firm eMarketer estimated that Google would claim 78 percent of US search ad revenues in 2017, totaling more than $28.5 billion.[83] Google and Facebook collectively snapped up 77 percent of all US online ad growth in 2016, leaving scraps for ravaged news organizations to pursue.

Some observers have used the term "duopoly" to describe the tight grip on digital ads held by Google and Facebook.[84] But the companies may argue that although their collective market share in digital ads is high, they compete with each other for marketing dollars. Plus, advertisers have plenty of offline options for reaching consumers. These arguments, while possibly imperfect, could prove convincing if the companies ever face off with antitrust lawyers in court.

One additional prospect for regulation is the chance that Google and Facebook could be forced to accept government oversight of political ads. This possibility grew more realistic after Facebook admitted that Russian forces had surreptitiously advertised on its platform to disrupt American politics.[85] In October 2017, Alphabet also admitted that Russian forces had placed advertisements on Google in an attempt to influence the presidential election.[86]

Around the same time, US senators Mark Warner (D-VA) and Amy Klobuchar (D-MN) began seeking support on Capitol Hill for a bill that would force Facebook to "disclose more information about who is buying political ads on its platform and whom those ads target," according to business news site Quartz.[87] Senator John McCain (R-AZ) had signed on to the bill by the time this book went to print, signaling potentially bipartisan interest in transparency and accountability.[88]

Yet aside from a smattering of angst in the journalism and political worlds about the girth of Google and Facebook, there was no indication of a significant threat of regulatory oversight or antitrust action as of this writing. Forcing them to provide information on their political ad buyers would be de minimis for their massive businesses. And even if the regulatory tide someday begins to turn against them in a meaningful way, both companies have significant influence in Washington as an extra layer of insurance against anything particularly intrusive. Alphabet spent $15.4 million on lobbying in 2016, the fourth most of any individual company and ahead of spending titans Comcast, Lockheed Martin, and Exxon Mobil. Facebook was twenty-third among individual companies in lobbying, spending $8.7 million, just ahead of General Motors, Coca-Cola, and Chevron.[89]

With significant government oversight unlikely, Epstein proposed that activists take it upon themselves to monitor the companies and expose any potential biases to the public. Those revelations "could be utilized by authorities if they so choose, even in the absence of regulation or antitrust action," he said.[90] For example, congressional investigators could raise a fuss about any algorithmic actions perceived as inappropriate. As we learned from Facebook's reactionary approach to politically charged criticism of its trending-news curation team, public scrutiny makes Silicon Valley uncomfortable.

Nonetheless, for the foreseeable future the public is largely reliant on the tech industry's leaders and algorithm creators to use their incredible power to color the public's perception of the world with caution.

HEALTHY CONNECTIVITY

One method to cope with the way technology has disrupted our lives would be to disconnect altogether. But that would be pointless, unrealistic, and just plain dumb. If used cautiously, social media can indeed have a positive impact on our lives. There's no denying it.

By fostering ways for friends and family to connect online, Facebook has certainly improved people's ability to better understand each other in some respects. For example, the Pew Research Center's Lee Rainie speculated that the rise of social media may have contributed to the nation's change of heart on marriage equality.[91]

Social media can expose people to societal injustices, as exemplified by the widespread sharing of video footage revealing police brutality against African Americans. In this way, access to information about other people's challenges has never been easier. And that's a good thing.

Yet despite social media's ability to help people stay in touch, its fundamental character as a tool for personal broadcasting remains a serious impediment to cultural and political unity. When individuals have the power to strategically polish their public personas through the distribution of content on social media, the result is often a skewed reality. And the natural consequences—isolation, depression, misunderstanding—often push people apart instead of drawing them together, thus deepening social divides.

"I'm not saying every social experience in the virtual world is bad—I'm a social media user too," said Brian Primack, a researcher at the University of Pittsburgh who has shown that increased social media use is associated with increased rates of depression. "There are certain things that make us laugh, that make us really happy" on social media.[92]

But, he said, people should limit the amount of time they spend on social media. They would also benefit from capping the number of digital friends they accumulate because research has shown that it's even harder to tell when strangers or peripheral connections are perpetuating skewed portrayals of their lives online. "Try to remain friends with mostly or just about solely people you know in real life," Primack said. And "realize that this is a medium where it's very, very easy to be misinterpreted."[93]

In Facebook's defense, the company has taken steps to try to help people get assistance when they need it. For example, Facebook-owned Instagram in 2016 introduced a tool that allows anyone who fears a friend may harm himself or herself to anonymously report those concerns. That action triggers a private message sent directly to the potentially troubled user: "Someone saw one of your posts and thinks you might be going through a difficult time. If you need support, we'd like to help." That is followed by access to resources, such as a professional helpline and the nudge to talk to a friend.[94]

"We listen to mental health experts when they tell us that outreach from a loved one can make a real difference for those who may be in distress. At the same time, we understand friends and family often want to offer support but don't know how best to reach out," Instagram chief operating officer Marne Levine told *Seventeen* after consulting with groups such as the National Eating Disorders Association and the National Suicide Prevention Lifeline. "These tools are designed to let you know that you are surrounded by a community that cares about you, at a moment when you might most need that reminder."[95] In addition, the company partnered with the teen magazine to promote National Body Confidence Day through posts with the hashtag #PerfectlyMe.[96]

Unquestionably, the immense impact of social media on daily life makes it impossible to proactively defuse all of its explosive interpersonal implications. Regardless, permanently and prominently bolstering the presence of healthcare providers on social media could help people who are facing depression or considering hurting themselves. It should be just as easy for people to find digital counseling services as it is for them to post about their weekend.

Among Zuckerberg's top priorities following the election was putting greater emphasis on "meaningful groups" on Facebook, which he said had already accumulated more than one hundred million members. Real-life community groups, he said, are crucial to the social fabric of America but have been deteriorating for decades.[97] "Online communities are a bright spot, and we can strengthen existing physical communities by helping people come together online as well as offline," Zuckerberg said in his manifesto.[98]

There is definitely value in helping people connect with meaningful groups. But giving them the tools to more easily migrate to cloistered digital islands actually risks promoting further political and social isolation, since the natural human tendency is to drift into communities with like-minded people and then to ignore, reject, or twist alternative perspectives.

"Technology makes it easy for us to find each other and form that community," said Indiana's Menczer, who developed a software model showing that, over time, people congregate into disparate groups on social media. "Once that community is formed, then you have group dynamics that make it more likely that we will gang together and discount people who are challenging the opinions of the group. We can support each other, we can reinforce each other, and then we can be more skeptical of outsiders who come in and tell us that what we're thinking is wrong."[99]

The most helpful and immediate action Facebook and other social media outlets could take would be to promote bonds between individuals instead of promoting personal broadcasting and public debates. Fostering more one-on-one communication and interaction among small circles of people brings out personal authenticity and genuinely thoughtful conversations about serious issues. People are also less likely to be phony in direct conversation with each other than when hundreds of friends are watching.

In this way, Facebook rival Snapchat has much to offer. Despite considerable handwringing over its ephemeral nature, Snapchat may actually promote more authentic communication for a healthier experience overall. The fact that content circulating on the app disappears soon after it's viewed is, in fact, a better reflection of fleeting real-life interactions, which are not permanently recorded for hundreds, or thousands, to see, parse, and share.

Perhaps this is why young people are drawn to it. While older folks, including even my subgeneration of older millennials, often confess that they don't understand the appeal of an app that allows people to distort their faces and send wacky photos to their friends, that's irrelevant. What's important is that Snapchat does not require its users to put on a performance for the masses in the same way as Facebook and Instagram.

"I would definitely agree with that," said Noelle Lilley, the Arizona State University student featured in chapter 5. "At least in my experience, the reason why Snapchat feels more genuine is simply because most people don't have as many friends on Snapchat as they would followers on Instagram."[100]

On Instagram, she had accumulated about nine hundred followers after rejoining the platform. On Snapchat, she had only about thirty. "Because of that I'm more likely to share something on Snapchat than I will on Instagram, whether that's me just goofing around and being silly or maybe saying something that I wouldn't feel comfortable just putting out there otherwise," she said. "Snapchat feels a little safer because I know, for myself, I don't have as many people on it. And another big factor of Snapchat is the fact that the posts expire after a certain time limit."[101]

Although empirical research on Snapchat's impact remains limited because it's still relatively new, Cornell University experts on information science, communication, and psychology published a paper in 2016 based on interviews with the app's users. The experts concluded that Snapchat encourages more authentic interactions than typical social media, "where automatic archiving of data is the default."[102]

Snapchat promotes "features that facilitate a network of mostly close relations," and "default deletion affords everyday, mundane talk and reduces self-consciousness while encouraging playful interaction," the Cornell researchers wrote. "Further, although receivers can save content through screenshots, senders are notified; this selective saving with notification supports complex information norms that preserve the feel of ephemeral communication while supporting the capture of meaningful content. This dance of giving and taking, sharing and showing, and agency for both senders and receivers provides the basis for a rich design space of mechanisms, levels, and domains for ephemerality."[103]

For Facebook, the lesson to be learned from Snapchat is to promote more one-on-one communication and downplay personal broadcasting. In March 2017, the company introduced a similar feature to Snapchat's that allows the posting of photos that disappear after twenty-four hours.[104] That could help somewhat. But completely reorienting Facebook toward more authentic communication would require a fundamental shift in the company's business model. And that is unlikely.

CONCLUSION
CRAVING AUTHENTICITY

With misinformation, misdirection, and misbeliefs swirling, authenticity is in short supply. Which is why people are naturally so hungry for something genuine. Chances are you can remember the most recent, candid post in your Facebook feed—in part because it's so impactful but also because it's so rare.

On social media, when someone displays vulnerability, support often comes pouring onto the screen. For example, after model Chrissy Teigen tweeted a close-up photo of her stretch marks several months after giving birth—captioned "Whatevs"—her followers were overwhelmed with gratitude.[1]

"Thank you from this girl who is super body conscious right now," one Arkansas woman wrote.[2]

"Thank you for being real, we need more public figures who aren't afraid to show their perfect imperfections," another fan replied.[3]

The allure and concrete benefits of authenticity extend far beyond social media, however. In business, simply admitting mistakes is rare, but when it happens, it often helps more than it hurts. I've witnessed this in companies I've covered as a journalist. When I was covering General Motors (GM) for the *Detroit Free Press*, CEO Mary Barra directed the automaker to unearth details about how engineers, executives, and lawyers had concealed a deadly ignition-switch defect for more than a decade.[4] Instead of defending GM's actions and obfuscating information to minimize legal liabilities, she swiftly apologized, ordered the public release of the company's comprehensive internal investigation, and authorized compensation for victims.[5] Admitting mistakes and taking action to help victims were key steps toward restoring trust with the public, which never stopped buying GM vehicles.

In government, increased transparency often bolsters trust. As the cliché goes, the cover-up is often worse than the crime. Similarly, political stonewalling is often counterproductive.

In a study designed to gauge how the release of government records affects the public's perception of the truth, a group of researchers led by Dartmouth's Brendan Nyhan found that documents with redacted information fostered conspiracy theories. That might not surprise you. But the study also concluded that un-redacted documents "consistently lowered conspiracy beliefs."[6] In other words, when people encountered the whole truth, they were more trusting of the government. Although there are good reasons for officials to withhold certain information, such as preserving national security, redacting material is often rather pointless.[7]

Finally, in journalism, readers and viewers respond positively to transparency, as well. Amid discontent with the news media over its role in provoking conflict, sensationalism, and distrust for the sake of web traffic, ratings, and political influence, outlets that are still committed to the truth would benefit from better explaining their processes to the public.

To its credit, newswire Reuters in 2017 launched an initiative designed to give readers more information about the company's journalism. The feature, dubbed Backstory, was aimed at revealing the inner workings of the Reuters news process and introducing readers to the real-life people involved.[8]

This type of commitment to transparency would help show readers that journalists at responsible news organizations are generally honest, hardworking folks. It's a much more practical step to restore faith in our industry than simply asking consumers to trust faceless bylines, which foster distance and breed suspicion.

"One of the things that troubles me and people in the industry is that we are a profession with professional standards, trying to be accurate, carefully sourced, unbiased, get fair comment, and the question is does the public understand that?" asked Reuters editor in chief Stephen Adler, who made the moves to bolster transparency after Trump ramped up his fake-news allegations. "Or because of the accusations, do they think we just make things up, not care how good the sources are, or publish things for the sake of it? What we are trying to do is show people that's not what we do, that we have a professional set of standards, and these are the insights that show how we go about getting information."[9]

The public's positive response to authenticity and transparency in social media, business, politics, and journalism is an encouraging sign because it suggests that many people still want to distinguish between fact and fiction. But the problem is that identifying genuine authenticity is extremely difficult in the misinformation age. In fact, it's a key reason why Donald Trump was elected president. To his supporters, Trump exemplified authenticity.

Online, especially, "people will gravitate toward those who feel authentic even when they're not. People just crave that," said David Berkowitz, chief strategy officer for social media analytics firm Sysomos, which has studied how readers consumed news about Trump during the election. "Unfortunately you can get away with being a bad actor out there and just totally manipulating your audience."[10]

Trump's willingness to buck conventional political standards, skew the truth by sounding authoritative, communicate openly and directly with followers on social media, and treat journalists with disdain all achieved a strategic outcome—giving him the perception of trustworthiness in a world overwhelmed by falsehoods.

As sociologist Erving Goffman wrote in 1956, it is possible for someone "to create intentionally almost any kind of false impression without putting himself in the indefensible position of having told a clear-cut lie. Communication techniques such as innuendo, strategic ambiguity, and crucial omissions allow the misinformer to profit from lies without, technically, telling any."[11]

So we should not be surprised that Trump's ability to mimic authenticity found a welcome audience. The groundwork had already been laid for someone to capitalize on our collective susceptibility to deception, regardless of our political persuasion. "We're all human beings, and we all engage in directionally motivated reasoning. It's part of who we are," Nyhan said. "I want to be understanding of the reality of human psychology. We're all vulnerable to this, and we all make mistakes as a result."[12]

It's rare for us to endorse facts that contradict our entrenched viewpoints because our first priority is to find a place of acceptance. Rejecting the prevailing belief among our friends and family brands us with an enduring mark of disloyalty. That's a price most people are not willing to pay—because ultimately we crave a sense of belonging more than the unvarnished truth.

"There are lots of areas where people are perfectly willing to say, 'I screwed up. I was wrong,'" Nyhan said. "But on these issues that are especially emotional or salient or essential to our identity, that can be much harder."[13]

Technology has simply aggravated this predisposition. "I think the problem," said computer scientist Panagiotis Takis Metaxas, "is really the human race."[14]

"A GRAIN OF TRUTH"

As I researched and wrote this book, I was repeatedly reminded of what Neil McGinness, editor in chief of the supermarket tabloid *Weekly World News*, told me about the appeal of fake news. Reality, he said in this book's introduction, is often inconvenient—so people seek out their own version of the truth.

To them, the *Weekly World News* is the essence of authenticity because it does not pretend to be something other than what it is. "I think detractors of *Weekly World News* would say, 'Hey, wink, wink, *Weekly World News*, are you serious?'" McGinness said. "And we would say, 'No, we're not serious.' We've always viewed seriousness as a form of stupidity in a very uncertain and incongruous world."[15]

As the media landscape has evolved and fabricated content has proliferated online, the *Weekly World News* suddenly looks less ridiculous. The gap between stories in the *Weekly World News* and content in the professional press and on social media—not to mention the difference between fake happenings and actual events—has narrowed.

"What we traffic in is very similar to what the *New York Post* or *Daily Mail* or [others] traffic in, which is the embrace of the flippant, bold headlines, almost Lynchian-type descriptions of morbid events or unusual occurrences," McGinness said, using a term used to describe cryptic film director David Lynch's propensity for presenting altered states of reality. "And it would certainly be my position that what we would have thought, in this country, to be the purveyors of the most credible information that people could hope to read have been very misleading."[16]

What the *Weekly World News* demonstrated, years before bogus news stories disrupted the 2016 presidential campaign, was that the allure of sensational content is universal.

"The most interesting thing about tabloids is there's always a grain of truth in their stories," said Alison Head, executive director of Project Information Literacy, who completed her doctoral dissertation on supermarket tabloids at the University of California, Berkeley, nearly three decades ago. "If you were a lawyer, you would say that's how they escape not all but a lot of their lawsuits—because there is some sort of grain of truth."[17]

That grain of truth keeps people coming back for more because they are seeking out something—or someone—to help explain the chaotic world that surrounds them. In that respect, the pursuit of the truth is no less fervent than it's ever been. For supermarket tabloids, "the formula is a good narrative that often has some sort of remedy or, in the end, some sort of solution that makes the world right," Head said.[18]

But usually the solution is just too good to be true.

On October 1, 2012, with real-life doomsday believers predicting the imminent end of the world based on a dubious interpretation of Mayan mythology, the *Weekly World News* published an online story headlined, "Facebook Will End on May 15th, 2013!"[19] The piece has since shattered the site's record for most discussed stories, with more than twenty-seven thousand comments.

The spoof article quoted a fake Mark Zuckerberg as saying the site had "gotten out of control" and "I need to put an end to all the madness." "And to be honest," the phony Zuckerberg continued, "I think it's for the better. Without Facebook, people will have to go outside and make real friends. That's always a good thing."[20]

One can dream.

But even the *Weekly World News* has limits to its imagination. "We've been covering Trump forever," McGinness said, noting "a pretty well-received story about Donald Trump buying the town of Scranton, Pennsylvania."[21]

Yet even that development wasn't completely unbelievable. "As out there as any of the Trump coverage has been from *Weekly World News*," McGinness said, "it never reached the level of him taking possession of the White House."[22]

ACKNOWLEDGMENTS

This book is dedicated to my parents, Randy and Deanna Bomey, who taught me that it's okay to not have an opinion about everything. It's okay to say, "I don't know." Thank you to them, to my brother, Dan Bomey, and to my in-laws, Lynn and Ben Blazier, for their endless support and love.

Ultimately, this book would not have been possible without my wife, Kathryn Bomey, whose unwavering encouragement, love, and strength provided all of the inspiration I needed. As it happens, Kathryn is also the best editor I've ever met—and her editing as I worked on this was truly impeccable.

Since this book is predicated on the idea that it's important to continuously seek out, consider, and vet a wide range of ideas and perspectives, I tried to approach my research, interviews, and writing with an open mind. Likewise, to ensure that I was treating all sides fairly, I asked friends and colleagues from a wide range of viewpoints for input throughout the process.

Thank you especially to Jason Idalski, Dan Meisler, Caleb Cohen, Kyle Lady, and Joe Guillen for sharing outstanding insights on the draft manuscript. Thank you also to Caleb and his company, Mockingbird Productions, for designing and maintaining my website, NathanBomey.com. Jason was also very helpful with an early round of copyediting.

I am especially appreciative of all the people I interviewed for this book. This effort would not have been possible without their achievements, wisdom, and generosity.

I conducted all of my interviews on the record with the exception of two: the former Facebook executives who agreed to speak on the condition of anonymity because of the sensitivity of the situation. I'd like to take this chance to thank them for sharing, as well.

To my talented colleagues and editors at *USA Today*, thank you for supporting me. I am grateful for the opportunity to work at an organization that is committed to meaningful journalism in a world overwhelmed with frivolous and misleading content.

ACKNOWLEDGMENTS

Of course, for the sake of eliminating all doubt, any perspectives or mistakes in this book are solely my own.

I owe a debt of gratitude to the supportive folks at Prometheus Books, but especially to Steven L. Mitchell, who believed in the concept of this book long before the topic exploded. I also can't say thank you enough to Jeffrey Curry for his exceptional editing. And I'd also like to thank my agent, Karen Gantz, for providing excellent feedback as I shaped the book proposal and for her continued support in my endeavors.

Lastly, I am grateful for you, the reader. If you made it this far, you are likely more committed than most to the free flow of ideas and the discovery of truth regardless of your preexisting biases. I hope, however, that you didn't reflexively agree with everything here. Rather, I hope that this book generates a productive conversation about the effects of social media, journalism, politics, and technology on our perception of reality. This, ultimately, is vital to our democracy.

NOTES

PROLOGUE: THE NEW GATEKEEPERS

1. Adam Schrader, interview with the author, May 1, 2017.
2. Ibid.
3. Ibid.
4. Benjamin Fearnow, interview with the author, April 26, 2017.
5. Schrader, interview with the author.
6. Fearnow, interview with the author.
7. Ibid.
8. Schrader, interview with the author.
9. Former Facebook executive A, interview with the author, May 23, 2017.
10. Michael Nunez, "Former Facebook Workers: We Routinely Suppressed Conservative News," *Gizmodo*, May 9, 2016, http://gizmodo.com/former-facebook-workers-we-routinely -suppressed-conser-1775461006 (accessed June 12, 2017).
11. US Senate Committee on Commerce, Science, and Transportation, "Thune Seeks Answers from Facebook on Political Manipulation Allegations," press release, May 10, 2016, https://www.commerce.senate.gov/public/index.cfm/pressreleases?ID=2BA05D9F-EAAD -4043-B195-B8D91FF690B4 (accessed December 15, 2017).
12. Former Facebook executive B, interview with the author, March 29, 2017.
13. Ibid.
14. Colin Stretch, General Counsel, Facebook, to John Thune, US Senate Committee on Commerce, Science, and Transportation, May 23, 2016, https://www.commerce.senate.gov/ public/_cache/files/93a14e98-2443-4d27-bf04-1fc59b8cf2b4/22796A1389F52BE16D225F9 A03FB53F8.facebook-letter.pdf (accessed December 15, 2017).
15. Ibid.
16. Ibid.
17. Schrader, interview with the author.
18. Stretch to Thune.
19. Ibid.
20. "John Wanamaker," PBS.org, http://pbs.org/wgbh/theymadeamerica/whomade/ wanamaker_hi.html (accessed January 9, 2018).
21. Schrader, interview with the author.
22. Ibid.

23. "Search FYI: An Update to Trending," Facebook Newsroom, August 26, 2016, https://newsroom.fb.com/news/2016/08/search-fyi-an-update-to-trending/ (accessed September 23, 2017).

24. "Facebook, Inc. Shareholder/Analyst Call," S&P Global Capital IQ, June 20, 2016.

25. Abby Ohlheiser, "Three Days after Removing Human Editors, Facebook Is Already Trending Fake News," *Washington Post*, August 29, 2016, https://www.washingtonpost.com/news/the-intersect/wp/2016/08/29/a-fake-headline-about-megyn-kelly-was-trending-on -facebook/?utm_term=.bc1c55f99048 (accessed June 12, 2017).

26. Adrien Friggeri et al., "Rumor Cascades," in *Proceedings of the Eighth International Conference on Weblogs and Social Media* (2014): 109.

27. Ibid., p. 105.

28. Ibid., p. 108.

29. Ibid., p. 109.

30. Panagiotis Takis Metaxas, interview with the author, May 25, 2017.

31. Ibid.

32. Giulia Segreti, "Facebook CEO Says Group Will Not Become a Media Company," Reuters, August 29, 2016, https://www.reuters.com/article/us-facebook-zuckerberg/facebook -ceo-says-group-will-not-become-a-media-company-idUSKCN1141WN (accessed September 23, 2017).

33. Former Facebook executive A, interview with the author.

34. Mike Nowak and Guillermo Spiller, "Two Billion People Coming Together on Facebook," Facebook Newsroom, June 27, 2017, https://newsroom.fb.com/news/2017/06/ two-billion-people-coming-together-on-facebook/ (accessed December 15, 2017).

35. "Facebook, Inc. FQ1 2016 Earnings Call Transcripts," S&P Capital IQ, April 27, 2016.

36. Former Facebook executive A, interview with the author.

37. Marshall McLuhan, *Understanding Media: The Extensions of Man* (New York: McGraw-Hill, 1964), p. 8.

38. Former Facebook executive A, interview with the author.

39. Craig Silverman, "This Analysis Shows How Viral Fake Election News Stories Outperformed Real News on Facebook," BuzzFeed, November 16, 2016, https://www.buzzfeed .com/craigsilverman/viral-fake-election-news-outperformed-real-news-on-facebook?utm_term =.ocQjZa7v5V#.fqWjnB49Av (accessed June 12, 2017).

40. Fearnow, interview with the author; Schrader, interview with the author.

41. Fearnow, interview with the author.

42. Silverman, "This Analysis."

43. Deepa Seetharaman, "Facebook Profit Jumps 79%, Revenue Up," *Wall Street Journal*, November 1, 2017, https://www.wsj.com/articles/facebook-profit-jumps-79-revenue-up -1509568694?tesla=y (accessed November 2, 2017).

44. Schrader, interview with the author.

45. Fearnow, interview with the author.

INTRODUCTION: THE POST-FACT ERA

1. George Will, "The Wisdom of Pat Moynihan," *Washington Post*, October 3, 2010, http://www.washingtonpost.com/wp-dyn/content/article/2010/10/01/AR2010100105262 .html (accessed June 16, 2017).

2. "The 'King of Whoppers': Donald Trump," FactCheck.org, December 21, 2015 (accessed January 9, 2018). https://www.factcheck.org/2015/12/the-king-of-whoppers-donald -trump/ (accessed January 9, 2018).

3. Brendan Nyhan, interview with the author, April 6, 2017.

4. Ibid.

5. Donald Trump and Tony Schwartz, *Trump: The Art of the Deal* (New York: Ballantine, 1987), p. 58.

6. "Word of the Year 2016 Is . . .," *Oxford Dictionaries*, November 16, 2016, https:// en.oxforddictionaries.com/word-of-the-year/word-of-the-year-2016 (accessed September 24, 2017).

7. Erving Goffman, *The Presentation of Self in Everyday Life* (Edinburgh: University of Edinburgh, 1956), pp. 38–39.

8. Fred Vultee, interview with the author, February 21, 2017.

9. Nikki Usher, interview with the author, February 28, 2017.

10. Neil McGinness, interview with the author, May 1, 2017.

11. Ibid.

12. Eli Pariser, *The Filter Bubble: What the Internet Is Hiding from You* (New York: Penguin Press, 2011).

13. Leonard Saxe, interview with the author, May 10, 2017.

14. Katharine Hayhoe, interview with the author, June 8, 2017.

15. Dan Kahan, interview with the author, May 4, 2017.

16. Ibid.

17. Jim Norma, "Americans' Confidence in Institutions Stays Low," Gallup, Washington, DC, June 13, 2016, http://www.gallup.com/poll/192581/americans-confidence-institutions -stays-low.aspx (accessed August 6, 2017).

18. Shanto Iyengar and Sean J. Westwood, "Fear and Loathing across Party Lines: New Evidence on Group Polarization," *American Journal of Political Science* 59, no. 3 (July 2015): 697–98, http://doi.org/10.1111/ajps.12152 (accessed December 15, 2017).

19. Ibid., p. 698.

20. Ibid., p. 699.

21. Ibid., p. 701.

22. Ibid., p. 699.

23. Neil Garrett et al., "The Brain Adapts to Dishonesty," *Nature Neuroscience* 19, no. 12 (2016), https://www.ncbi.nlm.nih.gov/pubmed/27775721 (accessed December 15, 2017).

24. Ibid.

25. Ibid.

26. "The Churchill Spirit—In His Own Words," *New York Times*, August 2, 1964, http://www.nytimes.com/1964/08/02/the-churchill-spiritin-his-own-words.html (accessed August 11, 2017).

CHAPTER 1: MISINFORMATION OVERLOAD

1. Howard Rheingold, interview with the author, March 16, 2017.

2. Ibid.

3. Ibid.

4. Black openly discussed his "white patriot" views and his connection to the King site at https://www.stormfront.org/dblack/, which I accessed on August 12, 2017, before his StormFront page was deactivated sometime in the following weeks.

5. Rheingold, interview with the author.

6. Google.com, search for "Martin Luther King Jr.," conducted June 21, 2017.

7. Antoine Harary, David Bersoff, and Sarah Adkins, *2017 Edelman Trust Barometer: Global Report* (New York: Edelman Insights, January 2017), https://www.edelman.com/global-results/ (accessed December 15, 2017).

8. Rheingold, interview with the author.

9. Varol Kayhan, interview with the author, March 2, 2017.

10. Barbara Demick, "In an Age of 'Alternative Facts,' a Massacre of Schoolchildren Is Called a Hoax," *Los Angeles Times*, February 3, 2017, http://www.latimes.com/nation/la-na-sandy-hook-conspiracy-20170203-story.html (accessed August 10, 2017).

11. Joshua Gillin, "How Pizzagate Went from Fake News to a Real Problem for a DC Business," PolitiFact, December 5, 2016, http://www.politifact.com/truth-o-meter/article/2016/dec/05/how-pizzagate-went-fake-news-real-problem-dc-busin/ (accessed August 11, 2017).

12. Faiz Siddiqui and Susan Svrluga, "NC Man Told Police He Went to DC Pizzeria with Gun to Investigate Conspiracy Theory," *Washington Post*, December 5, 2017, https://www.washingtonpost.com/news/local/wp/2016/12/04/d-c-police-respond-to-report-of-a-man-with-a-gun-at-comet-ping-pong-restaurant/?utm_term=.5a4d3e824cad (accessed August 11, 2017).

13. Brendan Nyhan, interview with the author, April 6, 2017.

14. Ibid.

15. Graham Lanktree, "Alex Jones Refuses to Apologize for Sandy Hook Conspiracy Theory," *Newsweek*, June 19, 2017, http://www.newsweek.com/alex-jones-megyn-kelly-sandy-hook-infowars-627129 (accessed August 12, 2017).

16. Nyhan, interview with the author.

17. Ryen White, "Beliefs and Biases in Web Search," in *Proceedings of the 36th*

International ACM SIGIR Conference on Research and Development in Information Retrieval (2013): 3–12, https://doi.org/10.1145/2484028.2484053 (accessed December 15, 2017).

18. Ibid.

19. Ibid.

20. Ibid.

21. Kayhan, interview with the author.

22. Ibid.

23. Ibid.

24. Panagiotis Takis Metaxas, interview with the author, May 25, 2017.

25. "Periodic Table of SEO Success Factors—Chapter 9: Violations & Search Engine Spam Penalties," *Search Engine Land*, https://searchengineland.com/guide/seo/violations -search-engine-spam-penalties (accessed January 9, 2018).

26. Rebecca Maynes, "How Do Consumers Conduct Searches on Google Using a Mobile Device?" Mediative, March 2016, http://www.mediative.com/whitepaper-how-do-consumers -conduct-searches-on-google-using-a-mobile-device/ (accessed December 15, 2017).

27. Ibid.

28. Kayhan, interview with the author.

29. James Vincent, "Google Is Removing Ads from the Right-Hand Side of Search Results," *Verge*, February 20, 2016, https://www.theverge.com/2016/2/20/11077472/google -search-ads-change-position (accessed June 12, 2017).

30. Ibid.

31. Maynes, "How Do Consumers Conduct Searches."

32. Kristi Kellogg, "How Mobile Has Changed the Way We Search, Based on 10+ Years of Eye-Tracking Studies," *Search Engine Land*, October 3, 2016, http://searchengineland.com/mobile -impacted-way-search-based-10-years-eye-tracking-studies-260052 (accessed June 13, 2017).

33. Maynes, "How Do Consumers Conduct Searches."

34. Alison Head, interview with the author, May 11, 2017.

35. Sam Wineburg, interview with the author, March 2, 2017.

CHAPTER 2: RULE BY METRICS

1. Fred Vultee, interview with the author, February 21, 2017.

2. "Newspapers Fact Sheet," Pew Research Center, Washington, DC, June 1, 2017. http://www.journalism.org/fact-sheet/newspapers/ (accessed August 11, 2017), using US Bureau of Labor Statistics inflation calculator at https://data.bls.gov/cgi-bin/cpicalc.pl.

3. "Newspapers Fact Sheet."

4. FCC Working Group on the Information Needs of Communities, *The Media Landscape* (Washington, DC: Federal Communications Commission, June 9, 2011), https:// transition.fcc.gov/osp/inc-report/INoC-1-Newspapers.pdf (accessed December 15, 2017).

5. Nikki Usher, interview with the author, February 28, 2017.

6. Lauren Johnson, "US Digital Advertising Will Make $83 Billion This Year, Says EMarketer," *Adweek*, March 14, 2017, http://www.adweek.com/digital/u-s-digital-advertising -will-make-83-billion-this-year-says-emarketer/ (accessed August 13, 2017).

7. Matt Hardigree, interview with the author, April 25, 2017.

8. Ibid.

9. "Newspaper Publishers Lose over Half Their Employment from January 2001 to September 2016," US Department of Labor, Bureau of Labor Statistics, April 3, 2017, https:// www.bls.gov/opub/ted/2017/newspaper-publishers-lose-over-half-their-employment-from -january-2001-to-september-2016.htm (accessed June 22, 2017).

10. FCC Working Group, *Media Landscape*.

11. John Wihbey, interview with the author, June 6, 2016.

12. Mark Jurkowitz, "The Growth in Digital Reporting: What It Means for Journalism and News Consumers," Pew Research Center, Washington, DC, March 26, 2014. http://www .journalism.org/2014/03/26/the-growth-in-digital-reporting/ (accessed June 22, 2017).

13. "Newspapers Fact Sheet," Pew.

14. Center for Advanced Social Research at the University of Missouri-Columbia School of Journalism Donald W. Reynolds Journalism Institute, "*2013 Community Newspaper Readership Survey*" (Columbia, MO: National Newspaper Association, December 2013).

15. Amy Mitchell, Jesse Holcomb, and Rachel Weisel, "State of the News Media 2016," Pew Research Center, Washington, DC, June 2016, https://assets.pewresearch.org/wp-content/ uploads/sites/13/2016/06/30143308/state-of-the-news-media-report-2016-final.pdf (accessed December 15, 2017).

16. Jack Nissen, "A Small-Town Michigan Newspaper Said Goodbye. Then Readers Stepped In," *Bridge*, October 5, 2017, http://www.bridgemi.com/success/small-town-michigan -newspaper-said-goodbye-then-readers-stepped (accessed October 5, 2017).

17. Ibid.

18. Sam Schulhofer-Wohl and Miguel Garrido, "Do Newspapers Matter? Short-Run and Long-Run Evidence from the Closure of the *Cincinnati Post*," *Journal of Media Economics* 26, no. 2 (2013): 65, http://doi.org/10.1080/08997764.2013.785553 (accessed December 15, 2017).

19. Ibid., p. 61.

20. Ibid., p. 64.

21. James M. Snyder Jr. and David Strömberg, "Press Coverage and Political Account- ability," *Journal of Political Economy* 118, no. 2 (2010): 355. https://doi.org/10.1086/ 652903 (accessed December 15, 2017).

22. Amy Mitchell and Rachel Weisel, "Political Polarization and Media Habits: From *Fox News* to Facebook, How Liberals and Conservatives Keep up with Politics," Pew Research Center, Washington, DC, October 2014, http://assets.pewresearch.org/wp-content/uploads/ sites/13/2014/10/Political-Polarization-and-Media-Habits-FINAL-REPORT-7-27-15.pdf (accessed December 15, 2017).

23. Ibid.

24. Craig Silverman, Jane Lytvynenko, Lam Thuy Yo, and Jeremy Singer-Vine, "Inside the Partisan Fight for Your News Feed," BuzzFeed, August 8, 2017, https://www.buzzfeed.com/craigsilverman/inside-the-partisan-fight-for-your-news-feed?utm_term=.tsRq7eoA0B#.cnlekBnmx3 (accessed August 25, 2017).

25. R. Kelly Garrett, Brian E. Weeks, and Rachel L. Neo, "Driving a Wedge between Evidence and Beliefs: How Online Ideological News Exposure Promotes Political Misperceptions," *Journal of Computer-Mediated Communication* 21, no. 5 (2016): 331–48. http://doi.org/10.1111/jcc4.12164 (accessed December 15, 2017).

26. Amy Hollyfield, "Obama's Birth Certificate: Final Chapter," PolitiFact, June 27, 2008, http://www.politifact.com/truth-o-meter/article/2008/jun/27/obamas-birth-certificate-part-ii/ (accessed September 28, 2017).

27. Garrett, "Driving a Wedge," p. 340.

28. Ibid., p. 342.

29. Ibid., p. 343.

30. Usher, interview with the author.

31. John Saroff, interview with the author, May 5, 2017.

32. Ibid.

33. Ibid.

34. Ibid.

35. Ibid.

36. Ibid.

37. Caitlin Petre, interview with the author, March 21, 2017.

38. Hardigree, interview with the author.

39. Ibid.

40. Ibid.

41. Ibid.

42. Steve Rayson, "We Analyzed 100 Million Headlines. Here's What We Learned (New Research)," BuzzSumo, June 26, 2017, http://buzzsumo.com/blog/most-shared-headlines-study/ (accessed September 28, 2017).

43. Vultee, interview with the author.

44. Petre, interview with the author.

45. Nathan Bomey and John Gallagher, "How Detroit Went Broke: The Answers May Surprise You—and Don't Blame Coleman Young," *Detroit Free Press*, September 15, 2013, https://www.freep.com/story/news/local/michigan/detroit/2013/09/15/how-detroit-went-broke-the-answers-may-surprise-you-and/77152028/ (accessed January 9, 2018).

46. Saroff, interview with the author.

47. Petre, interview with the author.

48. Ibid.

49. Donald Trump and Tony Schwartz, *Trump: The Art of the Deal* (New York: Ballantine, 2017), p. 56.

50. Donald Trump, interview by Chris Hayes, "*All in with Chris Hayes*, NBC News, September 14th, 2015," http://www.nbcnews.com/id/57864602/ns/msnbc-all_in_with_chris _hayes/#.VfiKM2RVhBd (accessed August 25, 2017).

51. Mary Harris, "A Media Post-Mortem on the 2016 Presidential Election," mediaQuant (blog), November 14, 2016, https://www.mediaquant.net/2016/11/a-media-post-mortem-on -the-2016-presidential-election/ (accessed April 20, 2017).

52. Paul Senatori, interview with the author, April 26, 2017.

53. Ibid.

54. Ibid.

55. Aaron Pickrell, interview with the author, May 4, 2017.

56. Ibid.

57. Linda A. Henkel and Mark E. Mattson, "Reading Is Believing: The Truth Effect and Source Credibility," *Consciousness and Cognition* 20, no. 4 (2011): 1705–21, http://doi.org/ 10.1016/j.concog.2011.08.018 (accessed December 15, 2017).

58. Linda Henkel, interview with the author, May 17, 2017.

59. Senatori, interview with the author.

60. Ibid.

61. Ibid.

62. David Berkowitz, interview with the author, May 12, 2017.

63. Cohen Peart, "Rank These 25 Donald Trump Campaign Scandals," *Denver Post*, October 28, 2016, http://www.denverpost.com/2016/10/28/rank-these-25-donald-trump -campaign-scandals/ (accessed August 8, 2017).

64. Trump and Schwartz, *Trump: The Art of the Deal*, p. 57.

65. Thomas E. Patterson, "News Coverage of the 2016 General Election: How the Press Failed the Voters" (working paper no. RWP16-052, Harvard Kennedy School, Harvard University, Cambridge, MA, December 2016), http://dx.doi.org/10.2139/ssrn.2884837 (accessed December 15, 2017).

66. Wihbey, interview with the author.

67. Patterson, "News Coverage."

68. Ibid.

69. Jonathan Chait, "The Case against the Media. By the Media," *New York*, July 25, 2016, http://nymag.com/daily/intelligencer/2016/07/case-against-media.html (accessed August 8, 2017).

70. Art Swift, "Americans' Trust in Mass Media Sinks to New Low," Gallup, Washington, DC, September 14, 2016, http://www.gallup.com/poll/195542/americans-trust-mass-media -sinks-new-low.aspx (accessed December 15, 2017).

71. "ASNE Releases 2016 Diversity Survey Results," American Society of News Editors, September 9, 2016, http://asne.org/diversity-survey-2016 (accessed December 15, 2017).

72. "More than Three Decades of Commitment to Diversity," American Society of News Editors, http://asne.org/content.asp?contentid=28 (accessed September 14, 2017).

73. Jack Shafer and Tucker Doherty, "The Media Bubble Is Worse than You Think," *Politico Magazine*, May/June 2017, http://www.politico.com/magazine/story/2017/04/25/media-bubble-real-journalism-jobs-east-coast-215048 (accessed June 23, 2017).

74. Chait, "Case Against."

75. Elizabeth Stoycheff, interview with the author, February 13, 2017.

76. Dataminr, "We're Working with Slack to Transform How News Teams Collaborate in Real-Time," press release, January 31, 2017, https://www.dataminr.com/press/we-re-working -with-slack-to-transform-how-news-teams-collaborate-in-real-time (accessed October 12, 2017).

77. "The World's Real-Time Information Discovery Company," Dataminr, 2017, https://www.dataminr.com/about (accessed October 12, 2017).

CHAPTER 3: DIGITAL MANIPULATION

1. Veerender Jubbal, interview with the author, May 25, 2017.

2. Ibid.

3. Ibid.

4. Nick Wingfield, "Feminist Critics of Video Games Facing Threats in 'GamerGate' Campaign," *New York Times*, October 15, 2014, https://www.nytimes.com/2014/10/16/technology/gamergate-women-video-game-threats-anita-sarkeesian.html?mcubz=1 (accessed September 23, 2017).

5. Jubbal, interview with the author.

6. Ibid.

7. Ibid.

8. Ibid.

9. Ibid.

10. Ibid.

11. The user who posted this tweet has since been banned from Twitter. The tweet, which was viewed via a third-party screen shot for this book, is no longer online.

12. Jubbal, interview with the author.

13. Jennifer Rankin and Jon Henley, "Islamic State Claims Attacks at Brussels Airport and Metro Station," *Guardian*, March 22, 2016, https://www.theguardian.com/world/2016/mar/22/brussels-airport-explosions-heard (accessed January 9, 2018).

14. Ibid.

15. Dan Austin, "*Detroit News* Building," HistoricDetroit.org, 2017, http://historicdetroit.org/building/detroit-news-building/ (accessed June 25, 2017).

16. Former Facebook executive B, interview with the author, March 29, 2017.

17. Ibid.

18. Former Facebook executive A, interview with the author, May 23, 2017.

19. "Facebook, Inc. Shareholder/Analyst Call," S&P Global Capital IQ, June 20, 2016.

20. Former Facebook executive B, interview with the author.

21. Former Facebook executive A, interview with the author.

22. Benjamin Markines, Ciro Cattuto, and Filippo Menczer, "Social Spam Detection," in *Proceedings of the 5th International Workshop on Adversarial Information Retrieval on the Web* (2009): 41–48, http://doi.org/10.1145/1531914.1531924 (accessed December 15, 2017).

23. Filippo Menczer, interview with the author, May 11, 2017.

24. Ibid.

25. Ibid.

26. Ibid.

27. Brendan Nyhan, interview with the author, April 6, 2017.

28. Craig Silverman and Lawrence Alexander, "How Teens in the Balkans Are Duping Trump Supporters with Fake News," BuzzFeed, November 3, 2016, https://www.buzzfeed.com/craigsilverman/how-macedonia-became-a-global-hub-for-pro-trump-misinfo?utm_term=.lxOBkm0PYA#.ohKdMBZ0Gr (accessed June 25, 2017).

29. Craig Silverman, "This Is How Your Hyperpartisan Political News Gets Made," BuzzFeed, February 27, 2017, https://www.buzzfeed.com/craigsilverman/how-the-hyperpartisan-sausage-is-made?utm_term=.kgq4mzkGqA#.taqdAOLzmq (accessed June 25, 2017).

30. Scott Shane, "From Headline to Photograph, a Fake News Masterpiece," *New York Times*, January 18, 2017, https://www.nytimes.com/2017/01/18/us/fake-news-hillary-clinton-cameron-harris.html (accessed June 25, 2017).

31. Caitlin Dewey, "Facebook Fake-News Writer: 'I Think Donald Trump Is in the White House Because of Me,'" *Washington Post*, November 17, 2016, https://www.washingtonpost.com/news/the-intersect/wp/2016/11/17/facebook-fake-news-writer-i-think-donald-trump-is-in-the-white-house-because-of-me/?tid=sm_tw&utm_term=.627a79e2eea3 (accessed June 25, 2017).

32. Jonathan Albright, interview with the author, May 23, 2017.

33. Jonathan Albright, "The #Election2016 Micro-Propaganda Machine," Medium, November 18, 2016, https://medium.com/@d1gi/the-election2016-micro-propaganda-machine-383449cc1fba (accessed May 23, 2017).

34. See a full list of the sites Albright analyzed at https://pastebin.com/BTY9iFJf (accessed December 15, 2017).

35. Albright, interview with the author.

36. Bence Kollanyi, Philip N. Howard, and Samuel C. Woolley, "Bots and Automation over Twitter during the US Election," (working paper, Computational Propaganda Project, Oxford, UK, 2016), http://comprop.oii.ox.ac.uk/wp-content/uploads/sites/89/2016/11/Data-Memo-US-Election.pdf (accessed December 15, 2017).

37. Ibid.

38. Ibid.

39. *Hearing on Disinformation: A Primer in Russian Active Measures and Influence*

Campaigns, Before US Senate Select Committee on Intelligence, 115th Cong. (2017) (statement of Clint Watts, Robert A. Fox Fellow at the Foreign Policy Research Institute and Senior Fellow at the Center for Cyber and Homeland Security, George Washington University), https:// www.intelligence.senate.gov/sites/default/files/documents/os-cwatts-033017.pdf (accessed December 15, 2017).

40. Ibid.

41. Ibid.

42. Ibid.

43. Ibid.

44. Ibid.

45. Benjamin Fearnow, interview with the author, April 26, 2017.

46. "Facebook Could Have Data Relevant to the Trump/Russia Investigation, but It's Not Releasing It (Yet)," *Media Matters* (blog), May 22, 2017, https://www.mediamatters.org/ blog/2017/05/22/Facebook-could-have-data-relevant-to-the-TrumpRussia-investigation-but -its-not-releasing-i/216589 (accessed January 9, 2017).

47. Panagiotis Takis Metaxas, interview with the author, May 25, 2017.

48. Donie O'Sullivan and Dylan Byers, "Exclusive: Even Pokémon Go Used by Extensive Russian-Linked Meddling Effort," CNN, October 12, 2017, http://money.cnn.com/2017/ 10/12/media/dont-shoot-us-russia-pokemon-go/index.html (accessed October 12, 2017).

49. Metaxas, interview with the author.

50. Jen Weedon, William Nuland, and Alex Stamos, *Information Operations and Facebook* (Menlo Park, CA: Facebook, April 27, 2017), https://fbnewsroomus.files.wordpress.com/ 2017/04/facebook-and-information-operations-v1.pdf (accessed December 15, 2017).

51. Ibid.

52. Ibid.

53. Office of the Director of National Intelligence, *Assessing Russian Activities and Intentions in Recent US Elections* (Washington, DC: National Intelligence Council Intelligence Community Assessment, January 6, 2017), https://www.dni.gov/files/documents/ ICA_2017_01.pdf (accessed December 15, 2017).

54. Jessica Guynn, "Facebook Expands Scope of Russian Influence on Americans for Second Time," *USA Today*, November 1, 2017, https://www.usatoday.com/story/tech/ 2017/11/01/facebook-says-146-million-americans-targeted-russia-campaign/821306001/ (accessed November 3, 2017).

55. Elliot Schrage, "Hard Questions: Russian Ads Delivered to Congress," Facebook Newsroom, October 2, 2017, https://newsroom.fb.com/news/2017/10/hard-questions -russian-ads-delivered-to-congress/ (accessed October 6, 2017).

56. Ibid.

57. Joel Kaplan, "Improving Enforcement and Transparency of Ads on Facebook," Facebook Newsroom, October 2, 2017, https://newsroom.fb.com/news/2017/10/improving -enforcement-and-transparency/ (accessed October 14, 2017).

58. "Facebook, Inc. FQ3 2017 Earnings Call Transcripts," S&P Capital IQ, November 1, 2017.

59. Facebook Investor Relations, "Facebook Reports Fourth Quarter and Full Year 2016 Results," press release, February 1, 2017, https://investor.fb.com/investor-news/press-release -details/2017/facebook-Reports-Fourth-Quarter-and-Full-Year-2016-Results/default.aspx (accessed December 15, 2017).

60. "Facebook, Inc. FQ2 2016 Earnings Call Transcripts," S&P Capital IQ, July 27, 2016.

61. Schrage, "Hard Questions."

62. Ibid.

63. Metaxas, interview with the author.

64. Albright, interview with the author.

65. Menczer, interview with the author.

66. Ibid.

67. Ibid.

68. Ibid.

69. Ibid.

70. Albright, interview with the author.

71. Menczer, interview with the author.

72. Michael Barthel, Amy Mitchell, and Jesse Holcomb, "Many Americans Believe Fake News Is Sowing Confusion," Pew Research Center, Washington, DC, December 15, 2016, http://www.journalism.org/2016/12/15/many-americans-believe-fake-news-is-sowing -confusion/ (accessed September 29, 2017).

73. Jessica Guynn, "Mark Zuckerberg: Facebook Fake News Didn't Sway Election," *USA Today*, November 10, 2016, https://www.usatoday.com/story/tech/news/2016/11/10/mark -zuckerberg-facebook-fake-news-didnt-sway-election/93622620/ (accessed June 27, 2017).

74. Eytan Bakshy, Solomon Messing, and Lada A. Adamic, "Exposure to Ideologically Diverse News and Opinion on Facebook," *Science* 348, no. 6239 (2015): 1130–32, http://doi .org/10.1126/science.aaa1160 (accessed December 15, 2017).

75. Ibid.

76. "Facebook, Inc. Shareholder/Analyst Call," S&P Global Capital IQ, June 20, 2016.

77. Christian Sandvig, "What Facebook's 'It's Not Our Fault' Study Really Means," *Wired*, May 8, 2015, https://www.wired.com/2015/05/facebook-not-fault-study/ (accessed June 28, 2017).

78. Eszter Hargittai, "Why Doesn't Science Publish Important Methods Info Promi- nently?" *Crooked Timber* (blog), May 7, 2015, http://crookedtimber.org/2015/05/07/why -doesnt-science-publish-important-methods-info-prominently/ (accessed June 28, 2017).

79. Nathan Jurgenson, "Facebook: Fair and Balanced," Society Pages, May 7, 2015, https://thesocietypages.org/cyborgology/2015/05/07/facebook-fair-and-balanced/ (accessed June 28, 2017).

80. Carl I. Hovland and Walter Weiss. "The Influence of Source Credibility on

Communication Effectiveness," *Public Opinion Quarterly* 15, no. 4 (1951): 635, https://doi
.org/10.1086/266350 (accessed December 15, 2017).

81. Linda Hankel, interview with the author, May 17, 2017.

82. Hovland and Weiss, "Influence of Source Credibility," p. 635.

CHAPTER 4: DIVIDING AND DENYING

1. Bob Inglis, interview with the author, April 20, 2017.

2. Ibid.

3. Ibid.

4. Ibid.

5. "Raise Wages, Cut Carbon Act of 2009," H.R. 2380, 111th Cong. (May 13, 2009),
https://www.congress.gov/bill/111th-congress/house-bill/2380 (accessed December 15, 2017).

6. Inglis, interview with the author.

7. Ibid.

8. Ibid.

9. Ibid.

10. Ibid.

11. Ibid.

12. Gordon Gauchat, "Politicization of Science in the Public Sphere: A Study of Public
Trust in the United States, 1974 to 2010," *American Sociological Review* 77, no. 2 (2012): 167,
https://doi.org/10.1177/0003122412438225 (accessed December 15, 2017).

13. Aaron M. McCright, Chenyang Xiao, and Riley E. Dunlap, "Political Polarization
on Support for Government Spending on Environmental Protection in the USA, 1974–2012,"
Social Science Research, 48 (2014): 258, https://doi.org/10.1016/j.ssresearch.2014.06.008
(accessed December 15, 2017).

14. Ibid.

15. Aaron McCright, interview with the author, March 20, 2017.

16. Ibid.

17. Ibid.

18. Riley E. Dunlap, Aaron M. McCright, and Jerrod H. Yarosh, "The Political Divide on
Climate Change: Partisan Polarization Widens in the US," *Environment: Science and Policy for
Sustainable Development* 58, no. 5 (2016): 8, http://dx.doi.org/10.1080/00139157.2016.1208
995 (accessed December 15, 2017).

19. Ibid.

20. Ibid., p. 11.

21. Ibid., p. 10.

22. John Cook et al., "Consensus on Consensus: A Synthesis of Consensus Estimates on
Human-Caused Global Warming," *Environmental Research Letters* 11, no. 4 (2016), http://doi
.org/10.1088/1748-9326/11/4/048002 (accessed December 25, 2017).

23. *Washington Post* Live, "Tennessee Congresswoman Marsha Blackburn and ClearPath Founder Jay Faison Talk about Energy and the Republican Party at the RNC," Facebook video, July 19, 2016, https://www.facebook.com/washingtonpostlive/videos/1051971188186199/ (accessed December 15, 2017).

24. Phil McKenna, "Educators Decry Conservative Group's Climate 'Propaganda' Sent to Schoolteachers," *Inside Climate News*, April 10, 2017, https://insideclimatenews.org/news/07042017/heartland-institute-climate-change-denial-science-education (accessed June 30, 2017).

25. Juliet Eilperin, "Climate Skeptic Group Works to Reverse Renewable Energy Mandates," *Washington Post*, November 24, 2012, https://www.washingtonpost.com/national/health-science/climate-skeptic-group-works-to-reverse-renewable-energy-mandates/2012/11/24/124faaa0-3517-11e2-9cfa-e41bac906cc9_print.html (accessed July 1, 2017).

26. Seth Shulman, *Smoke, Mirrors, & Hot Air: How ExxonMobil Uses Big Tobacco's Tactics to Manufacture Uncertainty on Climate Science* (Cambridge, MA: Union of Concerned Scientists, January 2007), http://www.ucsusa.org/sites/default/files/legacy/assets/documents/global_warming/exxon_report.pdf (accessed December 15, 2017).

27. Jim Norman, "Democrats Drive Rise in Concern about Global Warming," Gallup, Washington, DC, March 17, 2017, http://www.gallup.com/poll/206513/democrats-drive-rise-concern-global-warming.aspx (accessed July 1, 2017).

28. Gauchat, "Politicization of Science," p. 174.

29. Mark Romeo Hoffarth and Gordon Hodson, "Green on the Outside, Red on the Inside: Perceived Environmentalist Threat as a Factor Explaining Political Polarization of Climate Change," *Journal of Environmental Psychology*, 45 (2016): 46. https://doi.org/10.1016/j.jenvp.2015.11.002 (accessed December 15, 2017).

30. Josh Pasek, interview with the author, March 28, 2017.

31. Gregory King, "14 of Trump's Most Outrageous 'Birther' Claims—Half from after 2011," CNN.com, http://www.cnn.com/2016/09/09/politics/donald-trump-birther/index.html (accessed January 12, 2018).

32. Ibid.

33. Dan Kahan, interview with the author, May 4, 2017.

34. Dan M. Kahan, "Ideology, Motivated Reasoning, and Cognitive Reflection: An Experimental Study," *Judgment and Decision Making*, 8, no. 4 (2013): 407, http://dx.doi.org/10.2139/ssrn.2182588 (accessed December 15, 2017).

35. "Major Gaps between the Public, Scientists on Key Issues," Pew Research Center, Washington, DC, July 1, 2015, http://www.pewinternet.org/interactives/public-scientists-opinion-gap/ (accessed July 2, 2017).

36. Ibid.

37. Rush Holt, interview with the author, May 2, 2017.

38. Ibid.

39. Ibid.

40. Alexa Tullett, interview with the author, February 24, 2017.

41. Alexa Tullett et al., "Is Ideology the Enemy of Inquiry? Examining the Link between Political Orientation and Lack of Interest in Novel Data," *Journal of Research in Personality* 63 (2016): 123–32, https://doi.org/10.1016/j.jrp.2016.06.018 (accessed December 15 2017).

42. Tullett, interview with the author.

43. Ibid.

44. Ibid.

45. Karen Ernst, interview with the author, May 1, 2017.

46. Ibid.

47. Ibid.

48. Ibid.

49. Ibid.

50. Ibid.

51. Ibid.

52. "About," Voices for Vaccines, https://www.voicesforvaccines.org/about/ (accessed August 13, 2017).

53. Ernst, interview with the author.

54. Ibid.

55. Ibid.

56. Vaccine Resistance Movement, Facebook, https://www.facebook.com/groups/VaccineResistanceMovement/ (accessed July 1, 2017).

57. Ibid.

58. Ibid.

59. Ernst, interview with the author.

60. Ibid.

61. Brendan Nyhan, interview with the author, April 6, 2017.

62. Ibid.

63. Brendan Nyhan and Jason Reifler, "Does Correcting Myths about the Flu Vaccine Work? An Experimental Evaluation of the Effects of Corrective Information," *Vaccine* 33, no. 3 (2015): 459, http://doi.org/10.1016/j.vaccine.2014.11.017 (accessed December 15, 2017).

64. Ibid.

65. Nyhan, interview with the author.

66. Kahan, interview with the author.

67. Ernst, interview with the author.

68. Ibid.

69. Ibid.

70. Ibid.

71. Kahan, interview with the author.

72. Nyhan, interview with the author.

73. Dan M. Kahan, Ellen Peters, Erica Cantrell Dawson, and Paul Slovic, "Motivated

Numeracy and Enlightened Self-Government," *Behavioural Public Policy* 1, no. 1 (2017): 54–86, https://doi.org/10.1017/bpp.2016.2 (accessed December 15, 2017).

74. Ibid., p. 54.

75. Ibid.

76. Kahan, interview with the author.

77. Lee Rainie, interview with the author, May 15, 2017.

78. Ibid.

CHAPTER 5: "THE CONTEMPORARY FACE OF ISOLATION"

1. Noelle Lilley, interview with the author, June 6, 2017.

2. Ibid.

3. Ibid.

4. Ibid.

5. Ibid.

6. Ibid.

7. Ibid.

8. Ibid.

9. Erving Goffman, *The Presentation of Self in Everyday Life* (Edinburgh: University of Edinburgh, 1956), pp. 6–7.

10. Catalina Toma, interview with the author, February 27, 2017.

11. Ibid.

12. Ibid.

13. Ibid.

14. Ibid.

15. Ibid.

16. Donna Freitas, *The Happiness Effect: How Social Media Is Driving a Generation to Appear Perfect at Any Cost* (New York: Oxford University Press, 2017), p. 13.

17. Ibid., p. 126.

18. Hui-Tzu Grace Chou and Nicholas Edge, "'They Are Happier and Having Better Lives than I Am': The Impact of Using Facebook on Perceptions of Others' Lives," *Cyberpsychology, Behavior, and Social Networking* 15, no. 2 (2012): 117, https://doi.org/10.1089/cyber.2011.0324 (accessed December 15, 2017).

19. Ibid., p. 118.

20. Susan T. Fisk, "Envy Up, Scorn Down: How Comparison Divides Us," *American Psychologist* 65, no. 8 (2010): 698–706, https://www.ncbi.nlm.nih.gov/pmc/articles/PMC3825032/ (accessed December 15, 2017).

21. Ibid.

22. Motahhare Eslami et al., "I Always Assumed That I Wasn't Really That Close to [Her]: Reasoning about Invisible Algorithms in News Feeds," in *Proceedings of the 33rd Annual ACM Conference on Human Factors in Computing Systems* (2015): 153, http://doi.org/10.1145/2702123.2702556 (accessed December 15, 2017).

23. Adam D.I. Kramer, Jamie E. Guillory, and Jeffrey T. Hancock, "Experimental Evidence of Massive-Scale Emotional Contagion through Social Networks," *Proceedings of the National Academy of Sciences* 111, no. 24 (2014): 8788–90, http://doi.org/10.1073/pnas.1320040111 (accessed December 15, 2017).

24. Mary L. Gray, "MSR Faculty Summit 2014 Ethics Panel Recap," Microsoft Research Labs Social Media Collective Research (blog), August 19, 2014, https://socialmediacollective.org/2014/08/19/msr-faculty-summit-2014-ethics-panel-recap/ (accessed July 3, 2017).

25. Ibid.

26. "Facebook Manipulates Emotions: Business as Usual for Social Media Giant," NBC News, June 30, 2014. http://www.nbcnews.com/tech/internet/facebook-manipulates-emotions-business-usual-social-media-giant-n144811 (accessed January 12, 2018).

27. Ibid.

28. Toma, interview with the author.

29. Ibid.

30. Rachel Monroe, "#VanLife, The Bohemian Social-Media Movement," *New Yorker*, April 24, 2017, http://www.newyorker.com/magazine/2017/04/24/vanlife-the-bohemian-social-media-movement (accessed July 2, 2017).

31. "Wheresmyofficenow," Instagram, https://www.instagram.com/wheresmyofficenow/ (accessed July 2, 2017).

32. Monroe, "#VanLife."

33. Annalisa Merelli, "Socality Barbie Hits Uncomfortably Close to Home," *Atlantic*, September 9, 2015, https://www.theatlantic.com/entertainment/archive/2015/09/hipster-socality-barbie-shows-the-cliche-of-instagram-authenticity/404431/ (accessed July 2, 2017).

34. "Socality Barbie," Instagram, November 4, 2015, https://www.instagram.com/p/9rFl36HjIc/ (accessed July 2, 2017).

35. Philippe Verduyn et al., "Passive Facebook Usage Undermines Affective Well-Being: Experimental and Longitudinal Evidence," *Journal of Experimental Psychology* 144, no. 2 (2015): 480–88, http://dx.doi.org/10.1037/xge0000057 (accessed December 18, 2017).

36. Ibid.

37. Ibid.

38. Ibid.

39. Brian Primack, interview with the author, February 24, 2017.

40. Ibid.

41. Ibid.

42. Ibid.

43. Tobias Greitemeyer, Dirk O. Mügge, and Irina Bollermann, "Having Responsive Facebook Friends Affects the Satisfaction of Psychological Needs More than Having Many Facebook Friends," *Basic and Applied Social Psychology* 36, no. 3 (2014): 256, http://dx.doi.org/10.1080/01973533.2014.900619 (accessed December 18, 2017).

44. Paolo Parigi and Warner Henson, "Social Isolation in America" (paper; Stanford University, Stanford, CA, 2012), https://funginstitute.berkeley.edu/wp-content/uploads/2013/11/2012-Parigi--26-Henson_Social-Isolation2.pdf (accessed December 18, 2017).

CHAPTER 6: BLINDED

1. Beth Howard, "Colleges Tackle Free Speech, Trigger Warnings, Safe Spaces," *US News & World Report*, September 21, 2017, https://www.usnews.com/education/best-colleges/articles/2017-09-21/colleges-tackle-free-speech-trigger-warnings-safe-spaces (accessed October 8, 2017).

2. Conor Friedersdorf, "The New Intolerance of Student Activism," *Atlantic*, November 9, 2015, https://www.theatlantic.com/politics/archive/2015/11/the-new-intolerance-of-student-activism-at-yale/414810/ (accessed July 8, 2017).

3. Ibid.

4. Ibid.

5. Zachary Young, "How the Yale Halloween Vigilantes Finally Got Their Way," *Wall Street Journal*, June 3, 2016, https://www.wsj.com/articles/how-the-yale-halloween-vigilantes-finally-got-their-way-1464992297 (accessed October 9, 2017).

6. Friedersdorf, "New Intolerance."

7. Young, "How the Yale."

8. Emily Bohatch, "Is There a Protest Near You Today? Rallies against Hate, Trump Pop Up across USA in Wake of Charlottesville," *USA Today*, August 15, 2017, http://www.usatoday.com/story/news/2017/08/15/there-protest-near-you-today-rallies-against-hate-trump-across-usa/569275001/ (accessed January 12, 2018).

9. David Wasserman, "Purple America Has All but Disappeared," FiveThirtyEight, March 8, 2017, https://fivethirtyeight.com/features/purple-america-has-all-but-disappeared/?ex_cid=politicsnewsletter (accessed July 15, 2017).

10. Ibid.

11. Josh Pasek, interview with the author, March 28, 2017.

12. Shanto Iyengar and Sean J. Westwood, "Fear and Loathing across Party Lines: New Evidence on Group Polarization," *American Journal of Political Science* 59, no. 3 (2015): 691, http://doi.org/10.1111/ajps.12152 (accessed December 18, 2017).

13. Iyengar and Westwood, "Fear and Loathing," p. 692.

14. Allison Crimmins et al., "The Impacts of Climate Change on Human Health in the United States: A Scientific Assessment," Global Change Research Program, Washington, DC, 2016, http://dx.doi.org/10.7930/J0R49NQX (accessed December 18, 2017).

15. Ibid.

16. Bob Inglis, interview with the author, April 20, 2017.

17. Ibid.

18. Val Giddings, R. Atkinson, and John Wu, "Suppressing Growth: How GMO Opposition Hurts Developing Nations," Information Technology and Innovation Foundation, 2016, http://www2.itif.org/2016-suppressing-innovation-gmo.pdf (accessed December 18, 2017).

19. Ibid.

20. Nobel Laureates to the Leaders of Greenpeace, the United Nations, and Governments around the World, June 29, 2016, Support Precision Agriculture, http://supportprecisionagriculture.org/nobel-laureate-gmo-letter_rjr.html (accessed July 12, 2017).

21. Ibid.

22. Joel Achenbach, "107 Nobel Laureates Sign Letter Blasting Greenpeace over GMOs," Washington Post, June 30, 2016, https://www.washingtonpost.com/news/speaking-of-science/wp/2016/06/29/more-than-100-nobel-laureates-take-on-greenpeace-over-gmo-stance/?utm_term=.2d767c10671a (accessed July 11, 2016).

23. Ibid.

24. Jacqueline Howard, "Anti-Vaccine Groups Blamed in Minnesota Measles Outbreak," CNN.com, May 8, 2017, http://www.cnn.com/2017/05/08/health/measles-minnesota-somali-anti-vaccine-bn/index.html (accessed July 10, 2017).

25. Ibid.; Fiona Godlee, Jane Smith, and Harvey Marcovitch, "Wakefield's Article Linking MMR Vaccine and Autism Was Fraudulent," British Medical Journal 342, no. 7452 (2011), https://doi.org/10.1136/bmj.c7452 (accessed December 18, 2017).

26. Karen Ernst, interview with the author, May 1, 2017.

27. Ibid.

28. P. J. Hotez, "Texas and Its Measles Epidemics," PLoS Medicine 13, no. 10 (2016): e1002153, https://doi.org/10.1371/journal.pmed.1002153 (accessed December 18, 2017).

29. Brad Allenby and Joel Garreau, "Weaponized Narrative Is the New Battlespace," Defense One, January 3, 2017, http://www.defenseone.com/ideas/2017/01/weaponized-narrative-new-battlespace/134284/ (accessed July 15, 2017).

30. Ibid.

31. Ibid.

32. Carolin Rapp, "Moral Opinion Polarization and the Erosion of Trust," Social Science Research 58 (2016): 34–45, http://dx.doi.org/10.1016/j.ssresearch.2016.02.008 (accessed December 18, 2017).

33. Ibid., p. 43.

34. Tal Kopan, "Donald Trump: Syrian Refugees a 'Trojan Horse,'" CNN.com, November 16, 2015, http://www.cnn.com/2015/11/16/politics/donald-trump-syrian-refugees/index.html (accessed January 20, 2018).

35. Molly O'Toole, "Are Refugees Really a 'National Security Threat to America?"

Atlantic, October 9, 2015, http://www.theatlantic.com/international/archive/2015/10/us-policy-syrian/refugees/409822 (accessed January 12, 2018).

36. These figures were obtained by cross-referencing stats from multiple public data sources: US Bureau of Labor Statistics, "Volunteering in the United States," news release," February 25, 2016, https://www.bls.gov/news.release/volun.htm (accessed December 18, 2017); US Bureau of Labor Statistics, "Volunteering in the United States—2013," news release, February 25, 2014, https://www.bls.gov/news.release/archives/volun_02252014.pdf (accessed December 18, 2017); US Bureau of Labor Statistics, "Volunteering in the United States, 2005," news release, December 9, 2005, https://www.bls.gov/news.release/archives/volun_12092005.pdf (accessed December 18, 2017); US Bureau of Labor Statistics, "Volunteering in the United States, 2003," news release, December 17, 2003, https://www.bls.gov/news.release/archives/volun_12172003.pdf (accessed December 18, 2017).

37. Diane Swanbrow, University of Michigan, "Empathy: College Students Don't Have as Much as They Used To," press release, May 27, 2010, http://ns.umich.edu/new/releases/7724-empathy-college-students-don-t-have-as-much-as-they-used-to (accessed December 18, 2017).

38. Sara H. Konrath, Edward H. O'Brien, Courtney Hsing, "Changes in Dispositional Empathy in American College Students over Time: A Meta-Analysis," *Personality and Social Psychology Review* 15, no. 2 (2011): 180, http://doi.org/10.1177/1088868310377395 (accessed December 18, 2017).

39. Ibid., p. 187.

40. Swanbrow, "Empathy: College Students."

41. This quote and the others that follow come from University of Michigan Institute for Social Research's condensed Interpersonal Reactivity Index survey, https://umich.qualtrics.com/jfe/form/SV_bCvraMmZBCcov52?SVI (accessed January 20, 2018).

42. Take the University of Michigan's condensed Interpersonal Reactivity Index survey: https://umich.qualtrics.com/jfe/form/SV_bCvraMmZBCcov52?SVI (accessed December 18, 2017).

43. Robert Putnam, *Bowling Alone: The Collapse and Revival of American Community* (New York: Simon & Schuster, 2000).

44. Konrath et al., "Changes in Dispositional Empathy," p. 188.

CHAPTER 7: FABRICATION NATION

1. R. Bookwalter, "Why Adobe Max Is the Premier Conference for Creatives," *Macworld*, January 2, 2015, https://www.macworld.com/article/2840393/tech-events-dupe/why-adobe-max-is-the-premier-conference-for-creatives.html (accessed January 18, 2018).

2. "#VoCo. Adobe MAX 2016 (Sneak Peeks) | Adobe Creative Cloud," YouTube video, 7:20, filmed November 2016 in San Diego, California, posted by "Adobe Creative Cloud," November 4, 2016, https://www.youtube.com/watch?v=I3l4XLZ59iw (accessed December 18, 2017).

3. Ibid.

4. Ibid.

5. Ibid.

6. Ibid.

7. Ibid.

8. Ibid.

9. David A. Fahrenthold, "Trump Recorded Having Extremely Lewd Conversation about Women in 2005," *Washington Post*, October 9, 2016, https://www.washingtonpost.com/ politics/trump-recorded-having-extremely-lewd-conversation-about-women-in-2005/2016/ 10/07/3b9ce776-8cb4-11e6-bf8a-3d26847eeed4_story.html (accessed August 19, 2017).

10. This quoted comment along with the next several comments are from "#VoCo. Adobe MAX 2016."

11. "VoCo: Text-Based Insertion and Replacement in Audio Narration," YouTube video, 6:02, posted by "Adam Finkelstein," May 11, 2017, https://www.youtube.com/ watch?v=RB7upq8nzIU (accessed December 18, 2017).

12. Ibid.

13. Ibid.

14. Ibid.

15. Zeyu Jin, Gautham J. Mysore, Stephen DiVerdi, Jingwan Lu, and Adam Finkelstein, "VoCo: Text-Based Insertion and Replacement in Audio Narration," *ACM Transactions on Graphics* 36, no. 4, article 96 (July 2017) http://doi.org/10.1145/3072959.3073702 (accessed December 18, 2017).

16. "Adobe Voco 'Photoshop-for-Voice' Causes Concern," BBC News, November 7, 2016, http://www.bbc.com/news/technology-37899902 (accessed January 18, 2018).

17. Mark Randall, "Peek behind the Sneaks: Controversy and Opportunity in Innovation," *Adobe Perspectives* (blog), December 12, 2016, https://blogs.adobe.com/ conversations/2016/12/peek-behind-the-sneaks-controversy-and-opportunity-in-innovation .html (accessed July 16, 2017).

18. Ibid.

19. Ibid.

20. Ibid.

21. Ibid.

22. Lori Dorn, "Lyrebird, Remarkable Speech Synthesis Technology That Can Learn and Mimic Voices in Seconds," *Laughing Squid* (blog), April 24, 2017, https://laughingsquid.com/ lyrebird-remarkable-speech-synthesis-technology-that-can-learn-and-mimic-voices-in-seconds/ (accessed January 20, 2018).

23. Lyrebird, "Copy the Voice of Anyone," SoundCloud, https://lyrebird.ai/demo (accessed July 16, 2017).

24. Jeff Clune, interview with the author, April 28, 2017.

25. Ibid.

26. Ibid.

27. Ibid.

28. James Vincent, "This App Uses Neural Networks to Put a Smile on Anybody's Face," *Verge*, January 27, 2017, https://www.theverge.com/tldr/2017/1/27/14412814/faceapp -neural-networks-ai-smile-image-manipulation (accessed July 16, 2017).

29. Clune, interview with the author.

30. Anh Nguyen, Jeff Clune, Yoshua Bengio, Alexey Dosovitskiy, et al., "Plug & Play Generative Networks: Conditional Iterative Generation of Images in Latent Space," in *Computer Vision and Pattern Recognition* (November 30, 2016), https://arxiv.org/abs/1612.00005 (accessed December 18, 2017).

31. Clune, interview with the author.

32. Ibid.

33. Ibid.

34. Ibid.

35. Justus Thies, Michael Zollhofer, Marc Stamminger, Christian Theobalt, et al., "Face2Face: Real-Time Face Capture and Reenactment of Rgb Videos," in *Proceedings of the IEEE Conference on Computer Vision and Pattern Recognition* (2016): 2387–95, https://www .cv-foundation.org/openaccess/content_cvpr_2016/papers/Thies_Face2Face_Real-Time_Face _CVPR_2016_paper.pdf (accessed December 18, 2017).

36. Justus Thies, email interview with the author, May 8, 2017.

37. Ibid.

38. Linda Henkel, interview with the author, May 17, 2017.

39. Isabel Lindner and Linda A. Henkel, "Confusing What You Heard with What You Did: False Action-Memories from Auditory Cues," *Psychonomic Bulletin & Review* 22, no. 6 (2015): 1791–97, http://doi.org/10.3758/s13423-015-0837-0 (accessed December 18, 2017).

40. Ibid.

41. Henkel, interview with the author.

42. Ibid.

43. Ken Doctor, "Trump Bump Grows into Subscription Surge—and Not Just for the *New York Times*," *TheStreet*, March 3, 2017, https://www.thestreet.com/story/14024114/1/ trump-bump-grows-into-subscription-surge.html (accessed December 18, 2017).

44. Clune, interview with the author.

45. Donald J. Trump (@realDonaldTrump), "So they caught Fake News CNN cold, but what about NBC, CBS & ABC? What about the failing @nytimes & @washingtonpost? They are all Fake News!" Twitter, June 22, 2017, 5:47 a.m., https://twitter.com/realdonaldtrump/ status/879682547235651584?lang=en.

46. For example, see https://twitter.com/freeborn1983/status/954156437550370818; https://twitter.com/SantaMackly2/status/954192369678725120; and https://twitter.com/ CommonS2017/status/851936246557540352.

47. "Fight the Fake News," Donald J. Trump Campaign Website, https://donate .donaldjtrump.com/fight-the-fake-news (accessed July 21, 2017).

48. US Securities and Exchange Commission, "SEC: Payments for Bullish Articles on Stocks Must Be Disclosed to Investors," press release, April 10, 2017, https://www.sec.gov/news/press-release/2017-79 (accessed July 21, 2017).

49. Ibid.

50. Derek S. Bentsen, "SEC Complaint: Lidingo Holdings, Kamilla Bjorlin, Andrew Hodge, Brian Nichols," US District Court Southern District of New York Case No. 17-2540, April 10, 2017, https://www.sec.gov/litigation/complaints/2017/comp-pr2017-79-a.pdf (accessed December 18, 2017).

51. Brent J. Fields, "SEC Order: Ciaran Thornton," United States of America before the Securities and Exchange Commission, Order Instituting Cease-and-Desist Proceedings Pursuant to Section 8A of the Securities Act of 1933 and Section 21C of the Securities Exchange Act of 1934, Making Findings, and Imposing a Cease-and-Desist Order, April 10, 2017. https://www.sec.gov/litigation/admin/2017/33-10344.pdf (accessed December 18, 2017).

52. Bentsen, "SEC Complaint: Lidingo Holdings."

53. Fields, "SEC Order: Ciaran Thornton."

54. Lydia Polgreen, "Introducing HuffPost Opinion And HuffPost Personal," *HuffPost*, January 18, 2018, https://www.huffingtonpost.com/entry/huffpost-opinion-huffpost-personal_us_5a5f6a29e4b096ecfca98edb (accessed January 19, 2018).

55. Matt Friedman, interview with the author, February 14, 2017.

56. Ibid.

57. Ibid.

58. Ibid.

59. Alex T. Williams, "The Growing Pay Gap between Journalism and Public Relations," Pew Research Center, Washington, DC, August 11, 2014, http://www.pewresearch.org/fact-tank/2014/08/11/the-growing-pay-gap-between-journalism-and-public-relations/ (accessed December 18, 2017).

60. *Occupational Outlook Handbook: Reporters, Correspondents, and Broadcast News Analysts* (Washington, DC: US Bureau of Labor Statistics, December 17, 2015), https://www.bls.gov/ooh/media-and-communication/reporters-correspondents-and-broadcast-news-analysts.htm (accessed December 18, 2017).

61. *Occupational Outlook Handbook: Public Relations* (Washington, DC: US Bureau of Labor Statistics, December 17, 2015), https://www.bls.gov/ooh/media-and-communication/public-relations-specialists.htm (accessed December 18, 2017).

62. James V. Schnurr, "Remarks before the 12th Annual Life Sciences Accounting and Reporting Congress," US Securities and Exchange Commission, March 22, 2016, https://www.sec.gov/news/speech/schnurr-remarks-12th-life-sciences-accounting-congress.html (accessed December 18, 2017).

63. Ibid.

64. Robert Weissman, Kristen Strader, Josh Golin, and Jeffrey Chester, to the Federal Trade Commission, November 30, 2016, https://www.citizen.org/sites/default/files/followup-instagram-letter-to-the-ftc.pdf (accessed December 18, 2017).

65. Ibid.

66. Lindsay Stein, "One in Four Influencers Asked Not to Disclose Paid Promotion," *Advertising Age*, August 10, 2016, http://adage.com/article/cmo-strategy/influencers-asked-disclose-arrangement/305389/ (accessed July 18, 2017).

67. Weissman to the FTC.

68. Ibid.

69. Young Min Baek, Young Bae, and Hyunmi Jang, "Social and Parasocial Relationships on Social Network Sites and Their Differential Relationships with Users' Psychological Well-Being," *Cyberpsychology, Behavior, and Social Networking* 16, no. 7 (2013): 512–17, http://doi.org/10.1089/cyber.2012.0510 (accessed December 18, 2017).

70. Adam Hughes and Onyi Lam, "Highly Ideological Members of Congress Have More Facebook Followers than Moderates Do," Pew Research Center, Washington, DC, August 21, 2017, http://www.pewresearch.org/fact-tank/2017/08/21/highly-ideological-members-of-congress-have-more-facebook-followers-than-moderates-do/ (accessed August 25, 2017).

71. China Xinhua News (@XHNews), Twitter, http://twitter.com/XHNews (accessed January 23, 2018).

72. Linjuan Rita Men and Wan-Hsiu Sunny Tsai, "Public Engagement with CEOs on Social Media: Motivations and Relational Outcomes," *Public Relations Review* 42, no. 5 (2016): 932, https://doi.org/10.1016/j.pubrev.2016.08.001 (accessed December 18, 2017).

73. David Weigel, "House Science Committee Chairman: Americans Should Get News from Trump, Not Media," *Washington Post*, January 25, 2017, https://www.washingtonpost.com/news/powerpost/wp/2017/01/25/house-science-committee-chairman-americans-should-get-news-from-trump-not-media/?utm_term=.f9e1fe6c4cea (accessed July 24, 2017).

CHAPTER 8: CRAP DETECTION 101

1. Stanford Undergraduate Admission page, Stanford University, last updated August 11, 2017, http://admission.stanford.edu/apply/selection/profile16.html (accessed December 18, 2017).

2. Sam Wineburg, interview with the author, March 2, 2017.

3. Sam Wineburg, Joel Breakstone, Sarah McGrew, and Teresa Ortega, "From History Assessments to Assessments of News Literacy," Stanford History Education Group, 2016.

4. Ibid.

5. Ibid.

6. Wineburg, interview with the author.

7. Wineburg et al., "From History Assessments."

8. Ibid.

9. Ibid.

10. Ibid.

11. Ibid.

12. Ibid.

13. Ibid.

14. Ibid.

15. Wineburg, interview with the author.

16. Ibid.

17. Ibid.

18. Ibid.

19. Ibid.

20. Ibid.

21. Alison J. Head, "Staying Smart: How Today's Graduates Continue to Learn Once They Complete College," Project Information Literacy, University of Washington, January 5, 2016, http://dx.doi.org/10.2139/ssrn.2712329 (accessed December 18, 2017).

22. Ibid.

23. Alison Head, interview with the author, May 11, 2017.

24. Ibid.

25. Ibid.

26. Douglas Belkin, "Exclusive Test Data: Many Colleges Fail to Improve Critical-Thinking Skills," *Wall Street Journal*, June 5, 2017, https://www.wsj.com/articles/exclusive-test-data-many-colleges-fail-to-improve-critical-thinking-skills-1496686662 (accessed July 29, 2017).

27. Stuart Rojstaczer, "Grade Inflation at American Colleges and Universities," GradeInflation.com, last updated July 7, 2016, http://www.gradeinflation.com (accessed May 1, 2017).

28. Stuart Rojstaczer, interview with the author, May 1, 2017.

29. Ibid.

30. Ibid.

31. Ibid.

32. Ibid.

33. Andrew Rotherham, interview with the author, June 2, 2017.

34. "Sputnik Spurs Passage of the National Defense Education Act," US Senate Historical Office, October 4, 1957, https://www.senate.gov/artandhistory/history/minute/Sputnik_Spurs_Passage_of_National_Defense_Education_Act.htm (accessed July 29, 2017).

35. Ibid.

36. Wineburg, interview with the author.

37. Ibid.

38. Nathan Bomey, "Special Report: Automation Puts Jobs in Peril," *USA Today*, February 2, 2017, https://www.usatoday.com/story/money/2017/02/06/special-report-automation-puts-jobs-peril/96464788/ (accessed July 14, 2017).

39. Michael Chui et al., "Where Machines Could Replace Humans—And Where They

Can't (Yet)," *McKinsey Quarterly*, July 2016, http://www.mckinsey.com/business-functions/digital-mckinsey/our-insights/where-machines-could-replace-humans-and-where-they-cant-yet (accessed December 18, 2017); Thomas Torlone et al., *Organize Your Future with Robotic Process Automation* (London: PricewaterhouseCoopers, 2016), http://www.pwc.com/us/en/outsourcing-shared-services-centers/assets/robotics-process-automation.pdf (accessed December 18, 2017).

40. Torlone et al., *Organize Your Future.*

41. Bomey, "Special Report: Automation Puts Jobs in Peril."

42. Nathan Bomey, "Walmart to Cut 7,000 Back-Office Accounting, Invoicing Jobs," *USA Today*, September 1, 2016, https://www.usatoday.com/story/money/2016/09/01/walmart-jobs/89716862/ (accessed July 29, 2017).

43. Torlone et al., *Organize Your Future.*

44. Aaron Smith, "Public Predictions for the Future of Workforce Automation," Pew Research Center, Washington, DC, March 10, 2016, http://www.pewinternet.org/2016/03/10/public-predictions-for-the-future-of-workforce-automation/ (accessed December 18, 2017).

45. Lee Rainie, interview with the author, May 15, 2017.

46. Bomey, "Special Report: Automation Puts Jobs in Peril."

47. Associated Press, "Dunkin' Donuts Testing Removal of Non-Breakfast Sandwiches from Menu," *USA Today*, July 27, 2017. https://www.usatoday.com/story/money/2017/07/27/dunkin-donuts-testing-removal-non-breakfast-sandwiches-menu/516633001/ (accessed July 29, 2017).

48. Dan Kahan, interview with the author, May 4, 2017.

49. Ibid.

50. Ibid.

51. Lee Rainie and Janna Anderson, "The Future of Jobs and Jobs Training," Pew Research Center, Washington, DC, May 3, 2017, http://www.elon.edu/docs/e-web/imagining/surveys/2016_survey/Future%20of%20Jobs%20Skills%20Education%205_3_17%20Elon%20Pew.pdf (accessed December 18, 2017).

52. Ibid.

53. Ibid.

54. Ibid.

55. Mary Beth Hertz, interview with the author, February 21, 2017.

56. Ibid.

57. Howard Rheingold, "Crap Detection Mini-Course," Rheingold.com, February 20, 2013, http://rheingold.com/2013/crap-detection-mini-course/ (accessed October 12, 2017).

58. Robert Manning, "Hemingway in Cuba," *Atlantic*, August 1965, https://www.theatlantic.com/past/docs/issues/65aug/6508manning.htm (accessed December 18, 2017).

59. Rheingold, "Crap Detection."

60. Ibid.

61. Howard Rheingold, interview with the author, March 16, 2017.

62. Ibid.

63. Jeff Clune, interview with the author, April 28, 2017.

64. Rheingold, interview with the author.

65. Ibid.

66. "Wikipedia: Principles," *Wikipedia*, https://en.wikipedia.org/wiki/Wikipedia :Principles (accessed January 18, 2017).

67. Wineburg, interview with the author.

68. Ibid.

69. Paul English, interview with the author, February 17, 2017.

70. Ibid.

71. Ibid.

72. Ibid.

73. Ibid.

74. Marc Chun, interview with the author, June 20, 2017.

75. Ibid.

76. Ibid.

77. Ibid.

78. Kristina Zeiser, "Three Studies Show Impact of Deeper Learning," American Institutes for Research Policy Center, August 31, 2016, http://www.air.org/resource/three-studies-show -impact-deeper-learning (accessed December 18, 2017).

79. Chun, interview with the author.

80. Peter Bobkowski, *Civic Engagement among High School Journalists* (Lawrence: University of Kansas, November 2015), http://civicsandjournalists.org/wp-content/uploads/ 2015/11/Results-handout.pdf (accessed December 18, 2017).

81. Peter Bobkowski, interview with the author, May 19, 2017.

82. Ibid.

83. Ibid.

84. Ibid.

85. Clune, interview with the author.

86. Neal Goff, interview with the author, May 4, 2017.

87. Ibid.

88. Rotherham, interview with the author.

89. Ibid.

90. "English Language Arts Standards," Common Core State Standards Initiative, http:// www.corestandards.org/ELA-Literacy/ (accessed August 6, 2017).

91. Goff, interview with the author.

92. Rotherham, interview with the author.

93. Ibid.

94. Ibid.

95. Ryan J. Foley, "Efforts Grow to Help Students Evaluate What They See Online,"

Associated Press, December 31, 2017. https://apnews.com/64b5ce49f58940eda86608f3
eac79158/Alarmed-by-fake-news,-states-push-media-literacy-in-schools (accessed January 19,
2018).

CHAPTER 9: FINDING COMMON GROUND

1. Katharine Hayhoe, interview with the author, June 8, 2017.

2. Ibid.

3. "SXSL: President Obama Participates in SXSL Discussion," YouTube video, 1:02:18,
posted by "The Obama White House," October 3, 2016, https://www.youtube.com/watch?v
=_orUiJKf9qI (accessed December 18, 2017).

4. Hayhoe, interview with the author.

5. Ibid.

6. Ibid.

7. Ibid.

8. Ibid.

9. Ibid.

10. Ibid.

11. Ibid.

12. Ibid.

13. Ibid.

14. Bob Inglis, interview with the author, April 20, 2017.

15. Ibid.

16. Ibid.

17. Ibid.

18. Ibid.

19. Ibid.

20. Ibid.

21. Ibid.

22. Ibid.

23. Ibid.

24. Ibid.

25. Ibid.

26. Ibid.

27. Karen Ernst, interview with the author, May 1, 2017.

28. Ibid.

29. Ibid.

30. Amy Parker, "Growing Up Unvaccinated," Voices for Vaccines, 2013, https://www
.voicesforvaccines.org/growing-up-unvaccinated/ (accessed July 30, 2017).

31. Ibid.

32. Ibid.

33. Ibid.

34. Ernst, interview with the author.

35. Ibid.

36. Ibid.

37. Voices for Vaccines, Facebook, https://www.facebook.com/VoicesForVaccines/ (accessed December 18, 2017).

38. Ernst, interview with the author.

39. Sam Abrams, "The Blue Shift of the New England Professoriate," Heterodox Academy, July 6, 2016, https://heterodoxacademy.org/2016/07/06/the-blue-shift-of-the-new-england -professoriate/ (accessed July 31, 2017).

40. Paul Krugman, "Academics and Politics," *New York Times*, January 4, 2016, https:// krugman.blogs.nytimes.com/2016/01/04/academics-and-politics/?_r=0/ (accessed July 31, 2017).

41. Sam Abrams, "Professors Moved Left since 1990s, Rest of Country Did Not," Heterodox Academy, January 9, 2016, https://heterodoxacademy.org/2016/01/09/professors -moved-left-but-country-did-not/ (accessed July 31, 2017).

42. Ibid.

43. "Sharp Partisan Divisions in Views of National Institutions," Pew Research Center, Washington, DC, July 10 2017, http://www.people-press.org/2017/07/10/sharp-partisan -divisions-in-views-of-national-institutions/ (accessed December 18, 2017).

44. "Public Opinion on Higher Education," Public Agenda, September 12, 2016, https:// publicagenda.org/pages/public-opinion-higher-education-2016 (accessed July 31, 2017).

45. Lee Rainie and Janna Anderson, "The Future of Jobs and Jobs Training," Pew Research Center, Washington, DC, May 3, 2017, http://www.elon.edu/docs/e-web/imagining/ surveys/2016_survey/Future%20of%20Jobs%20Skills%20Education%205_3_17%20 Elon%20Pew.pdf (accessed December 18, 2017).

46. Ibid.

47. "Catholics, Muslims Highlight Shared Beliefs for Social and Political Life," Vatican Radio, May 4, 2016, http://en.radiovaticana.va/news/2016/05/07/catholics,_muslims _highlight_shared_beliefs_for_common_good/1227793 (accessed July 31, 2017).

48. Ibid.

49. Ibid.

CHAPTER 10: RECONNECTING WITH REALITY

1. Nikki Usher, interview with the author, February 28, 2017.

2. John Saroff, interview with the author, May 5, 2016.

3. Ibid.

4. Shane Bauer, "My Four Months as a Private Prison Guard," *Mother Jones*, July/August 2016, http://www.motherjones.com/politics/2016/06/cca-private-prisons-corrections-corporation-inmates-investigation-bauer/ (accessed August 1, 2017).

5. Graeme Wood, "What ISIS Really Wants," *Atlantic*, March 2015, https://www.theatlantic.com/magazine/archive/2015/03/what-isis-really-wants/384980/ (accessed September 9, 2017).

6. "Who Will Win the Presidency?" FiveThirtyEight, November 8, 2016. https://projects.fivethirtyeight.com/2016-election-forecast/ (accessed September 9, 2017).

7. Saroff, interview with the author.

8. Ibid.

9. Ibid.

10. Ibid.

11. Amy Mitchell, Jeffrey Gottfried, Elisa Shearer, and Kristine Lu, "How Americans Encounter, Recall, and Act Upon Digital News," Pew Research Center, Washington, DC, February 9, 2017, http://www.journalism.org/2017/02/09/how-americans-encounter-recall-and-act-upon-digital-news/ (accessed December 18, 2017).

12. Saroff, interview with the author.

13. Ibid.

14. Kristina Eriksson, "*Financial Times* Rolls Out 'Cost Per Hour' Advertising Metric," *Financial Times*, May 18, 2015, https://aboutus.ft.com/en-gb/announcements/financial-times-rolls-out-cost-per-hour-advertising-metric/#axzz3du (accessed October 14, 2017).

15. Ibid.

16. Caitlin Petre, interview with the author, March 21, 2017.

17. John Wihbey, interview with the author, June 6, 2017.

18. Ibid.

19. Institute for Nonprofit News Member Directory, https://inn.org/members/ (accessed August 1, 2017).

20. "What Wouldn't You Know, If Not for Nonprofit News Media?" Institute for Nonprofit News, https://inn.org/2017/01/2016-nonprofit-news-top-stories/ (accessed August 1, 2016).

21. Nathan Bomey, "Panama Papers Read Like Who's Who of World Power," *USA Today*, April 4, 2016, https://www.usatoday.com/story/news/world/2016/04/04/panama-papers-list/82607516/ (accessed August 1, 2017).

22. John Bebow, "Collaborating Instead of Competing: New *Crain's* Joint Venture Helps *Bridge* Serve Michigan Readers and Leaders," *Bridge Magazine*, April 28, 2015, http://www.bridgemi.com/center-michigan/collaborating-instead-competing-new-crains-joint-venture-helps-bridge-serve-michigan (accessed January 18, 2018).

23. "Partners," ProPublica, https://www.propublica.org/partners/ (accessed January 19, 2018).

24. Stephen King, interview with the author, June 16, 2017.

25. Michael Hudson, "Panama Papers Wins Pulitzer Prize," International Consortium of Investigative Journalists, April 10, 2017, https://www.icij.org/blog/2017/04/panama-papers -wins-pulitzer-prize (accessed August 1, 2017).

26. King, interview with the author.

27. "Omidyar Network Invests in Rappler," Rappler, November 5, 2015, http://www .rappler.com/about-rappler/about-us/109992-omidyar-network-invests-rappler (accessed August 1, 2017).

28. King, interview with the author.

29. Benjamin Mullin, "Can Trust in the News Be Repaired? Facebook, Craig Newmark, Mozilla, and Others Are Spending $14 Million to Try," Poynter, April 3, 2017, http://www .poynter.org/2017/can-trust-in-the-news-be-repaired-facebook-craig-newmark-mozilla-and -others-are-spending-14-million-to-try/454330/ (accessed August 1, 2017).

30. Ibid.

31. Ken Doctor, "Newsonomics: Craig Newmark, Journalism's New Six Million Dollar Man," Nieman Lab, February 16, 2017, http://www.niemanlab.org/2017/02/newsonomics -craig-newmark-journalisms-new-six-million-dollar-man/ (accessed August 1, 2017).

32. Alexios Mantzarlis, "Why CNN's Fact-Checking Chyron Is a Big Deal—and Why It Isn't," Poynter, June 3, 2016, https://www.poynter.org/news/why-cnns-fact-checking-chyron -big-deal-and-why-it-isnt (accessed January 19, 2018).

33. Alexios Mantzarlis, interview with the author, May 16, 2017.

34. Chengcheng Shao, Giovanni Luca Ciampaglia, Alessandro Flammini, and Filippo Menczer, "Hoaxy: A Platform for Tracking Online Misinformation," in *Proceedings of the 25th International Conference Companion on World Wide Web* (2016): 745–50, https://doi .org/10.1145/2872518.2890098 (accessed December 18, 2017).

35. Kim LaCapria, "Blogs Claim Obama Dropped Leaflets Warning ISIS of Upcoming Airstrikes," *Snopes*, November 23, 2015, http://www.snopes.com/2015/11/23/obama-dropped -leaflets-warning-isis-airstrikes/ (accessed August 6, 2017).

36. Mark Zuckerberg, "I want to share some thoughts on Facebook and the election," Facebook, November 12, 2016, https://www.facebook.com/zuck/posts/10103253901916271 (accessed December 18, 2017).

37. Petre, interview with the author.

38. Akos Lada, James Li, and Shilin Ding, "News Feed FYI: New Signals to Show You More Authentic and Timely Stories," Facebook Newsroom, January 31, 2017, https:// newsroom.fb.com/news/2017/01/news-feed-fyi-new-signals-to-show-you-more-authentic-and -timely-stories/ (accessed December 18, 2017).

39. Mark Zuckerberg, "Building Global Community," Facebook, February 16, 2017, https://www.facebook.com/notes/mark-zuckerberg/building-global-community/ 10154544292806634/ (accessed August 2, 2017).

40. Ibid.

41. Ibid.

42. Ibid.

43. Sara Su, "Rolling out Related Articles More Broadly," Facebook Newsroom, August 25, 2017, https://newsroom.fb.com/news/2017/04/news-feed-fyi-new-test-with-related -articles/ (accessed August 6, 2017).

44. Ibid.

45. Filippo Menczer, interview with the author, May 11, 2017.

46. Ibid.

47. Ibid.

48. Ibid.

49. Jeff Clune, interview with the author, April 28, 2017.

50. Larry Greenemeier, "When Will Computers Have Common Sense? Ask Facebook," *Scientific American*, June 20, 2016, https://www.scientificamerican.com/article/when-will -computers-have-common-sense-ask-facebook/ (accessed November 10, 2017).

51. Clune, interview with the author.

52. Ibid.

53. "Facebook, Inc. (FB)," Yahoo! Finance, https://finance.yahoo.com/quote/FB/ (accessed October 14, 2017).

54. Benjamin Fearnow, interview with the author, April 26, 2017.

55. Ibid.

56. Lada et al., "News Feed FYI."

57. Adam Mosseri, "News Feed FYI: Bringing People Closer Together," Facebook Newsroom, January 11, 2018, https://newsroom.fb.com/news/2018/01/news-feed-fyi -bringing-people-closer-together/ (accessed January 17, 2018).

58. Ibid.

59. Adam Mosseri, "News Feed FYI: Helping Ensure News on Facebook Is from Trusted Sources," Facebook Newsroom, January 19, 2018, https://newsroom.fb.com/news/2018/01/ trusted-sources/ (accessed January 19, 2018).

60. Amy Mitchell and Rachel Weisel, "Political Polarization and Media Habits: From Fox News to Facebook, How Liberals and Conservatives Keep up with Politics," Pew Research Center, October 2014, http://assets.pewresearch.org/wp-content/uploads/sites/13/2014/10/ Political -Polarization-and-Media-Habits-FINAL-REPORT-7-27-15.pdf (accessed January 19, 2018).

61. Former Facebook executive A, interview with the author, May 23, 2017.

62. Nick Wingfield, Mike Isaac, and Katie Benner, "Google and Facebook Take Aim at Fake News Sites," *New York Times*, November 14, 2016, https://www.nytimes.com/2016/ 11/15/technology/google-will-ban-websites-that-host-fake-news-from-using-its-ad-service.html (accessed January 19, 2018).

63. Jen Weedon, William Nuland, and Alex Stamos, "*Information Operations and Facebook*," (Menlo Park, CA: Facebook, April 27, 2017), https://fbnewsroomus.files.wordpress .com/2017/04/facebook-and-information-operations-v1.pdf (accessed December 18, 2017).

64. Satwik Shukla and Tessa Lyons, "Blocking Ads from Pages That Repeatedly Share False News," Facebook Newsroom, August 28, 2017, https://newsroom.fb.com/news/2017/08/blocking-ads-from-pages-that-repeatedly-share-false-news/ (accessed December 18, 2017).

65. Menczer, interview with the author.

66. "Alphabet Inc. (GOOG)," Yahoo! Finance, https://finance.yahoo.com/quote/GOOG/ (accessed October 14, 2017).

67. Robert Epstein, interview with the author, March 14, 2017.

68. Karen Gilchrist and Anita Balakrishnan, "EU Hits Google with a Record Antitrust Fine of $2.7 Billion," CNBC, June 27, 2017, https://www.cnbc.com/2017/06/27/eu-hits-google-with-a-record-antitrust-fine-of-2-point-7-billion.html (accessed August 3, 2017).

69. Varol Kayhan, interview with the author, March 2, 2017.

70. Megan Rose Dickey, "Algorithmic Accountability," TechCrunch, April 30, 2017, https://techcrunch.com/2017/04/30/algorithmic-accountability/ (accessed January 19, 2018).

71. Kara Swisher and Kurt Wagner, "Facebook Has Hired Former NYT Public Editor Liz Spayd as a Consultant in a 'Transparency' Effort," *Recode*, August 25, 2017, https://www.recode.net/2017/8/25/16202992/facebook-taps-former-nyt-public-editor-transparency-effort (accessed August 25, 2017).

72. Panagiotis Takis Metaxas, interview with the author, May 25, 2017.

73. Mediaite, Facebook, https://www.facebook.com/mediaite (accessed September 9, 2017).

74. Fearnow, interview with the author.

75. Petre, interview with the author.

76. Matt Hardigree, interview with the author, April 25, 2017.

77. Ibid.

78. Ibid.

79. David McCabe, "One Idea for Regulating Google and Facebook's Control over Content," Axios, August 18, 2017, https://www.axios.com/one-proposal-for-regulating-giant-web-platforms-2474462034.html (accessed August 25, 2017).

80. Ibid.

81. Dickey, "Algorithmic Accountability."

82. Epstein, interview with the author.

83. "Google, Facebook Increase Their Grip on Digital Ad Market," eMarketer, March 14, 2017, https://www.emarketer.com/Article/Google-Facebook-Increase-Their-Grip-on-Digital-Ad-Market/1015417 (accessed October 14, 2017).

84. Lara O'Reilly, "The Race Is on to Challenge Google-Facebook 'Duopoly' in Digital Advertising," *Wall Street Journal*, June 19, 2017, https://www.wsj.com/articles/the-race-is-on-to-challenge-google-facebook-duopoly-in-digital-advertising-1497864602 (accessed October 14, 2017).

85. Adam Entous, Craig Timberg, and Elizabeth Dwoskin, "Russian Operatives Used Facebook Ads to Exploit America's Racial and Religious Divisions," *Washington Post*, September

25, 2017, https://www.washingtonpost.com/business/technology/russian-operatives-used
-facebook-ads-to-exploit-divisions-over-black-political-activism-and-muslims/2017/09/
25/4a011242-a21b-11e7-ade1-76d061d56efa_story.html (accessed October 14, 2017).

86. Daisuke Wakabayashi, "Google Finds Accounts Connected to Russia Bought Election
Ads," *New York Times*, October 9, 2017, https://www.nytimes.com/2017/10/09/technology/
google-russian-ads.html (accessed October 14, 2017).

87. Heather Timmons and Keith Collins, "How Congress Could Regulate Facebook
vs. How Mark Zuckerberg Wants to Do It Himself," Quartz, September 22, 2017, https://
qz.com/1085176/facebooks-russian-political-ads-senators-klobuchar-and-warner-want
-regulation-but-zuckerberg-has-his-own-proposals/ (accessed October 14, 2017).

88. Ashley Gold, "McCain Signs on to Democrats' Facebook Ad Disclosure Bill," *Politico*,
October 18, 2017, https://www.politico.com/story/2017/10/18/facebook-ad-disclosure
-bill-243914 (accessed November 3, 2017).

89. Megan R. Wilson, "Lobbying's Top 50: Who's Spending Big," *Hill*, February 7, 2017,
http://thehill.com/business-a-lobbying/business-a-lobbying/318177-lobbyings-top-50-whos
-spending-big (accessed October 14, 2017).

90. Epstein, interview with the author.

91. Lee Rainie, interview with the author, May 15, 2017.

92. Brian Primack, interview with the author, February 24, 2017.

93. Ibid.

94. Kate Storey, "These New Instagram Tools Could Actually Help Save Lives," *Seventeen*,
October 17, 2016, http://www.seventeen.com/life/news/a43281/new-instagram-tools
-perfectlyme/ (accessed August 3, 2017).

95. Ibid.

96. Ibid.

97. Mark Zuckerberg, "Building Global Community," Facebook, February 16, 2017.
https://www.facebook.com/notes/mark-zuckerberg/building-global-community/
10154544292806634/ (accessed August 2, 2017).

98. Ibid.

99. Menczer, interview with the author.

100. Noelle Lilley, interview with the author, June 6, 2017.

101. Ibid.

102. Bin Xu, Pamara Chang, Christopher L. Welker, Natalya N. Bazarova, et al., "Automatic
Archiving versus Default Deletion: What Snapchat Tells Us about Ephemerality in Design," in
*Proceedings of the 19th ACM Conference on Computer-Supported Cooperative Work & Social Com-
puting* (2016): 1662, https://doi.org/10.1145/2818048.2819948 (accessed December 18, 2017).

103. Ibid.

104. Casey Newton, "Facebook Launches Stories to Complete Its All-Out Assault on
Snapchat," *Verge*, March 28, 2017, https://www.theverge.com/2017/3/28/15081398/facebook
-stories-snapchat-camera-direct (accessed January 19, 2018).

CONCLUSION: CRAVING AUTHENTICITY

1. Blake Bakkila, "Chrissy Teigen Gets Honest with Fans by Sharing another Photo of Her Stretch Marks: 'Whatevs,'" *People*, January 19, 2017, http://people.com/bodies/fans-praise -chrissy-teigen-after-posting-sharing-stretch-marks-pic/ (accessed August 5, 2017).

2. Casey Marie (@MissCaseyMarie), Twitter, January 18, 2017, 8:51 p.m., https:// twitter.com/MissCaseyMarie/status/821943057956438017 (accessed December 18, 2017).

3. Marisa (@DivaMarisa73), Twitter, January 18, 2017, 8:59 p.m., https://twitter.com/ DivaMarisa73/status/821945203544248324 (accessed December 18, 2017).

4. "GM CEO Mary Barra's Remarks to Employees on Valukas Report Findings," General Motors Corporate Newsroom, June 5, 2014, http://media.gm.com/media/us/en/gm/news .detail.html/content/Pages/news/us/en/2014/Jun/060514-mary-remarks.html (accessed January 19, 2018).

5. Ibid.

6. Brendan Nyhan, Franklin Dickinson, Sasha Dudding, Enxhi Dylgjeri, et al., "Classified or Coverup? The Effect of Redactions on Conspiracy Theory Beliefs," *Journal of Experimental Political Science* 3, no. 2 (2016): 109, https://doi.org/10.1017/XPS.2015.21 (accessed December 18, 2017).

7. Ibid.

8. Stephen J. Adler, "To Our Readers, from the Editor-in-Chief," Reuters, April 6, 2017, http://www.reuters.com/article/us-backstory-editor-idUSKBN178208 (accessed August 5, 2017).

9. Caroline Scott, "Reuters Launched Backstory to Provide More Transparency around Its Reporting Process," Journalism.co.uk, April 21, 2017, https://www.journalism.co.uk/news/ reuters-launched-initiative-to-provide-more-transparency-around-its-reporting-process/s2/ a703027/ (accessed August 5, 2017).

10. David Berkowitz, interview with the author, May 12, 2017.

11. Erving Goffman, *The Presentation of Self in Everyday Life* (Edinburgh: University of Edinburgh, 1956), p. 41.

12. Brendan Nyhan, interview with the author, April 6, 2017.

13. Ibid.

14. Panagiotis Takis Metaxas, interview with the author, May 25, 2017.

15. Neil McGinness, interview with the author, May 1, 2017.

16. Ibid.

17. Alison Head, interview with the author, May 11, 2017.

18. Ibid.

19. J. B. Smitts, "Facebook Will End on May 15th, 2013!" *Weekly World News*, October 1, 2012, http://weeklyworldnews.com/headlines/27321/facebook-will-end-on-ma-15th/ (accessed August 7, 2017).

20. Ibid.

21. McGinness, interview with the author.

22. Ibid.

INDEX

INDEX

INDEX